The War Correspondent

The War Correspondent

Fully updated second edition

Greg McLaughlin

PlutoPress
www.plutobooks.com

First published 2002
Fully updated second edition first published 2016 by Pluto Press
345 Archway Road, London N6 5AA

www.plutobooks.com

British Library Cataloguing in Publication Data
A catalogue record for this book is available from the British Library

ISBN   978 0 7453 3319 9   Hardback
ISBN   978 0 7453 3318 2   Paperback
ISBN   978 1 7837 1758 3   PDF eBook
ISBN   978 1 7837 1760 6   Kindle eBook
ISBN   978 1 7837 1759 0   EPUB eBook

Typeset by Stanford DTP Services, Northampton, England

Simultaneously printed in the European Union and United States of America

To Sue with love

Contents

APPENDICES

Acknowledgements

Warm thanks and appreciation to the people who helped me see this book through to completion and into production:

At Pluto Press, commissioning editor, David Castle, for his priceless patience and wise counsel; managing editor, Robert Webb, for his expert supervision of the book's production; copy editor Nuala Ernest for her guidance and advice; and Melanie Patrick and her colleagues, Emily Orford, Kieran O'Connor and Chris Browne, for their superb cover design and promotional work.

At the University of Ulster, my good friends and colleagues Martin McLoone, for his constructive comments on early drafts, and Stephen Baker for his valuable review of the final manuscript; Head of School, Colm Murphy, for giving me time and space when most needed; and Carol, Sally and Lisa for their amazing admin support and for keeping me grounded.

Thanks once again to the journalists who provided such great interview material for the first edition: Christiane Amanpour, Martin Bell, Victoria Brittain, Robert Fisk, Nik Gowing, Lindsey Hilsum, Mark Laity, Jacques Leslie, Jake Lynch, Mike Nicholson, Maggie O'Kane, John Pilger, John Simpson, Alex Thomson and Mark Urban; and to NATO press secretary, Jamie Shea. Their insights and arguments have stood the test of time so many years later. Special thanks also to Mary Dejevsky and Alex Thomson for giving me such rich interview material for this new edition.

On the home front, the love and faith of my mum, brothers and sisters was as crucial as always. But I don't think I would have made it to the end without Sue and her endless love, belief and support.

Míle buíochas do gach duine.

Abbreviations

ABC	American Broadcasting Company
AP	Associated Press
APTN	Associated Press Television News
BBC	British Broadcasting Corporation
BEF	British Expeditionary Force
CBS	Columbia Broadcasting System
CINCLANT	Commander-in-Chief of the US Atlantic Fleet
CNN	Cable News Network
CPJ	Committee to Protect Journalists
DoD	Department of Defense (US)
FEC	Far Eastern Command
IDF	Israel Defence Forces
IED	Improvised Explosive Device
INSS	Institute for National Security Studies
IPI	International Press Institute
ITN	Independent Television News
MoD	Ministry of Defence (UK)
NATO	North Atlantic Treaty Organization
NBC	National Broadcasting Company
PAG	Public Affairs Guidance
PTSD	post-traumatic stress disorder
RTLM	Radio-Television Libre des Milles Collines
SAS	Special Air Service
SORH	Syrian Observatory for Human Rights
UN	United Nations

1

Introduction

William Howard Russell is widely regarded as one of the first war correspondents to write for a commercial daily newspaper. He became famous for his dispatches from the Crimean War, 1854–56, for *The Times* and he seemed to appreciate that he was blazing a trail for a new breed of journalist, calling himself the 'miserable parent of a luckless tribe'. Charles Page, an American contemporary of Russell, also seemed to see the miserable and luckless side of the job. In an article entitled *An Invalid's Whims...The Miseries of Correspondents*, he compared himself and his colleagues to invalids, 'proverbially querulous and unreasonable. They may fret and scold, abuse their toast and their friends, scatter their maledictions and their furniture' (1898, p. 143). The war correspondent, he warned, 'will inevitably write things that will offend somebody. Somebody will say harsh things of you, and perhaps seek you out to destroy you. Never mind. Such is a part of the misery of correspondents' (ibid., p. 146). During the Anglo Zulu war of 1879, a 'Special Correspondent' for the *Natal Witness* (19 June) complained that '[To] enthusiastic persons, the position of War Correspondent may be a very pretty one... but a little practical experience of such work will rub off a great deal of its gloss' (Laband and Knight, 1996, p. *v*).

More recent and contemporary accounts suggest these impressions have changed little since the nineteenth century. In *Dispatches*, Michael Herr recalls some of the things political commentators and newspaper columnists called him and his colleagues during the course of the Vietnam War. They were called 'thrill freaks, death-wishers, wound-seekers, war-lovers, hero-worshippers, closet queens, dope addicts, low-grade alcoholics, ghouls, communists [and] seditionists [...]' (1978, p. 183). With the growth of media journalism in the 1990s, the media reporting the media, war reporting has become a story itself. Coverage of war is bound to feature articles and TV programmes looking at various issues that reporters face in the war zone. As the first bombs fell on Afghanistan in October, 2001, the *Independent* carried a special feature item on 13 October, highlighting the conditions experienced by journalists who were not even in the country a week but were already missing their home comforts: 'Reporters live on bread, onions and water from gutter'; 'Foreign correspondents are down to one lavatory per 45 people'. The capture by the Taliban of the *Sunday Express* reporter Yvonne Ridley seemed to put these discomforts into perspective, if we were to believe 'a world exclusive' in the *Daily Express*, published just after her eventual release on 8 October 2001. The front-page splash highlighted Ridley's 'Taliban Hell', in which she lay captive in a 'filthy, rat-infested prison cell', 'went on hunger strike' and 'fought with vicious guards'. She even 'risked death to keep secret diary for *Express* readers' (9 October 2001). According to Ridley, the true story was rather less dramatic. She told the media that the prison conditions were bearable and that the Taliban treated her well.[1] In coincidence with Ridley's release, the British Broadcasting Corporation's (BBC's) chief news correspondent, Kate Adie, was being pilloried by the British popular press for allegedly revealing embargoed information about Prime Minister Tony Blair's itinerary in the Middle East, where he was undertaking a tour to drum up Arab support for the war in Afghanistan. In fact, she inadvertently confirmed a leading question from her news anchor about Blair's next stop. Amid furious complaints from 10 Downing Street, the BBC failed to protect her from the flak even in the wake of a full front page headline from *The Sun*: 'Sack Kate Adie!'(10 October 2001). Adie threatened libel action against *The Sun* and suggested that the original breach of security, such that it was, lay with 10 Downing Street for the way in which they briefed the media. Some critics suspected sinister government spin because it seemed all too convenient that the row helped deflect public attention away from difficult domestic stories.[2]

There are other impressions and depictions of the war reporter in the wider culture. The movies usually depict journalists as hard-boiled, cynical or dissolute scoundrels; but in films such as *Salvador* (dir. Oliver Stone, 1983) or *The Killing Fields* (dir. Roland Joffé, 1984), the war correspondent is depicted as a hero, risking life and limb to report the story and 'telling truth to power' (McNair, 2010; pp. 57–133).[3] In Evelyn Waugh's newspaper satire, *Scoop* (1938), anti-hero William Boot of the *Beast*, goes off to report a war in the fictional African country of Ishmaelia, with no experience and for no other reason than he has been sent there by his editor, Lord Copper. In a situation that many experienced war correspondents today would recognise as an example of 'parachute journalism', Boot recalls his big moment with blasé wonderment and naivety:

> Two months ago, when Lord Copper summoned me from my desk in the *Beast* office, to handle the biggest news story of the century, I had never been to Ishmaelia, I knew little of foreign politics. I was being pitted against the most brilliant brains, the experience, and the learning of the civilized world. I had nothing except my youth, my will to succeed, and what – for want of a better word – I must call my flair.

The aim of this book is to provide a more complete, objective impression of the war correspondent than those available in personal memoirs and interviews or in fictional representations. Since journalism is often taken as 'the first draft of history', its claims to 'make sense' of reality with objectivity and authority would be of obvious interest to the critical media scholar. If the relationship between war reporter and military, from the Crimean War to the latest conflicts of the twenty-first century, is so crucial to the shaping of that same draft of history, and thus public understanding of war, then the scholar will want to inquire into the nature of that relationship in its historical, professional and political contexts. And, if ideology and ideological frameworks are so fundamental to how citizens perceive and make sense of war in a supposedly chaotic world, then those that construct and reproduce those frameworks, including journalists, are of obvious interest and concern to the sociologist and the cultural studies critic. There are two impulses, then, that drive this book: the need to inquire into and analyse one of the most interesting but controversial genres of mainstream journalism from a sociological and historical perspective; and to de-mythologise war correspondents, to get past the legends, the myths and cultural representations and get to the reality of who they are, what they do and why they do it.

This is the second edition of a book first published in 2002, and has been significantly updated and restructured to consider the various issues and debates that have surrounded the reporting of the major conflicts that have happened since then, such as those in Afghanistan, Iraq and Syria. It ends with an entirely new chapter that looks at the implications for western journalism of two recent reporting paradigms: the 'war on terror' frame that defined our understanding of conflict in the first decade of the new century and a newly-emerging Cold War frame that heralds the return of the Evil Empire: Vladimir Putin's Russia. To that end, it is divided into three thematic sections.

Part I examines the various issues and debates that surround the role of war correspondents. It acknowledges the very real risks and dangers that come with the job and, in that context, explores the motivations and journalistic traditions that compel them to accept those risks (Chapter 2). It examines the ethical problems that come with the practice of objectivity in the war zone (Chapter 3), and the challenges and opportunities that each new media technology has brought to the job (Chapter 4). Part II of the book shifts the focus of inquiry from the work of the war reporter as individual and examines the vexed relationship between journalist and the military, perhaps one of the key factors that have shaped and defined war reporting since the Crimean War and William Howard Russell. It puts the relationship into historical perspective, moving from the Crimean War to the Korean War (Chapter 5); from the Vietnam War to the Gulf War in 1991 (Chapter 6); and into the twenty-first century with the 'war on terror' conflicts in Afghanistan and Iraq (Chapter 7). It suggests that this controversial and problematical relationship has been one of evolution, leaving behind the traces of past practices and confrontations but also mutating and refining itself with each conflict. For the military, it has been about learning the lessons of the last war, fine tuning systems of control, censorship and propaganda in which war reporters and the media in general have a predetermined role: to sell war to domestic publics. Alas for the majority of war correspondents, it has been about forgetting the lessons except, perhaps, between the covers of their memoirs where they might express regret for how easily they conformed to the system for the sake of getting the story.

Telling the story, of course, is vital for the journalist on any beat, whether that be war, defence or diplomacy, and Part III examines the importance of historical and ideological frameworks for shaping and sometimes limiting the content and scope of the story as effectively as military censorship in the war zone. Of particular interest in this respect is the Cold War framework or paradigm (Chapter 8), with its meta-narrative of a bipolar world order of ideological oppositions, as well as the implications for journalism of its crisis after the fall of the Berlin Wall in 1989 and the collapse of the Soviet Union just two years later. Looking at the much less coherent framework that apparently replaced it, that of a 'new world order', the book closes with two more recent and competing frameworks for making sense of international conflict: the 'war on terror' that followed the attacks on America in 2001 (9/11); and the 'new Cold War' story that seems to be coming into play in the western media as a means of reporting the return of a familiar old enemy: Russia (Chapter 9). It is unlikely that we will see again anything like the global, imperial and ideological conflict of superpowers that ended in 1991. But even an analysis of the Cold War hysteria and rhetoric that has characterised the western media image of Vladimir Putin, and the reporting of his approach to the crisis in neighbouring Ukraine, suggests that the power of such frameworks, to shape and perhaps distort our understanding of complex wars and civil conflicts, is still considerable.

Part I

The War Correspondent in Historical Perspective

2

The War Correspondent: Risk, Motivation and Tradition

Most war reporters are brave, selfless types – more interested in the news story at hand than their own physical discomfort and fear. Not me.

Chris Ayres, *War Reporting for Cowards*, 2005

The job of the war correspondent is defined by the risks and dangers involved with getting the story: death, injury, kidnap, harassment and imprisonment, among others. This chapter considers the real extent of these risks, the kinds of training courses available to journalists reporting in hostile environments and the variable level of risk that a war reporter might face, depending on the size and resources of his or her news organisation. In that context, it explores the motivations by which war correspondents rationalise risk and danger: from the candid (the thrill and excitement of reporting war) to the pragmatic (getting the story) or the idealistic (reporting the truth or the human cost of war). It suggests that whatever the motivations might be and however writers and commentators might define them, today's war correspondents have little sense of commonality, of being part of Russell's 'luckless tribe' or some 'fellowship of danger' (Lambert, 1987, p. 13) other than just being journalists.

RISK

According to journalist organisations such as the International Press Institute (IPI) in Vienna and the Committee to Protect Journalists (CPJ) in New York,[1] up to 1,400 journalists and media workers have lost their lives in the period 1997–2014, the majority of them reporting wars or conflicts of some description. The IPI was founded in Vienna in 1950[2] and began monitoring death rates among journalists worldwide in 1992. Its definition of 'journalist' has always been a broad one and includes media workers such as producers, freelancers and local contacts. The CPJ was founded in New York in 1981 and began compiling data on journalists and risk in 1992. In its early life, it defined journalists as 'people who cover news or comment on public affairs through any media – including in print, in photographs, on radio, on television, and online'; and it still campaigns today on behalf of 'staff journalists, freelancers, stringers, bloggers, and citizen journalists' around the world.[3] However, in 2003, it broadened its definition along the lines of the IPI to include media support workers. The historical differences in methodology has resulted in various statistical discrepancies between these organisations, but a summary of their key data provides a vivid picture of the level and nature of the risks that war reporters and other journalists and media workers face on a daily basis.

The IPI's Death Watch Survey reports that 1,461 journalists have been killed in hostile situations around the world between 1997 and 2014, 824 of these since 2006 – an average of over 90 per year. The CPJ takes a longer sample period and reports that 1,102 journalists have been killed between 1992 and 2014, 657 of these murdered with impunity, an issue on which both organisations campaign strongly.

Most deadly countries

The IPI and CPJ websites also feature breakdowns of these statistics by country. The IPI's ten most deadly countries for journalists to work between 1997 and 2013 were:

1. Iraq (203)
2. The Philippines (122)
3. Colombia (85)
4. Mexico (81)
5. Pakistan (76)
6. Russia (64)
7. Syria (56)
8. Somalia (53)
9. India (49)
10. Brazil (39)

The CPJ includes figures for 20 countries but for sake of comparison with the IPI, its ten most deadly countries for journalists to work in the same period were:

1. Iraq (104)
2. The Philippines (75)
3. Syria (63)
4. Algeria (60)
5. Russia (56)
6. Pakistan (54)
7. Somalia (52)
8. Colombia (45)
9. India (32)
10. Mexico (30)

The interested reader may explore this data in detail on the IPI and CPJ websites, but it is worth considering here some of the most dangerous assignments and the different kinds of hazards they present to international and local correspondents alike.

Iraq's number one billing in both surveys is hardly surprising considering that since 1991 the country has suffered two major wars and following the US-led invasion in 2003, an insurgency against western occupation as well as sectarian warfare between the country's Sunni and Shi'a populations. Included in the high death toll among journalists are those killed in so-called 'friendly fire' or 'blue on blue' incidents, where military forces accidentally fire upon and kill or injure allied military forces or civilians. Independent Television News' (ITN's) Terry Lloyd was killed in such an incident on 22 March 2003 when reporting the early stages of the invasion as an independent, or what the military call 'unilateral', correspondent; in other words, working outside of the military's 'embed' system of media accreditation (for an analysis of the embed system, see Chapter 7). The circumstances of Lloyd's death and that of his cameraman, Fred Nérac, and Lebanese 'fixer', Hussein Osman, are still disputed. Were they simply unlucky to run into crossfire between the American and Iraqis, as official versions claim? Or was he deliberately targetted as an example to all foreign journalists of the dangers of working outside of military restrictions? In a film to mark the tenth anniversary of his death, his daughter, Chelsey, and ITN colleague,

Mark Austin, question the official version and also ask why, after a coroner's ruling in 2006 of 'unlawful killing', no one has been prosecuted or held accountable for his death.[4]

Similar questions have been asked about the deaths on 8 April 2003 of news cameramen Taras Protsyuk (Reuters) and José Couso (Telecinco), killed when American forces fired at the Palestine Hotel in Baghdad; or that of the Al Jazeera reporter Tariq Ayyoub, killed earlier that day when an American missile struck the network's Baghdad office. The BBC's veteran foreign correspondent, John Simpson, himself a victim of American friendly fire in the north of Iraq just before the US ground invasion, suggests that the targeting of journalists has become a new feature of American military operations around the world. What is disturbing for Simpson and many other journalists is the impunity enjoyed by those who do the targetting, whether deliberately or by accident.[5] Chris Paterson makes a strong case for seeing these incidents as part of US military strategy since the attacks on America in 2001, 9/11, designed above all to ensure a compliant media response to US military operations (2014, pp. 9–12, 21–22).

In cases like these, the US military insists that it does not target journalists and that it operates according to official rules of engagement but that accidents sometimes happen.[6] Such 'accidents' might include the killing by an Apache helicopter gunner on 12 July 2007 of Reuters photographer Namoor Noor-Eldeen, his driver Saeed Chmagh and ten civilians who tried to rescue their bodies; two children were wounded in the incident. The cockpit video (with crew audio) from the helicopter gunship was later leaked to WikiLeaks, but to date no one has been brought to account for what happened. In a strong address to an anti-war conference in 2010, US Ranger Ethan McCord explained the difference between the *official* rules of military engagement in Iraq and what soldiers were told *off record* to do when they came under fire:

If you feel threatened by anybody, you are able to engage [fire upon] that person. Many soldiers felt threatened just by the fact that you were looking at them so they fired their weapons at anyone who was looking at them. We were told that if we were to fire our weapons at people, and we were to be investigated, officers would take care of you. We were given orders for 360-degree rotational fire whenever we were hit by an IED [Improvised Explosive Device]. We were told by our commander to kill every motherfucker in the street.[7]

The most recent addition to these most deadly country lists has been Syria. From the beginning of the civil war there in 2011 up until the end of 2014, various sources have put the death toll at between 150,000 and 200,000, the majority being combatants.[8] Over 600 Syrian civilians lost their lives in the same period and the pictures of hundreds of thousands of refugees fleeing to neighbouring countries such as Turkey, Jordan and Lebanon have dominated news from the region. In what seems to be a brutal and unpredictable conflict without clear lines of opposition or rules of engagement, the figure of up to 63 journalists killed so far seems mercifully low but when expressed as an annual death rate, it represents an average of 25–30 per year over two years compared to 15–20 per year over ten years in Iraq. The Syrian Journalists Association includes in its statistics what it calls 'media activists and citizen reporters' and reported a death toll in December 2012 of just over 100, a much higher figure than that of either the IPI or CPJ.[9] The most high-profile casualty among western journalists in Syria has been Marie Colvin of the *Sunday Times*, killed on 21 February 2012 with French photojournalist Remi Ochlik, when the house where she was staying in the besieged city of Homs was hit by incoming artillery fire from the Syrian army. Three other journalists, including her colleague, photojournalist Paul Conroy, were wounded in the attack.[10] Conroy recounts the moment he found his dead colleagues in the aftermath of the shelling:

> There, in what had once been the entranceway to the house, lay the bodies of my two friends. Mercifully, I could not see Marie's face. Her head and legs were covered in fallen rubble and I recognize her only by her blue jumper and belt. Of Remi, I saw only his back through the thick layers of dust and fallen masonry. [...] The wonderful, smiling Remi – together we had dodged bullets and bombs as we pushed our way through the cities and deserts of Libya. [...] Marie who had given a face and voice to millions of people whose lives had been torn apart by war; Marie the Martha Gellhorn of our generation who now lay motionless in the ruins of Babr Amr. I gently lay my hand on her chest and checked she was dead. Farewell Chechen queen. (2013, p. 222).

The majority of journalists killed in the conflict have been from Syria and other countries in the Middle East. Ghaith Abd al-Jawad and Amr Badir al-Deen Junaid, news cameramen for the pro-opposition Qaboun Media Centre were killed by mortar shell on 10 March 2013. Syrian correspondent Yara Abbas was killed by sniper fire near the border with Lebanon on 26 May 2013. Hamza al-Hajj Hassan, cameraman Mohamed Muntich and technician Halim Alouh, were killed on 14 April 2014 while on assignment for Lebanon's Al-Manar TV; they died when the car they were in was sprayed with machine gunfire from 'unknown assailants'. The IPI has also estimated that, as of September 2013, at least 34 journalists from Syria and abroad have been kidnapped or reported missing since the conflict began.[11]

Both the IPI and CPJ identify the Philippines as the second most dangerous country for journalists. This 40-year conflict between the mainly Christian government and Islamic insurgents is barely reported in the international media, yet it has claimed up to 150,000 deaths and displaced over 2 million people.[12] The CPJ reports that 76 journalists were killed there between 1997 and 2013; out of those, 74 were murdered, 66 with impunity. The worst single incident was the death on 15 July 2012 of 32 mainly Filipino journalists and 26 other civilians in what has become known as the Maguindanao Massacre, which was not directly related to the wider military conflict but to a regional party political power struggle. In a special feature article to mark the second anniversary of the massacre, the IPI reported that to date no one had been brought to justice for the killings.[13] Elsewhere around the world, the drugs wars in Colombia and, in recent times, Mexico, as well as corruption and racketeering in Russia have made these countries particularly dangerous for investigative journalists. The murder of Russian journalist Anna Politkovskaya at her home in Moscow on 7 October 2006 has been variously blamed on the Russian mafia, the pro-Russian Chechen President, Ramzan Kadyrov, and on an unnamed, senior Russian politician. The Chechen connection seemed to the prosecution at least to be the most likely lead because of Politkovskaya's critical reporting of Russia's conduct in the two Chechen wars, between 1994–96 and 1999–2009, even though her investigations probed other aspects of Russian President Vladimir Putin's authoritarian regime (see for example, Politkovskaya 2001, 2004 and, posthumously, 2008 and 2011). In 2014, after a retrial, two men identified as Chechen criminals were convicted of her murder. However, crime reporter Elena Shmaraeva has examined the transcripts of the trial and concludes that the real assassins may still be at large.[14] At least 55 other journalists have been killed in Russia between 1992 and 2013, 32 of those with impunity.[15]

Another very real risk for war correspondents is psychological trauma, which can often have long term effects in their professional and personal lives. In the documentary film, *Reporters at War* (dir. Brian Woods, 2003),[16] former ITN cameraman, Jon Steele, tells how he developed post-traumatic stress disorder (PTSD) on return from assignment in Bosnia, where he filmed a fatally injured girl as she was being rushed to hospital:

> There was this little girl in a pool of blood, lying on her back. And I didn't go rush up to her. I didn't try to help. I ran to the truck and got my camera. And I started filming the situation. Some men picked her up and put her in the back of a car and they were actually blocking my shot. And I grabbed one of the men on the back of the shoulder, yanked him back and I went in with the camera. I was looking at her through the eyepiece. I don't know if she was conscious...but she just sort of looked into the lens and then her eyes just sort of lost focus and then the car took off [to the hospital].

On cleaning his camera some time later, he realised the implications of what he had done:

> I was looking into the glass of the lens...and the more I looked at the lens, the more something hit me. I was seeing myself in the lens and I was looking at my eyes in the lens and then I realised that that girl had seen herself in the lens as she was dying and bleeding. And it just hit me that the last thing she saw in her life was her own self, dying. I did that to her.

Wracked with guilt that he had put the needs of the job before those of the girl, he went off to film civilians under fire on Sarajevo's main boulevard, dubbed Sniper Alley, without wearing protective body armour. 'At that moment, I really wanted to die', he says. 'I wanted to take a bullet [...] for what I had just done and that's when I lost it completely. And everything was a bit of a blur for the next few days until I wound up having a nervous breakdown in Heathrow Airport.' On reflection, Steele thinks that the nature of the job of news cameraman, the imperative to keep looking, leaves him or her particularly vulnerable to psychological trauma:

A correspondent, a reporter, a scribbler, a soundman, even a stills cameraman, can turn away. The nature of television is that you have to let the action happen within the frame, which means you have to concentrate, which means you have to count, which means you have to stare. And you keep looking for pictures, looking for pictures, which means you have to look at this stuff. You have to look at the blood, you have to look at the carnage...you have to look at the faces screaming at you in pain. And you take that in. You are the camera. It goes through the lens, into the eyepiece, into your eyes, into your brain, into your heart and into your soul. And it never leaves. It stays there forever.[17]

Other war reporters with similar experiences resist the possibilities of psychological trauma. Anthony Lloyd of *The Times* has written two powerful memoirs of his first major assignment in Bosnia (Lloyd, 2007) and then Kosovo, Sierra Leone and Iraq (Lloyd, 2013). In the latter volume, *Another Bloody Love Letter*, he admits openly to his heroin addiction but dismisses any assumption of cause and effect, that somehow his addiction marks a traumatic response to his experience of war:

War had not produced my drug addiction, nor was I totally convinced by the platitudes of those suggesting it was an addiction in itself. I felt fairly grounded in my relationship with war. It was certainly an environment full of compulsion and attraction, and one that fired my imagination, but my inability to find tranquility in peace was more the question at stake. It would have been too simple to regard heroin as some sort of self-medication to the horrors I had seen. Instead I felt victim to nothing but self-execution. (2013, p. 63)[18]

As disturbing as these case studies in risk might be, it is important to offer some perspective here. First, while the dangers are obvious, it is difficult to establish whether war reporting today is proportionately more dangerous than it was before the 1990s when organisations such as the IPI and CPJ began gathering data. It is also important to note in the context of this book that the IPI and CPJ count journalists killed on various beats, for example crime, political or financial corruption and human rights, not just war and conflict. In any case, are the death tolls today higher because journalists have become targets more than ever before? Or is it simply because there are more journalists working in war zones, with their work and the risks they face daily as much a part of the media story as the conflict they report? And has that in turn raised the public profile of the job, making heroes and celebrities out of war reporters in a way not seen since Winston Churchill and other journalists during the Second Boer War (1899–1902)?[19] It is probably impossible to offer definitive answers to these questions, but the very perception of risk in war journalism has had consequences in recent times. In civil conflicts of the 1990s, such as those in Somalia, Rwanda, East Timor and Sierra Leone, most western journalists either left eventually or were called home by their employers when the risks were perceived to be too high. There are also financial considerations. The prohibitive costs of safety training and equipment as well as insurance cover are unaffordable for all but the larger international news organisations and agencies.

Training and support

Writing in 2001 for the IPI, News Editor-in-Chief of ITN, Richard Tait, acknowledged that war reporting had become 'unacceptably dangerous', but wanted to avoid sending 'a message to the teams on the frontline that we are no longer committed to enterprising, courageous and original journalism.' In response to these concerns, ITN joined with BBC, CNN, Reuters and APTN to set up a safety group and draw up guidelines on 'assignment, training, protective equipment, post-traumatic counseling and insurance' (ibid.; see Appendix 1). Such interventions led to the development of special training courses for journalists working in dangerous or hostile regions. A company in Britain, AKE, offers a 'Surviving Hostile Regions' course of between one and five days in length.[20] It also offers a range of insurance products covering 'Personal Accident and MedEvac' (premiums from £750 plus VAT per person), 'Kidnap and Ransom' (premium unspecified) and 'General Liability and Professional Indemnity' (premium unspecified).[21] Instructed by former Special Air Service (SAS) personnel, participants in the AKE course are trained in the awareness, anticipation, and avoidance of danger; as well as coping in the extreme conditions of 'weather, disease and war' (for the full syllabus, see Appendix 2).

AKE offers on its website an example of how its training course has helped journalists in difficult situations:

> During the height of the conflict in 1996 a team of four journalists crossed the border into rebel-held Goma (Democratic Republic of Congo). While interviewing civilians in the town a grenade exploded behind them, sending them running for cover. One journalist rounded a corner into oncoming rifle fire and was hit in the leg. His partner, *remembering his AKE training*, managed to administer first aid, constructed a tourniquet to stem the bleeding whilst in an exposed position and still under fire, and took control of the situation.
>
> After getting all safely across the border he summoned further assistance from an aid group before organising evacuation to Kigali. Here more medical aid was given to the wounded before both were airlifted home and to hospital in Europe. The surgeons at home ascribed the positive outcome to the actions of both journalists; both of them are sure that *without AKE's preparation* the outcome would have been very different. (Emphasis added)[22]

It is difficult to separate hype from heroics in this sales pitch, but most war correspondents accept the risks; some celebrate them, and others rationalise them in philosophical terms. 'I think I shall take chances all my life', wrote the French reporter Victor Franco, 'it's part of my trade' (1963, p. 2). ITN's reporter, Mike Nicholson, now retired, talks of 'that fatalism in the people who do the job that I do...the certainty that you're never going to get clobbered. It's never crossed my mind that I'd ever get hurt or killed or wounded in any way...I really do believe in a kind of immortality...otherwise I'd never want to do it again.'[23] Channel 4's international editor, Lindsey Hilsum, is particularly scathing of the risk angle:

> We're all supposed to be in danger all the time and we're all supposed to be traumatised and in need of psychotherapy because of all the dangerous things that we do. I mean, it's bollocks! We choose to do this and it is sometimes dangerous but so are lots of other jobs. Nobody forces me to do this.[24]

For most war correspondents, then, the impulse is to play down the dangers and get on with the job. American reporter Siobhan Darrow admits to an 'addiction to danger', an impulse among war reporters to 'push themselves to the limit of risk and endurance.' Echoing Lindsey Hilsum's disdain for the journalism safety culture, she reveals that 'lots of hardened journalists would never be caught dead in a flak-jacket, the wartime equivalent of a seat belt' (2000, p. 73). So what sort of journalist wants to become part of the 'luckless tribe'? What motivates them to take and accept these obvious risks?

MOTIVATION

At a very basic level, the job may satisfy the 'terrible show-off' in a journalist.[25] Some reporters talk about war reporting as 'something in our background, in our childhood, in our upbringing, which makes us feel slightly deficient somewhere, and makes us want to do something where we get noticed', and that require one 'to be tenacious, tenacious, tenacious to the point of being insufferable, being obsequious, being an absolute bastard' in order to get the story ahead of the competition.[26] For many reporters, most of them men, modern warfare provides the ultimate media spectacle and may even fulfill their dearest *Boy's Own* fantasies. A BBC defence correspondent remembers always being 'a complete fanatic about aircraft, military aircraft in particular.'[27] Richard Dowden of *The Independent* confesses to fascination as well as fear and revulsion: 'Half of me never wants to do anything like that ever again, and another part of me says, "Where's the next one? That was great!"'[28] Tony Clifton, editor of *Newsweek*, compares the Gulf War with sex: it was 'a hell of a lot of foreplay and one final orgasm that lasted eight and a half seconds.' And on a more psychedelic plane, Robert Fox of the *Daily Telegraph*, 'a kid of the sixties...brought up on Camus and the existen-tialists', admits to 'a mad, depersonalised' sense of excitement; it was 'the lunatic on the edge...the moment when things come together.'[29]

On one of his first assignments, reporting the civil war in El Salvador in the 1980s, the BBC's Jeremy Bowen was caught up in a crossfire and clearly remembers the mix of fear and exhilaration he felt afterwards:

It was hard to believe the bullets were real, even though...civilians, government soldiers and guerilla fighters were dying. Then, when it was over and I got through it and I wasn't dead, it was fantastically exciting. That was the first big burst of the war drug, pulling me towards addiction. It was also frightening, but to start with anyway, you forget the fear and remember the excitement. I liked it. It was an action movie and I was in it. (2006, p. 45)

This idea of the danger and excitement of war as an addiction comes up time and again when war reporters talk about their experiences. 'War is like hard drug abuse or a fickle lover', writes Anthony Lloyd, 'an apparently contradictory bolt of compulsion, agony and ecstasy that draws you back in the face of better judgment time and time again' (1999, p. 310). Alex Thomson of Channel 4 News talks of 'an enormous drive and an enormous excitement and an enormous addiction' to the job. It was the excitement and glamour that first caught his attention when watching the news as a child:

I watched people do it on TV and I thought, 'Jesus! That looks quite fun!' I mean really if I'm honest with you that is part of the motivation. I think that anyone who doesn't say that being a war correspondent is a glamorous way of making a living is bull-shitting you because it is and I'm no different from the person out there. You travel to interesting, different places. You are there at moments of history... . [It] is a fantastic opportunity, purely selfishly, leaving the job aside, to be at, to be present where things are happening.[30]

Mike Nicholson reported up to 16 wars in his career as a correspondent for Independent Television News (ITN). He says that it is 'not that you like going to war, though I do; it's the promise of excitement and...the knowledge and the certainty of getting all the big stories.' For him, the excitement and glamour are the driving motivations:

Obviously, travel is the main attraction. [...] I used to sit there [as a cub reporter] and see these guys going off to Africa or Australia, going off to all these wars and felt very jealous about it as every young blood did and probably still does. [...] I wanted to do all the exciting things I was watching other people do and eventually, and by luck really, it's usually luck, I was given the chance to [report] the Nigerian civil war. And once it's in the blood it's very hard to get rid of... . If a company spends a lot of money sending you to foreign places a long way away you can be guaranteed it's going to get pretty prominent place in the running order. So it's also that. You're going to get high profile. There's that glamour attached to being a foreign correspondent, a roving correspondent, or a fireman war correspondent.[31]

The abiding attraction for him, however, is a fascination with war:

I like going to war and you have to be very honest about it...which makes you sound rather inhuman; in fact you *do* sound inhuman... And you have to be honest... I did get quite a thrill from being under fire, being with soldiers, watching the fighting. It's a very exciting, exhilarating existence and I'd be dishonest if I didn't admit it.[32]

This is not to argue that all foreign or war correspondents are thrill seekers, 'parachutists' or 'ambulance chasers' after the quick scoop and then off to the next one. Talk to other war reporters at length and they reveal the conflicts and dilemmas that constantly haunt their efforts to 'get the story' more than their colleagues on political or diplomatic beats. Scratch the surface values of excitement, glamour, and even danger, and one reveals deeper motivations and even misgivings. Michael Herr writes that the glamour of being a war reporter in Vietnam may have been 'empty and lunatic but there were times when it was all you had, a benign infection that ravaged all but your worst fears and deepest depressions' (1978, p. 152). As well as 'curiosity and the desire to tell a story', Christiane Amanpour of CNN talks of being 'further motivated by a deep conviction that the stories I cover are important and absolutely need to be told...stories such as the genocide in Bosnia and Rwanda.'[33] The BBC's World Affairs editor, John Simpson, concedes the importance of a 'serious moral purpose' in one's work as a journalist but insists that he does not see himself 'as being on any kind of crusade to change the world.' The ultimate litmus test for him is telling the story and getting behind the news to look at 'what is really going on...the sort of underside of the whole thing, the submerged realities.' He does not so much go for the breaking news as for 'the sort of grander, broader stories and also to be the sweeper-up who tells you what's happened in places that you might think have dropped out of public attention.'[34]

Former war reporter, Maggie O'Kane, saw more to her job than dodging 1000 lb bombs on the Grozny road and living to tell the tale. 'I think in the beginning', she says, 'it was an exciting way to make a living and a very adventurous way to make a living [but] I suppose as I got more into it I began to believe and still believe that you can make a difference.'[35] The desire to 'make a difference', however, is sometimes tempered by a certain battle weariness, especially among more experienced correspondents. Anthony Lawrence (1972) reflects with some disillusionment on what the job of 'foreign correspondent' really added up to in the end:

> The rewards are elusive and related to memories. You had a chance to travel to strange places and sometimes have a seat booked in the spectator stands of great events...Then you remember fragments of talk in the small hours...long, deceitful news conferences, the baking concrete of innumerable airports, enormous bedrooms in old hotels; the jungle. (p. 9)

Reflecting on his reporting of the atom bomb tests on Bikini Atoll in 1947, James Cameron writes of how: 'One had tried; one had travelled 22,000 miles, one had stewed and steamed, one had fought for the words against the clock. But one was only a reporter, not a historian; one had suffered from the occupational delusion of importance. At home nobody gave a damn' (1967, p. 67). Mike Nicholson looks back on his long career and measures the ideals of his job against its potential to change things:

> I actually believe that we are one of the four cornerstones of democracy. It stands to reason. If we weren't here making public some of the misdemeanours of government...and all the other rottennesses in society, who would know about it? [...] One begins one's career as a young man really in a kind of cavalier fashion but underlying all that is a belief that your pen, your camera, your writing can help change the way the world is. By making it public, by showing suffering, by showing war, by showing corruption, by showing misdemeanour... you're going to help change it. But when the time comes to hang up your boots as I'm just about doing you realise that you've done very little to change the world. All you've really done is to advertise its ills. It's a very sad epitaph.[36]

A few correspondents profess utter confidence in their own convictions. Mark Urban, Diplomatic Editor for BBC *Newsnight*, professes to be guided in his work by 'Truth, the belief in the power of truth', even if that means perhaps complicating a delicate political process like the peace process in Northern Ireland or the Middle East.[37] John Pilger has long been a dissenting voice when the flags run full mast at wartime. There is no greater motivation for him than to pursue the truth and he applies two principles when reporting wars: 'to report them from the ground up, from the point of view of both civilian and combatants because most wars now are against civilians directly or indirectly', and to reveal the hidden agendas of war:

> It's a wider principle of do you report from the side of the powerful or do you report from the side of people? I think it's a choice many have to face...But I think it's essential to be with those who are either fighting the war, struggling for their lives in the war, or are victims of the war. I think the other motivation is to attempt to explain the war, to deconstruct it, to find out what the real agendas of the war are...The hidden agendas, which are really the truth of the wars, have only emerged later. That is true of all those wars. [We] found out that the Gulf War was not a war at all, it was a slaughter, and that the reporters were only playing theatrical bit parts in the slaughter, standing on top of hotel buildings, admiring the technology, or being captive members of press conferences, military people showed them video games of people being blown up on bridges...I mention all that because [revealing] that agenda...is the most important aspect of war reporting.[38]

Many of the journalists I spoke to talked about history or, as Martin Bell puts it, getting 'a front row seat in the making of history. There's nothing quite like the buzz of being there when important events are taking place.'[39] Robert Fisk of *The Independent* sees it as 'a job where we are uniquely witnesses to history', although for him history is something that should also *inform* the craft of reporting: 'One of the things I always say to some of my younger colleagues when they're going off on a story is take a history book. Don't just go there and report it as if it's a crime story. Take a history book!' When he arrived in Beirut in the 1970s to report the Middle East conflict he did so armed with a good working knowledge of the history of the area and the significance of the conflict. That has helped him to explain the reactions, responses and reflexes of the various protagonists both in his daily reporting and in his authored writing on conflict in the Middle East (Fisk, 2001 and 2006). For example, when reporting the Israel-Palestine conflict he is able to see it in a variety of historical contexts:

I was very conscious from the very start it was not just a story about Arabs and Israelis and conflict over one piece of real estate in particular, Palestine/Israel. It was also about the Jewish Holocaust in the Second World War. It was about the results of the Armenian genocide by the Turks, it was about the carving up of the Middle East by the victorious Allied powers at the end of the First World War in which my father fought, therefore had a direct connection to Sarajevo. Therefore I was aware when I went to Beirut, for example, that most of the countries which were invented or whose borders were created in the two years after the First world war, ended up with serious internal conflicts: Lebanon, Syria, Palestine, Yugoslavia, Northern Ireland and the Free State. All these borders we drew at the same time had been covered in blood. So when I started in Beirut, even though it was the height of the civil war, which was of course dramatic and so on...I knew at the start I was covering something with enormous historical perspective to it. It wasn't for me something to dip into for a few years and then go on somewhere else.[40]

A perspective such as this brings us closer to a sense of foreign and conflict reporting as part of something more idealistic and serious. Fisk talks of journalism as 'a vocation' and describes himself as 'a foreign correspondent, not a war reporter.' He eschews generalism and careerism in journalism for a lifetime of specialism. 'There's a problem', he says:

When a journalist starts to rise and he starts writing the truth, he's told that he can't see the wood for the trees. When he's there long enough to understand it, he's gone native. Well, I think both of those are rubbish. If you read up properly and start carefully you can be very good from the beginning and you can keep going. And as long as you don't ally yourself with one side or another – and my story's far too risky for any sane person to do that – I think you should stay there. I mean it's an investment for the paper. I have contacts I would never have if I started anywhere else. I understand the region, the culture and so on...I think in general it's time that correspondents thought more in terms of career in a particular location and becoming a specialist.[41]

Victoria Brittain's fascination with the Vietnam War was not just its currency as '*the* big foreign policy issue' of the times but also 'the broader issues [such as] the balance of power between third world countries [...] and the big powerful western countries.' This became the abiding specialism underpinning the rest of her reporting career. She based herself in Algiers in the 1970s, 'which at the time...was very much the centre of the third world movement – more economic equality and so on. Intellectually, it was a very important influence on the rest of the third world.' She was able to stop and look with some breadth and depth at 'the whole question of what South Africa was doing to the continent... and more interested in the other countries affected by that.' Brittain returned every year to look and see what was happening in the various countries across the continent. She was astonished that African countries were at one and the same time under-reported and misreported by the western news media, but she found them 'so fascinating I just wanted to know more and I wanted to write more so I kind of got stuck into that'. She agrees with Robert Fisk that the idea of the specialist corre-spondent has been compromised by media economics, or at least by the pretext that media organisations can no longer afford to commit area specialists to the Middle East or Africa. But she also points to 'a kind of a cultural shift', a generation gap in terms of aspirations and ambitions. Young journalists these days 'don't want to take the risk of going off and trying to hack it in some obscure place.' Instead, 'they are so aware that big careers in media now are either made in television or [writing] flashy columns about themselves because that's thought to be a very successful thing to do. I think for my generation what could possibly be duller?'[42]

The idea of the specialist correspondent sits uncomfortably with many news media who see the commercial realities of journalism impinging more and more on their ability to provide and maintain credible foreign news coverage. Alex Thomson thinks that in this respect newspapers have an advantage over television news:

Some newspapers for instance may send their...specialist[s] to those conflicts – he or she will speak the language and be very well versed in the politics and the history and traditions of the place. But of course no television company except possibly the BBC can afford that. So I think in terms of the heavy broadsheet newspaper, there *is* a pool of resources there for in-depth coverage and they undoubtedly have more time. They're like me, they've got the luxury of only one deadline a day.[43]

The importance of a good relationship between editor and war correspondent recalls the excellent friendship between William Howard Russell and John Delane, his editor at *The Times*. Throughout the Crimean War, Delane supported Russell and protected him from political and military pressures to have him recalled. It was a solid relationship of mutual trust in a powerful institution. In her time as foreign desk editor for the *Guardian*, Victoria Brittain would assume a 'facilitator' role – standing by her correspondents, fighting their corner in the newsroom and taking the chill off the 'cold calculations' that editors make about budgets and resources. In an interview for the first edition of this book, she said:

I love the correspondents. The best part of my day is talking to the correspondents and trying to work out with them what stories they want to do, how best we can place them in the paper, whether we should be concentrating more on this, more on that and so on...But of course above me is a whole layer of editors who are only interested as you say in budgets and what it's going to cost and do we really need a man in Harare, those sort of preoccupations...It's a very lonely business being a foreign correspondent and unless you're incredibly self-sufficient you need a friendly, understanding presence back at base to help you do those things and I hope that's what I do for a lot of people. It's certainly what I try to do.[44]

Robert Fisk talks of his relationship with his editor at *The Independent* and how important it is to have his friendship and trust:

Mine is my friend. I go to see him, I talk to him on the phone, I write to him...The editor must trust you. Don't fight your editor...We also have a lot of readers unprompted who write to the editor saying they want to read Bob Fisk. That helps too. It's very important.

He thinks that is why readers matter, too, but the commercial pressures which *The Independent* has faced throughout its short existence, including takeovers and revamps, provides a salutary lesson that the best newspapers with the best specialist correspondents and columnists cannot take reader loyalty for granted:

> When Murdoch deliberately [lowered] the price of *The Times* using money from elsewhere in his conglomerate, his attempt was to put us out of business. We were selling at 50p so he went down to 30 or 20. And we believed that our readers were loyal. Great readers of *The Independent*! And in one week we lost 20 per cent of them. Our loyal readers decided they wanted to pay 20p and not 50p. Big problem. And you can say we got this right and we got that right, and we tell the truth and we don't go along with the NATO briefings. They left and we still haven't got most of them back because they want a cheaper paper.[45]

And, as Nik Gowing points out, sending the best roving correspondent on a temporary assignment somewhere on the other side of the world 'happens less and less in some ways because more information is coming in more quickly from more parts of the world than ever before from people who are based in the region, and therefore you've got to work out where the value-added is [in] sending a correspondent and that's a cold calculation that only editors can take.'[46] Commercial realities such as these rather put into perspective the glamour and excitement of war reporting, and perhaps herald a news future in which instead of sending their best writers and reporters to Libya, Gaza or Syria, news organisations will choose to graze on various inflows of information, from the news agencies, satellite feeds and social media. Is it possible, then, that we are seeing the end of a tradition of war reporting, a sense and sensibility among some correspondents today that they are part of a line going back to William Howard Russell, Archibald Forbes or Richard Harding Davis?

TRADITION

The American journalist Walter Cronkite writes that 'nothing in the field of journalism is more glamorous than being a war correspondent' and recalls 'the model of the newspaper reporter dashing from one scene of action to the next, press badge tucked into his hatband, notebook in hand. His mandatory costume reeks of wartime experience – the trench coat with its vestigial epaulets' (Stenbuck, 1995, p. viii). This is a rather outdated model of the war correspondent at a time when some of the highest paid, highest profile war correspondents have been women such as Christiane Amanpour (CNN), Kate Adie (BBC) or Maggie O'Kane (*Guardian*). So when the war reporter John Burrowes (1984) dedicates his memoirs 'To reporters everywhere – and the women who have to suffer them', he rather misses the point. There is no doubting that the glamour and excitement of the job have attracted many to the ranks of the 'luckless tribe', regardless of gender or risk perception. Yet, among some older, more experienced war correspondents, there is a palpable sense also of being part of a tribe with a tradition and a history going back more than 160 years to their 'miserable parent', William Howard Russell.

Alan Hankinson refers to,

the sharpness of [Russell's] observation, an appraising intelligence which enabled him to find the truth in a welter of conflicting evidence, his broad historical sense of the struggle and the political implications of the events he had witnessed, the courage with which he set down his impressions and judgements. (1982, p. 269)

Unlike many of his journalist colleagues of the day, Russell was 'serious, not superficial...an observer of events, not a participant'. Opinionated but not prejudiced,

[his] judgements sprang from two strong and complimentary qualities: a realistic view, based on his reading of history and his maturing experience, of the way men and armies and nations behave in moments of stress; and high standards of what constituted decent, civilised, humane conduct. (Ibid.)

This was the tradition many think Russell set down – 'the uncompromising quest for the truth, and the belief that society can only hope to be just and healthy if it is blessed with an independent and critical and courageous press' (ibid., p. 270).

John Simpson is the ultimate public-service news journalist and John Pilger the radical independent, yet both place themselves in the tradition of Russell and they do so with considerable admiration. Pilger boasts as a 'prize possession' a copy of the first edition of Russell's *War Diaries*. Russell was, for Pilger and many others, *the* war correspondent, the one who 'stuck to his principles of reporting the blunders and the disasters, everything he saw and everything he knew to be true, without fear or favour.'[47] Simpson looks at Russell's reporting in the Crimea as,

the ultimate that you can do to cut through the [...] mystification that any government then or now tends to try to build up around its activities and tell what's really going on. He cut through all the 'gallantry of war' aspect of it, the idea that because the British government was doing something it must be [getting] done in a sensible and rational and good way, and he showed people what the reality was. I don't think there's anything better than that.[48]

In a study of the 'warcos', the war correspondents who reported on the Second World War, Collier mentions that even then reporters clung to an abiding image of the war correspondent as 'intrepid individualist, long on courage and short on introspection', an image very much inspired by correspondents like Russell and Richard Harding Davis: 'Such shining examples, along with hazy adolescent memories of Tennyson's *Charge of the Light Brigade* and Kipling's *Barrack Room Ballads*, had forged the war correspondent of 1939' (Collier, 1989, p. 20).

But there are other sources of inspiration. For former BBC journalist Mark Laity, it is British public service broadcast journalism – 'the style, the careful authoritative style, unsensational, concerned, ...just getting it right and eschewing bells and whistles.' Significantly for him, its origins lie in the reporting of the Second World War; all the BBC's war reporters inspired him in his work as the corporation's defence correspondent in the 1990s.[49] Martin Bell looks first to George Orwell whose journalism was characterised 'by plain speaking, by eye-witness and not being blinded by preconceptions' but he also speaks of his admiration for James Cameron.[50] Lindsey Hilsum believes that most reporters like her 'would want to be in the same tradition as Cameron and Martha Gellhorn...because those are journalists who are honourable, those are journalists who wrote incredibly well and were able to convey things' not normally conveyed by journalists in the warzones of today.[51] Cameron's name occurred almost as often as Russell in my interviews for this book. John Pilger refers back to Cameron's attempts to report the Vietnam War from the North, funding the assignment from his own pocket only to meet with opposition not from the frontline censors but from editors and producers within the BBC who refused to use his material. In the way he went about getting that footage and struggling to have it aired, Cameron demonstrated, 'All the initiative and curiosity and passion and all those things that make up a good maverick reporter.' It is this determination that inspires Pilger and reminds him when he watches journalists accept the propaganda line from Downing Street or the White House that 'it needn't be like this.'[52]

Other journalists are rather more reticent when talking about a specific tradition of war reporting and hesitate to single out particular journalists who have inspired them. They prefer to talk in terms of simply reporting and explaining the story and hoping, like John Simpson and Victoria Brittain, that as a result people will know more about the war in Afghanistan or Syria. Brittain stresses a 'tradition in which the reporter is of absolutely no importance [where] you certainly wouldn't use the word "I" or anything like that; you're kind of a transmission vehicle.' Nowadays, she thinks, 'there's a kind of a thing about reporters as stars and I'm not that, I'm not that tradition.'[53] Maggie O'Kane confesses some ambivalence about the idea of working within a tradition, 'because in a way I think a lot of the journalism...was very inhumane. A lot of the war correspondents were very much part of a particular class and a particular sex and were introduced to the war through positions within the army and military rank. So the accessibility to the story and the way that they did it was something I certainly didn't aspire to emulate because it didn't sound very exciting really.'[54]

There is a possible generation gap here that might even mark the end of tradition in war reporting in the face of new political and commercial realities in journalism. Alex Thomson talks not of some abstract notion of tradition, but of:

a deep-seated belief [that] any government that is talking to you is likely to be lying to you and that the establishment, the received view, is likely to be a bigger lie. And I think that is true in terms of war as in terms of many other things. Politics, I know, is all we've got but I certainly know that...politicians are not to be trusted, least of all when they're getting involved in the business of killing people.[55]

Mike Nicholson wishes he could look to the work of Richard Dimbleby and James Cameron and say he was part of that tradition but he cannot because, unlike newspaper reporting, television, the medium in which he has always reported, has developed beyond tradition in terms of technology and professional practice:

> We have to do things that newspaper reporters aren't often called upon to do. They don't need to be at the frontline. Because we stand alongside a camera, we always have to be where it's happening, or at least we have to try to be where it's happening, whereas newspaper reporters can actually sit in a bar, can't they, and pick up gossip. They can go to the AP line, they can talk to us; there's so much the newspaperman can do that we can't do. We simply have to be there with our lens.[56]

Nik Gowing agrees with much of this and argues that the newspaper reporting style of James Cameron is impossible for the broadcast journalist today because the technology and the immediacy makes the reporter instantly accountable:

> What you say is heard by people, seen by people, and in a transparent environment they know very quickly if you're not telling the truth, if you're being too florid in your language, you know, embellishing it because it sounds good.[57]

CONCLUDING REMARKS

War correspondents talk readily and easily about the motives and impulses that drive them to take so many obvious risks to report from the world's warzones; and what fascinates and excites them about what they see as a job or even a vocation. Few, if any, think about it as a 'career'. There seems to be less certainty about the notion of following in tradition, especially among younger journalists, and certainly among young broadcast journalists who see war reporting as no different than other journalism beats. It is simply about 'reporting the facts' and 'telling the story' as best and as honestly as they can. All this is very interesting and provides a good insight into the psyche of the war reporter. Yet in some ways, it is much too easy. Common to most memoirs by or interviews with contemporary war reporters is a self-conscious sense of glamour, offset by world-weary cynicism or self-deprecating humour. So it is important to handle their reflections with care and put them into some sort of critical perspective. In his polemical and sometimes savage critique of war reporting, Mick Hume attacks the self-regarding news articles and television documentaries that focus on the trials and tribulations of the war reporter-as-martyr (1997, pp. 18–19). He has a point. The BBC, for example, has broadcast special 45-minute programmes looking back at the work of reporters in the first Gulf War (*Tales from the Gulf*, BBC2, 1991) and the Bosnian civil war (*Tales from Sarajevo*, BBC2, 1993). And shortly after the Iraq War in 2003, both the BBC and Channel 4 aired programmes on the conflict from the perspective of a few of the hundreds of international journalists who covered the conflict.[58] It is much less common to read or watch insider stories about lobby correspondents at Westminster, and I have been unable to find a written memoir or television documentary anywhere that lays bare the challenges of the farming correspondent. Yet, for Hume, there is more to this than just good copy or good television. There is an ideological message in these kinds of news features and programmes that taps into our human curiosity about anything dramatic, dangerous and heroic. It acts as a catharsis, reassuring us in our helplessness that some will take risks on our behalf to bring the story home in a way that is comfortable, that does not disturb our moral universe. It is, in short, what Hume calls 'a twisted sort of therapy' – for the reporter and, by extension, for us (1997, pp. 17–21).

Hume's critique of the culture and psyche of today's war reporter comes as part of a focused attack on the idea of 'committed journalism' in the war zone or, as the BBC journalist Martin Bell put it while reporting the Bosnian civil war in the 1990s, 'the journalism of attachment'. This is the idea that in the face of atrocity or even genocide, the practice of journalistic objectivity and impartiality can get in the way of making an ethical, moral judgement on what is right or wrong, good or evil, in the conduct of war. The following chapter puts the debate into historical perspective and considers the various implications and difficulties of the journalism of attachment in the war zone.

3

Journalism, Objectivity and War

Strange as it may seem, a war correspondent is often good at what he
does because of a certain detachment. I mean, a journalist is not an
academic. He is a dilettante by definition.

Andrei Babitsky, Russian war correspondent[1]

The existence or possibility of objectivity and impartiality in journalism
has long been debated, but it seems to have most pressing relevance
in the reporting of war and conflict. Amid the propaganda and the
censorship, war reporters have had to don their metaphorical helmet and
flak jacket and protest their integrity as loudly as possible. So when the
BBC reporter Martin Bell raised his head above the parapet during the
Bosnian civil war (1992–95) and proclaimed that he could no longer be
impartial in the face of the daily atrocities of that conflict, he ignited a
heated and acrimonious public debate. His advocacy of what he called a
'journalism of attachment' placed emphasis on the moral duty to tell the
truth, however inconvenient, over and above the professional obligation
to be impartial (see Bell, 1998). The proposition attracted criticism from
all quarters, not least from some of his colleagues in Bosnia; but the most
sustained and withering critique came from Mick Hume, editor of the
Living Marxism magazine. For him, the journalism of attachment was
both a 'twisted sort of therapy' for reporters like Bell and 'a menace to
good journalism' (Hume, 1997).

This chapter will consider the debate in more detail later and offer
some explanation of why it emerged as it did. It will conclude with a
discussion of the flip side of the debate: the assumption of impartiality
in the reporting of grossly asymmetrical conflicts such as that between
Israel and the Palestinians. It is important first, though, to look at some
historical precedents and understand that what Martin Bell advocated in
Bosnia was nothing new.

THE COMMITTED WAR CORRESPONDENT:
HISTORICAL PRECEDENTS

There are many instances in history of war correspondents crossing the line between journalism and combat by taking part in the fighting they were there to report or setting themselves up as military or political advisors. During the Mexican War (1846–48), the newspaper reporter and owner George Wilkins Kendall rode with the Texan Rangers as both journalist and combatant. This dual role and the intelligence he drew from it gave him a decisive edge over his competitors (Lande, 1996, p. 51) but from a military point of view it set an unhealthy precedent for military–press relations in wartime. Lieutenant General Lord Chelmsford, commander of British forces in the Anglo–Zulu War (1879), complained bitterly about correspondents who were 'always ready without sufficient data for their guidance to express their opinions on every conceivable military subject ex cathedra' (Laband and Knight, 1996, p. *v*). During the Sioux Uprising in America (the Ghost Dance War, 1890), the *Chicago Inter Ocean* declared that 'the war correspondent ever was the most war-like personage [and] there is the stuff that makes a good brigadier in most good war correspondents' (Kolbenschlag, 1990, p. 41). As if to prove the point, the *Nebraska State Journal* declared its reporter, William Kelley, to be the 'champion Indian fighter among war correspondents' after he picked up a rifle from a dead union soldier and killed two Sioux warriors (ibid., p. 69). In the Spanish–American War (1898), journalists spied for the US army and navy, took part in combat operations, assumed quasi-officer roles and even hoisted the first flags to claim Cuba as part of America (Brown, 1967, p. *vii*). Richard Harding Davis was one of the most famous reporters of the war and saw no conflict of interest between reporting the war as a professional journalist and fighting it as a patriotic citizen. Much in the style of George Kendall, he rode with Theodore Roosevelt's Rough Riders and paid tribute to other American journalists for their part in the war, most notably for their 'reconnoitring, scouting, and fighting' (Lande, 1996, p. 165).

The trend for this kind of adventurism in war reporting continued well into the twentieth century. With the retreat of the German army in Europe in the Second World War, armed journalists accepted surrenders in what Richard Johnston called 'a manhunt with notebooks and cameras'

(Collier, 1989, pp. 193). Evelyn Irons of the *London Evening Standard*, for example, arrived in a small Bavarian village with three other reporters – all armed with revolvers – and apparently forced its surrender; while Ernest Hemingway packed a brace of pistols in breach both of army rules and of the Geneva Conventions (ibid.). Journalists had the honorary rank of captain and they could dress accordingly, but unless they actually enlisted they were still civilian and were not permitted to carry a weapon. Peter Arnett (1996) recalls his pistol-packing days reporting the Vietnam War when,

> ...it was tempting to play soldier. In the early years I carried a large revolver that I lovingly polished while relishing the approval of the GIs I was covering. I never did fire that pistol...and eventually threw it away while running for dear life...during a Vietcong rocket attack.

And in the wake of the Soviet invasion of Afghanistan in 1979, journalists such as Columbia Broadcasting System (CBS) reporter Kurt Lohbeck were roundly criticised from within their profession for associating themselves too closely with the Mujahideen rebels (Williams Walsh, 1990). In fact, it was suspected that Lohbeck was helping the rebels with their public relations and building contacts with western media outlets and arms dealers. Lohbeck had a rather murky career as a political lobbyist and journalist, but CBS were happy to hire him without vetting him because he came cheap – keeping a staff reporter in the region would cost the network anything up to US$200,000 per year – and because he boasted knowledge of the region and contacts with the Mujahideen (ibid., p. 28). He insisted that he was a reporter, not 'a player', but found it difficult to shake the allegations that he was 'a partisan in a holy war' (ibid., p. 36).

But it is the Spanish Civil War (1936–39) that puts into sharpest perspective the debate Martin Bell provoked in Bosnia. This was a conflict of stark ideological and political positions that presaged not only imminent world war but also the Cold War that followed. The correspondents who went to report it from Europe and North America were marked out by their partisanship in favour of one side or the other. Reporting on the Republican side were Claude Cockburn, Arthur Koestler, Ernest Hemingway, Herbert Matthews and Martha Gellhorn, 'at her happiest striding out alone on a journalist's cause' such as Spain

35

(Shakespeare, 1998, p. 225). Kim Philby reported for *The Times* on the Nationalist side but was also working as a Soviet spy (Knightley, 2004, p. 210). One of the most celebrated American journalists of the Spanish Civil War was Herbert Matthews. He recalled later what was behind this trend for committed journalism at the front in Spain:

> All of us who lived the Spanish Civil War felt deeply emotional about it...I always felt the falseness and hypocrisy of those who claimed to be unbiased, and the foolish, if not the rank stupidity of editors and readers who demand objectivity or impartiality of correspondents writing about the war... [In] condemning bias one rejects the only factors which really matter – honesty, understanding and thoroughness. A reader has the right to ask for all the facts; he has no right to ask that a journalist or historian agree with him. (Ibid., pp. 210–11; see also Matthews, 1971)

However, Philip Knightley argues that some correspondents in Spain forgot about the importance of facts altogether and became nothing more than propaganda mouthpieces for one side or the other. It is alleged, for example, that Arthur Koestler, of the *London News Chronicle*, and Claude Cockburn of *The Week* and the *Daily Worker*, mixed propaganda with fact and were not averse to inventing stories to further the Republican cause, which they championed with great passion as Communists first and reporters second. Knightley objects not so much to their partisanship as to the assumption that newspaper readers had no right to the truth if the truth damaged the cause of right against wrong (ibid., p. 213). Christopher Holme (1995) argues that with so much propaganda issuing forth from Spain, it was 'the straightforward news reporting' of correspondents such as Hugh Christopher Holme (Reuters), Noel Monks (*Daily Express*) and George Steer (*The Times*) that provoked the greatest emotional responses to outrages such as the German bombing of Guernica on 26 April 1937 (p. 47).

But there were early attempts to apply some notion of objectivity into war reporting. An early pioneer of the approach was James Gordon Bennett, publisher of the *New York Herald*, who put the emphasis of coverage on reporting and gathering facts and information rather than sensationalism and propaganda. This, he thought, distinguished the *Herald* in its coverage of such events as the Canadian Revolution in 1837.

The political sympathies of his reporters were their own, he said, but 'their facts belong to history' (Bjork, 1994, p. 857). James R. Gilmore, in his introduction to the collected letters of Charles Page, the famous American Civil War reporter, wrote that 'in the thick of the fight, where sabres clash, and minieballs whistle', or from a vantage point of 'a friendly tree, or on some commanding hill', the reporter could observe events first hand and achieve ultimate objectivity where even historians failed, dependent as they were on secondary sources. The reporter had only to 'be cool, truthful, and intrepid' to provide the readers with 'a living photograph of the tremendous conflict' (Page, 1898, p. *vii*).

'An attitude of clarity': journalism and historiography

This comparison between journalists and historians is a persistent theme in discussions of objectivity. Like history, journalistic objectivity can be discussed in terms of either pure method or, as Pierre Vilar puts it, 'an attitude of clarity'. Vilar was writing here about historiography, the method and the practice of history, but it could just as well apply to journalism. 'Can one be objective in writing contemporary history?' he asked:

> Differences among historians are to be found in their attitudes. There is a dishonest attitude: to call oneself objective, while knowing oneself to be partisan; there is the blind attitude: to be partisan while believing oneself to be objective; and then there is the attitude of clarity: to state one's position, while believing firmly that thorough analysis is the best way to buttress that position. It is pejorative to say of a work of history that it is a plea for a cause. Yet a good plea made by a good lawyer and for a worthy cause can become a model to the historian. (Southworth, 1977, p. *xvi*)

In *What is History?*, E. H. Carr considers R. G. Collingwood's philosophy of history as a model of development. This includes a number of principal axioms: that 'the facts of history never come to us "pure" [but] are always refracted through the mind of the recorder', so we must question the historian's position as much as the facts he or she presents (1986, p. 16); that the historian requires 'imaginative understanding for the minds of the people with whom [one] is dealing' as opposed to 'sympathy', which implies partiality (ibid., p. 18); that 'we can view the past, and achieve our understanding of the past, only through the eyes of the present'; that the very vocabulary we use to describe the great events of the past – 'democracy, empire, war, revolution' – have undeniable contemporary resonance from which we cannot escape (ibid., p. 19). 'The function of the past', according to Collingwood's idea of history, 'is neither to love the past nor to emancipate [oneself] from the past, but to master and understand it as the key to the understanding of the present' (ibid., p. 20).

However, Carr sees several dangers in adopting such a view. It encourages the belief that the historian does not require objectivity at all, that it is all subjective interpretation: ergo, 'history is what the historian makes' of it. This is 'a purely pragmatic (Nietzschean) view of the facts... that the criterion of a right interpretation is its suitability to some present purpose'. In other words, 'the facts of history are nothing, interpretation is everything' (ibid., p. 20ff). Carr believed the contrary, that objectivity was possible in history and that to call an historian objective meant two things: firstly, that one 'has a capacity to rise above the limited vision of [one's] own situation in society and in history'; and secondly, that one 'has the capacity to project [one's] vision into the future in such a way as to give [one] a more profound and more lasting insight into the past than can be attained by those...whose outlook is entirely bounded by their own immediate situation...The historian of the past can make an approach towards objectivity only as he approaches towards the under-standing of the future' (ibid., p. 117–18).

OBJECTIVITY UNDER FIRE

Objectivity in journalism has come under serious critique from academics (Glasgow University Media Group, 1976; Lichtenberg, 1996; Streckfuss, 1990; Parenti, 1993). They suggest in various ways that the news media do not simply report and reflect our social world but that they more or less play an active part in shaping, even constructing it; that they represent sectional interests rather than society as a whole.[2] When these criticisms are leveled at journalists, their traditional defence is their practice of objectivity but what does it mean to be objective in journalism in the first place? According to Michael Schudson (1978), objectivity is based on the assumption that a series of 'facts' or truth claims about the world can be validated by the rules and procedures of a professional community. The distortions and biases, the subjective value judgements of the individual or of particular interest groups, are filtered out so that among journalists at any rate, 'The belief in objectivity is a faith in "facts", a distrust of "values", and a commitment to their segregation' (p. 6). Gaye Tuchman refers to this method as 'a strategic ritual', a method of news-gathering and reporting that protects the journalist from charges of bias or libel (1972, p. 661ff).

Radical critiques measure journalistic claims to objectivity against analyses of how the news media produce and represent their version of reality according to sectional interests. Bias is not in the eye of the beholder but is structured within the entire news process; the news filters and constructs reality according to a dominant or institutional ideology (Glasgow University Media Group, 1976). 'What passes for objectivity', for American scholar Michael Parenti, 'is the acceptance of a social reality shaped by the dominant forces of society – without any critical examination of that reality's hidden agendas, its class interests, and its ideological biases' (1993, p. 52). It is the difference respectively between the journalist as the professional, instutionalised reporter and the journalist as the partial eyewitness and writer. John Pilger points to the transparency of this ideology of professionalism, especially in a public service broadcaster like the BBC whose coverage of domestic and foreign crises has demonstrated its true agenda and its true allegiances:

> These people waffle on about objectivity as if by joining that institution or any institution they suddenly rise to this Nirvana where they can consider all points of view and produce something in five minutes. It's nonsense and it's made into nonsense because the moment there's any kind of pressure on the establishment you find reporters coming clean, as they did after the Falklands. They were very truculent: 'These were our people, our side. And now we'll get back to being objective'. It's the same with the term 'balance'. I mean censorship for me always works by omission. That's the most virulent censorship and what we have is an enormous imbalance one way, ...the accredited point of view, the sort of consensus point of view which has nothing to do with objectivity, nothing to do with impartiality and very little to do with the truth.[3]

The pressure to pursue objectivity in reporting has had serious consequences for journalism as a form of factual writing. James Cameron thought that 'objectivity in some circumstances is both meaningless and impossible.' He could not see 'how a reporter attempting to define a situation involving some sort of ethical conflict can do it with sufficient demonstrable neutrality to fulfil some arbitrary concept of "objectivity".' This was not the acid test for Cameron who 'always tended to argue that objectivity was of less importance than the truth, and that the reporter whose technique was informed by no opinion lacked a very serious dimension' (1967, p. 72). There are, however, alternative forms of journalism that subvert the very notion of objectivity: the 'New Journalism' of the 1960s and what has been called 'honest journalism', described as a compromise between the blind assumption of impartiality and ideological commitment.

War and alternative journalisms

As practiced by writers such as Hunter S. Thompson, Ryszard Kapusciniski and Joan Didion,[4] the New Journalism emerged from the counterculture of the 1960s as a rebellion against the practices of mainstream journalism. It is journalism as art, the writer's moral vision and personal perspective always to the fore. The techniques of factual journalism (the use of the passive voice, the chronicling of events, the use of interviews) are blended with those of fiction (the authorial point of view or first person narrative, the use of style and imagination). Dan Wakefield argues that such writing is imaginative 'not because the author has distorted the facts, but because [she or] he has presented them in a full, rather than a naked manner, brought out the sights, sounds, and feel surrounding these facts and connected them by comparison with other facts of history, society, and literature in an artistic manner that does not diminish but gives greater depth and dimension to the facts' (1974, p. 41; see also Glasser, 1992). The New Journalism, therefore, rejects the notion of objectivity altogether and embraces subjectivity in its represen- tation of reality and, as Hollowell puts it, serves 'the function of fiction' by illuminating 'the ethical dilemmas of our time' (1977, p. 11).

Compare, for example, the ways in which Didion and Kapuscinski write about the nature of fear in a conflict situation. In her book, *Salvador* (1983), Didion reflects on the 'mechanism of terror' by which right-wing death squads subjugated El Salvador since the beginnings of the civil war there in 1979. Here she writes about her immediate impressions of the country when she arrived for the first time and took a taxi from the airport to the capital, San Salvador:

> Terror is the given of the place. Black-and-white police cars cruise in pairs, each with the barrel of a rifle extruding from an open window. Roadblocks materialise at random, soldiers fanning out from trucks and taking positions, fingers always on triggers, safeties clicking on and off. Aim is taken as if to pass the time. Every morning *El Diario de Hoy* and *La Prensa* carry cautionary stories...A mother and her two sons hacked to death in their beds by eight *desconocidos*, unknown men...the unidentified body of a young man, strangled, found on the shoulder of a road...the unidentified bodies of three young men, found on another road, their faces partially destroyed by bayonets, one face carved to represent a cross...The dead and pieces of the dead turn up in El Salvador everywhere, every day, as taken for granted as in a nightmare, or a horror movie...Bodies turn up in the brush of vacant lots, in the garbage thrown down ravines in the richest districts, in public rest rooms, in bus stations. (1983, pp. 14–15, 19)

Fear, in Didion's account of El Salvador, is a reign of terror, a 'given of the place.' But the late Polish journalist Kapuscinski saw it differently. His book, *Shah of Shahs* (1982), on the fall of the Shah of Iran to the Islamic revolution in 1979, explores the underlying impulses and dynamics that make a revolution and reveals fear as a voracious monster that must be slain if revolution is possible:

> Fear: a predatory, voracious animal living inside us. It does not let us forget it's there. It keeps eating at us and twisting our guts. It demands food all the time, and we see that it gets the choicest delicacies. Its preferred fare is dismal gossip, bad news, panicky thoughts, nightmare images. From a thousand pieces of gossip, portents, ideas, we always cull the worst ones – the ones that fear likes best. Anything to satisfy the monster and set it at ease...All books about all revolutions begin with a chapter that describes the decay of tottering authority or the misery and sufferings of the people. They should begin with a psychological chapter, one that shows how a harassed, terrified man suddenly

breaks his terror, stops being afraid. This unusual process, sometimes accomplished in an instant like a shock or a lustration, demands illuminating. Man gets rid of fear and feels free. Without that there would be no revolution. (pp. 110–11)

In Didion, fear defeats; in Kapuscinski, fear is defeated. Both, however, reject the constraints of the 'disciplined' and 'objective' report and seek truth and revelation in the subjective, the meditative. Taken several steps further, the Russian journalist, Artyom Borovyik (1990), seeks his truth about the war in Afghanistan in more surreal terms:

One time I woke from a nightmare in a cold sweat. In my dream I'd seen a field strewn with corpses. Even awake, I could smell the vivid violet-like odor of carrion. In the morning, I learned that my refrigerator was broken. It was shaking feverishly (it was afraid too, the bastard) in a gigantic pool of blood. The blood was still oozing out of the freezer, which my predecessor had packed tight with meat. Despite all my efforts to scrape the linoleum clean, the large bloodstain had remained on the floor ever since. Every time I saw the bloodstain it reminded me of the dream, as did the war itself – a running, real-life nightmare. To find out about the meaning of my nightmare, I once borrowed a dictionary of dreams from an acquaintance, but apparently no one else had ever dreamed such vileness. (p. 110)

It was Kapuscinski, however, who revealed the deeper, broader picture, and like all great writers he forged his own unique style. He did not assume absolute truth or prescribe a moral course but, as James Aucoin (2001) puts it, he took you there, showed you an incomplete picture and then challenged you to find the missing pieces. He implicitly passed responsibility on to the reader. It was not conventional, objective journalism, and it was not the journalism of attachment, but perhaps it was better journalism for that. This is close to the idea of 'honest journalism' in conventional reporting, whereby the journalist admits not just to the difficulties of objectivity, but to the constructed nature of journalism as a form. In his study of the US press corps in El Salvador during some of the worst years of its civil war in the 1980s, Mark Pedelty highlights a key difference between American and Salvadoran journalists in how they saw their job. The Americans insisted that they 'report' news as fact; the

Salvadorans talked in terms of 'making' news. The Americans adhered to notions of 'objectivity', while the Salvadorans thought the highest aspiration in journalism was 'honesty' (1995, p. 226–27). As Pedelty argues, the ethic of honest journalism comes somewhere between objective journalism and propaganda:

> Objective journalists deny their subjectivities, rather than acknowledge them and critically challenge them. They reduce complexities, rather than explain them. They evade contradiction, rather than letting the reader in on the inevitable doubts and difficulties encountered in any act of discovery. (ibid., p. 227)

Put in this kind of historical and theoretical context, then, the journalism of attachment debate in the 1990s resonates with the reporting of some of the major conflicts of the last two centuries, not least the Spanish Civil War, where the battle lines were most clearly drawn. When Martin Bell advocated a more committed, moral approach to reporting the conflict in Bosnia – condemning atrocity from whatever side and speaking out for the defenceless – he seemed to be invoking the spirit of Martha Gellhorn (1993) in her writings from Spain but the controversy he provoked was intense and sometimes hostile.

'A twisted sort of therapy'? The journalism of attachment debate

'I was trained in a tradition of objective and dispassionate journalism', said Bell. 'I believed in it once. I don't believe in it anymore.' Objective reporting was 'bystanders journalism' that ill-equipped the reporter for 'the challenges of the times.' While he still believed in impartiality and in the facts, he wondered about the meaning of objectivity and whether it really existed, not least in the midst of some brutal war or human calamity (1998, pp. 102–03). Bell proposed an alternative journalism, a journalism of attachment 'that cares as well as knows'. It does not take sides any more than aid agencies but it 'is aware of the moral ground on which it operates.' For him, reporting a conflict like Bosnia according to the traditional norms of objective journalism removes any sort of moral content from the story and leaves only an empty spectacle. He was by no means alone in rejecting 'bystander journalism'. The veteran ITN reporter Michael Nicholson argued that it missed the real stories of war:

All the great journalists that I've admired...were people who weren't afraid to show their emotions, afraid to show their humanity. There's this line isn't there that the reporter should stand on the sidelines. [...] They should be a spectator trying to objectively report a story without trying to get emotionally involved. Well I've always said...that you've got to get as close to a story as you can and sometimes that means becoming a casualty yourself, a physical casualty or, as I was in Sarajevo, an emotional casualty. But I see nothing wrong with that. [...] One of the things about Sarajevo was that it was one of the few instances...in which you were very much part of the scene because you couldn't get out of the place. You were under siege yourself... and therefore how could you be objective? No, I don't believe in this so-called objectivity. You can still report the facts. You can still be as close to the truth as any person can be and still show a commitment, an emotional anguish. I don't see them to be contradictory.[5]

Nicholson reported the story of the Bosnian War for the British company ITN, but decided to cross the line to become personally involved when he came across 200 orphans outside Sarajevo and helped organise a rescue mission to save them from the relentless Bosnian Serb bombardment of the city. In the end, he ended up adopting one of the children, nine-year-old Natasha Mihaljcic, and later wrote of the difficulty of staying detached and objective in this situation (Nicholson, 1993).[6]

Issues of 'objectivity' and 'attachment', and the dilemmas they present to the war correspondent, provoked some bitter exchanges of fire on the home front. The most sustained critique of the journalism of attachment has come from Mick Hume, editor of the now defunct *LM* (*Living Marxism*) magazine. His pamphlet, *Whose War Is It Anyway?* (1997), is strongly argued and stands as a coherent and significant contribution to the debate. Hume sees the trend of personalised, crusading reporting as a 'menace to good journalism – and to those whose lives it invades.' It neglects the historical and political context of the conflict it reports and portrays it instead as merely a metaphysical struggle between good and evil. Journalists who adhere to this kind of reporting set themselves up – intentionally or by default – as judge and jury. Their mission is not to explain and contextualise but to promulgate the morally correct line and this, says Hume, obscures and undermines their role as impartial and objective reporters. Hume is adamant. 'The journalism of attachment', he says, 'is self-righteous. Worse, it is repressive. Those who fall the wrong side of the line the press corps draws between Good and Evil...can expect to be on the receiving end of more than a bad press' (p. 4). Hume argues that there is nothing wrong with taking sides in a conflict. The problem is the tendency of reporters to mix emotion with the reporting of facts. When the facts are suppressed, when they do not fit the moral framework reporters have constructed for themselves, then the reader, the viewer, the listener, is the loser:

> There is a difference between taking sides and taking liberties with the facts in order to promote your favoured cause. There is a difference between expressing an opinion and presenting your personal passions and prejudices as objective reporting. And there is a difference between reporting from the midst of a conflict and writing as if you were the one at war, so that journalists and their feelings become the news. (p. 5)

Robert Fisk, special Middle East correspondent for *The Independent*, also suspects the ideological impulses of reporting steeped in moral outrage and says it is not what he understands by 'journalism':

> I can remember...in the Gulf, one of my colleagues, a normally very sensible, rational guy...became a bit odd. He said, 'We've got to smash Saddam. It's the only way to do it. The Arabs are with us!' He was cheerleading in print. It was a very serious problem and it happened in the Kosovo war. [One of the] reporters came in talking about, 'Here in Djakovice you can see evil and you can smell evil!' To which my reply is if a guy is talking like that either he needs a holiday or he should go into holy orders. This is ridiculous! This is not journalism, you know. It is the sort of journalism I'm totally against. There's another reporter who I have a lot of respect for but he's always looking into his own heart: 'Behind me, unimaginable horrors are taking place in our time.' Big problem![7]

While Martin Bell and reporters who share his general view insist that objectivity is still possible even if the reporter adopts a moral standpoint on the rights and wrongs of a conflict, Mick Hume and others argue that this is an untenable position. Stephen Ward (1998) wonders how it can inform reporting of civil conflicts like Northern Ireland or Bosnia (p. 124). It allows for no grey areas, no doubts, no skepticism and no questions. What happens when certain facts fail to fit the moral framework? What happens when the 'bad guys' tell the truth? Or when the 'good guys' tell lies?

The Bosnian War was reported as a titanic battle between good and evil in which journalists in general adopted a sustained anti-Serb narrative. Atrocity stories were reported with scant regard for their veracity – no checking, no official confirmations or denials, just the rush to instant judgement. Hume gives several examples of the Journalism of Attachment in action when reporting the war in Bosnia. Roy Gutman, reporter with *Newsday*, broke news of the existence of Serbian death camps, only to later admit that he got it wrong, that he neglected to check the story out in his rush to tell the world 'the truth' (Hume, 1997, p. 9). Media reports of the Sarajevo market place massacre of February 1994 blamed the Bosnian Serbs despite a UN investigation that pointed to Bosnian Muslim involvement, a possible attempt to attract worldwide sympathy and provoke a tough military response against the Serbs. Then there was the Bosnian Serb officer who was tried and convicted for war crimes yet allowed to tell his confession to the world's media; this was spun as testament to what the Serbs were capable of in Bosnia but much of it was unverified and based on half truths and exaggerations. In stories like these, Hume argues, 'The reporters and their editors imposed their own external agenda in deciding which facts did and did not qualify as news' (p. 11).

Maggie O'Kane filed up to 50 reports on the war in Bosnia for the *Guardian* yet only one of those tried to explain the Serbian position in the conflict. 'In retrospect', she admits, 'I could have seen more of the Serbian side...but you gravitate to where the bigger story is. We were all in Sarajevo writing human interest stories' (cited in Hume, 1997; p. 13). But O'Kane is unapologetic in her basic ethical approach to the Bosnia story and she draws a clear line between professional objectivity and telling the truth; the two in her view, and that of many of her colleagues, are not always the same:

I think the highest thing we can achieve is the truth. The truth is not objective sometimes [and] actually there's nothing very objective about a pogrom and a sweeping policy of ethnic cleansing across an entire country. It's very brutal, it's very calculated and it's very one-sided. [...] I think the interesting thing about objectivity is that the people who wave those banners are usually either people who've got something to hide as in the case of the Serbs who were criticising journalistic coverage and saying we weren't objective and were biased, that's one category. Secondly, political, establishment figures...were uncomfortable with the reporting and therefore attacked journalists for lacking objectivity. [...] So you have to ask where are they coming from? [...] I sort of feel that I try for the truth and sometimes the truth's a good story and sometimes it isn't and actually that's all that matters.[8]

Alex Thomson, for Channel 4 News, is of a similar view regarding his reporting of the Kosovo conflict in 1999. He is clear and unapologetic in his dismissal of objectivity in situations where it invalidates difficult or inconvenient truths or where it appears to legitimise torture, rape or ethnic cleansing:

I made no attempt to be objective in my reporting about the Serb pogrom which was being conducted in Kosovo...What is objectivity in that situation? What is objectivity!?...Do we mean by objectivity that there is essentially a kind of middle ground of explanation which can legitimately explain why these people are being raped and tortured and burned out of their houses? That's bullshit! You just tell people what's happening. You let them make their own moral judgement about it... But in my own personal feelings...I was overjoyed when they started bombing Novi Sad and wasting the Serb's infrastructure – absolutely overjoyed![9]

CNN's Christiane Amanpour thinks that in a story like the genocide in Rwanda, in 1994, reporters should certainly be fair but that does not mean treating the perpetrators on an equal basis with their victims equally or 'insisting on drawing a balance when no balance exists'. She attacks today's 'culture of moral equivalence', where 'journalism seems uncomfortable with identifying a victim and aggressor.' In Bosnia, for example, 'Britain and France kept insisting both sides in that conflict were equally guilty. They were not. That has been recognised in retrospect, but in the meantime it caused international inaction and unnecessary loss of life, not to mention a sense of political impotence on the part of the west.'[10]

This mode of reporting became the norm for covering conflicts elsewhere in the world, especially in Africa where, Hume argues, 'western journalists could give even freer rein to their prejudices and force the facts into their preconceived framework' (1997, p. 12). Furthermore, it should be noted that the journalism attachment debate was very specific to the reporting of the Balkan wars or other civil conflicts in the 1990s, where none of the NATO powers were directly involved as combatants on the ground in the way they were in the first Gulf War in 1991. In that conflict, the majority of Western journalists happily conformed to the pooling system of reporting, policed as it was by military minders, and barely considered or debated aloud the limits of objectivity and balance. In the prevailing control culture of the briefing rooms in that conflict and later in the Iraq War (2003), cheering on 'our boys' against 'evil Saddam' was a natural and unquestionable patriotic response. (Part II of this book will look at that control culture in more detail.)

EXPLAINING THE JOURNALISM OF ATTACHMENT

There are two principal explanations for the journalism of attachment in the 1990s. One is the rising number of women war correspondents, bringing to the job a less gung-ho, more human-oriented sensibility to their reporting; another is the postmodern, cultural zeitgeist that privileged the individual and celebrity.

There were two styles of reporting from the Crimean War in 1854: one that was concerned with the strategy and tactics of battle and another that focused on the human stories of war. The journalism of attachment as practiced in Bosnia tended to lean towards the latter which some say was influenced by the increasing number of women journalists reporting war and conflicts today. It is assumed that unlike their male colleagues, women journalists are keen to get beyond the obsession with military hardware and report the human costs of war: suffering, loss and bereavement, displacement and upheaval. But it is wrong to see the prominence of the woman war correspondent as a relatively new phenomenon (see for example Elwood-Akers, 1988; Sebba, 1994; Wagner, 1989), just as it is wrong to suggest that there is a strict gender difference in style between men and women reporters. Some women journalists see they have advantages over their male colleagues. Jan Goodwin, for example, reported on the Afghan resistance to the Russian occupation during the 1980s and recalls 'that as a woman, I was able to see a different side of guerrillas from the one that is normally shown to journalists – with me the freedom fighters could allow themselves to be vulnerable. And I in turn came to respect and care for these men' (1987, p. *xviii*). One has to wonder if this image of the caring woman journalist helping heavily armed yet apparently vulnerable 'freedom fighters' get in touch with their feelings in the mountain wilderness of Afghanistan does anything for the efforts of most women journalists to struggle for and win credibility in a still male-dominated occupation.

A better exemplar of the qualities of the woman war correspondent might be the crisis in East Timor in 1999. When Indonesia agreed to end its illegal, 25-year occupation of the country and allow a free referendum on independence, it promised to withdraw its troops. With its tacit support, however, pro-Indonesian militia set about a campaign of terror and intimidation against the majority of the population who wanted independence. They also lashed out at the United Nations and the assembled media, laying siege to the UN compound in the capital Dili. The UN eventually announced its intention to withdraw its western staff and advised journalists to do likewise. Three refused, choosing to stay with the local staff inside. Victoria Brittain thought it no accident that all three journalists were women. The Dutch freelance journalist and photographer, Irene Slegt, became 'the voice to the outside world of 1,500 desperate Timorese who had taken refuge in the compound and faced certain death if the UN plans to abandon them had been carried out'. A friend of Slegt described her as 'The kind of woman who's prepared to feel an emotional sympathy for the people she's working among, where a man would override that in the interests of common sense.' With her were Minka Nijhuis, a writer, and the late *Sunday Times* correspondent, Marie Colvin.[11] This presents quite a black and white picture that excludes the possibility of a man acting on emotion or sympathy and a woman acting on common sense but Brittain insists that:

> Of course there are plenty of careerist women for whom common sense comes first but I think that most people who are on a sharp career track tend to be men; women are much more likely not to be so interested in that. [The] kind of choices that Irene's made, you know to go after these unfashionable stories. East Timor turned out to be an unfashionable one but [Slegt] spent 20 years working on these kinds of

unfashionable stories. And she's a good example of the kind of woman who's not a journalist because she wants to make a big career or a big name or big money. She's a journalist because she wants to find out what makes the world tick and communicate that to other people and I think that's why I identify with her because that's what I have tried to do. Men, particularly younger men, they want to be big or they wouldn't go into journalism in the first place. They'd become primary school teachers.[12]

As Brittain wrote at the time, the gender gap is thrown into sharp relief in the 'intensity of war [when] even outsiders find themselves uncomfortably revealed, shorn of the props and mannerisms which allow most people, men in particular, to mask themselves most of the time.' Men respond to fear with bravado, she argued, and male war correspondents are no different: 'they become obsessed with weapons and start identifying with the military as role models, in the hope of feeling stronger and braver themselves'.[13] The response of the women correspondent to the extremes of the war correspondent, says Brittain, 'is to identify with the people whose intimate lives are shattered. Irene Slegt [had] no hesitation in saying about women journalists what many of us would hesitate to put into words: "We are more courageous...you see men losing it quicker". For young male correspondents coming up and taking on assignments in this war zone or that, 'the shape of journalism now is very much about your ego, your starring and general you-ness'. Male correspondents 'don't make great companions in difficult situations... whereas there's something about women, not that they're just sort of soft or anything. They're just able to be more attuned to what else is going on in the situation'. This is particularly the case with television, which is why Brittain stopped doing TV news and prefers print journalism. She 'couldn't stand the way it deformed what you were trying to see'. Television by its very nature, with its stand-ups to camera, projects the journalist and makes her very visible where maybe she prefers anonymity:

You know, you became the story whereas, particularly where you're doing very difficult things like civil wars, the kind of stories that I do a lot in Africa. Obviously you stand out for a kick off because you are white but beyond that you want to be as invisible as possible and I think most male journalists find that a bit difficult. They don't want to be invisible. The whole reason they're a journalist is because they want a picture byline on the front page. I just think that's a shame and it makes the work that much more difficult.[14]

Yet the image of the macho male correspondent and his soldier fantasies is also a caricature, immortalised by cartoonist Steve Bell's creation, Luke Hardnose (McLaughlin, 2002a, p. 174). Many male correspondents and cameramen take risks not for their own greater glory but for a story they care about. Maggie O'Kane praises the courage of a number of male correspondents in East Timor who took risks to report what was happening outside on the streets and on the island. Their fortunes were mixed. The news cameraman Max Stahl filmed footage of people being forced by the militias into West Timor, for which he received international plaudits but Sanders Thoenes of the *Financial Times*, was shot dead by pro-Indonesian militia and dumped in an alleyway.[15]

The BBC's Mark Urban also doubts that attachment can be wholly explained as part of the feminisation of war reporting. He prefers to see it as part of the cultural zeitgeist, a cultural condition 'in which victimhood is everything in these conflicts and where it's almost impossible in the reporting of somewhere like Bosnia or Kosovo for someone with a gun in their hand to be a hero in the way that it was, even in the early days of the Northern Ireland conflict or the Falklands.' Much of what passes for war reporting now 'is simply about how high you can crank the emotionometer.' But this, says Urban, does not come down to a 'feminisation of news values.' Rather, it is 'a view of conflict in which you simply concentrate on the civilian victims and you only interview the military protagonists through a heavy filter of cultural bias or aggressive...innuendo [which] is utterly self defeating.'[16] The assumption, that viewers and readers need to be led by the reporter through a minefield of moral distinctions, between good guys and the bad guys, good victims and bad victims, to be told whose side to take, is exactly what bothers critics such as Stephen Ward, who cautions against such moral leadership in 'a pluralistic society with few common standards' (1998, p. 124).

In an interview with the author in 1999, BBC journalist, John Simpson, attacked what he called 'look at me journalism'. 'It's not the purpose of being there', he argued. 'I don't think the BBC is that kind of organisation and I don't really want to impose those kind of views and attitudes on to people.' He explained that his approach was rooted in the tradition of

BBC public service journalism that focuses not on the storyteller but on telling the story. Viewers want to know about events on the ground in Beijing or Belgrade, not what John Simpson is thinking or feeling about those events because what he feels just gets in the way of their understanding and is 'of no value or of no interest to anybody.'[17] This is all the more essential when reporting complex events on which it is possible to take more than one perspective. People should be able to appreciate the complexity and not have their opinions directed or their minds made up for them:

> Nowadays you might say there's only one view that you could take about the Tiananmen Square massacre [in Beijing, 1989] and that probably is true. But as I found when I was there, there was more than one view you could take about the bombing of Belgrade [1999]. I think that one of the strengths of my position there was that I wasn't trying to tell people what to think and I wasn't trying to whip up feelings, and I wasn't telling people how I felt when I saw people dying or being killed. I was able simply to explain what was going on. Sometimes that was terrible and it was indeed – the death, the horrible death of people right in front of my eyes. I don't feel the requirement to rant on how I personally felt about it and the effect it had on my life because I didn't think that was what anybody else was interested in.[18]

Simpson's rejection of 'look at me journalism' was to backfire in 2001, when he reported on the invasion of Afghanistan and told BBC Radio 4 how he and the BBC liberated Kabul from Taliban control. 'It was only BBC people who liberated this city!' he claimed. 'We got in ahead of Northern Alliance troops. I can't tell you what a joy it was. I was very proud indeed to be part of an organisation that could push forward ahead of the rest' (12 November 2001). The idea of the BBC as a spearhead in a military invasion may have come as a surprise to the Northern Alliance and it certainly grated with Simpson's colleagues at ITN, Channel 4 News and other news outlets that could make equally valid claims to enter Kabul first. More to the point, the adverse publicity Simpson generated for himself and the BBC seemed to highlight the very phenomenon he identified in 1999: the trend for the reporter to become part of, or even more newsworthy than the story he or she is there to tell. In fairness, however, it should be noted that Simpson was one of the few journalists in the international media to follow the fate of Afghanistan in the 1990s, when the Soviet occupation ended and gave way to brutal civil war and the rise of Islamic fundamentalism.

The journalism of attachment is also said to encourage voluntary and moral self-censorship. Robert Fisk recalls a poem from Humbert Wolfe's *The Uncelestial City* (1930), which includes the lines: 'You cannot hope / to bribe or twist, / thank God! the / British journalist. / But, seeing what / the man will do / unbribed, there's no occasion to.'[19] Systematic censorship and control were largely absent from the Bosnian war because, says Mick Hume, it was not required. Nothing the international media said undermined the general propaganda framework as promoted in the West or threatened anyone's security. And there was no need to control the movements of reporters because they rarely if ever ventured behind Serb lines to get the story there. He concludes that,

> [those] who pursue the Journalism of Attachment...are playing a dangerous game for high stakes. The language of evil, genocide, and Holocaust can exact a high price from the accused. Such a substitution of emotion and histrionics for rational and critical analysis must also prove a major set-back for standards of journalism. (1997, p. 27)

Lindsey Hilsum remarks that after reporting on the mass killings in Rwanda in 1994, she read something in Primo Levi's work that she found herself disagreeing with:

> He said to understand is to justify and I don't think [that is always true]. The job of a journalist is to try and understand, not to understand emotionally, but to understand historically. And so I am not objective about the fact that a government had a policy of trying to exterminate all the Tutsis and all the moderate Hutus in Rwanda. That was a terrible, wicked thing to do. But my job as a journalist is to try and understand how this situation came about and to understand why those Hutus in those villages picked up their machetes and slaughtered people. [...] Now some people will then say I am justifying it because I try and understand what was going on in the minds of those people who did that [...]. But that's not the case at all. It's my job.[20]

Hilsum tells how she 'crossed the line to commitment' one day in 1997 when she testified at the United Nations International Criminal Tribunal for Rwanda. She was summonsed by the prosecution to support the case that what happened in Rwanda in 1994 'constituted crimes against humanity and genocide' (Hilsum, 1997, p. 29). Martin Bell and the *Guardian*'s Ed Vulliamy have both testified to the International Criminal Tribunal for the Former Yugoslavia (see Bell, 1993, and Vulliamy, 1993); others refused on the grounds that it is not for journalists to get involved in the story they report and that to testify against possible sources and contacts would be to erode a fundamental principle of journalism and destroy the credibility and effectiveness of the journalist. Who would talk to journalists again if they thought it might prejudice their position? But Hilsum argues that 'the normal rules of journalistic ethics are overwhelmed by murder' on the scale perpetrated in Rwanda. She was one of the very few western journalists actually there when it was all happening, so she felt it was her 'moral duty to use [her] unique position to influence the historical record in the court' (ibid., p. 30). She argues further for the 'need to find a balance between the practical and ethical demands of reporting, and our responsibility as citizens – or human beings – in the face of extreme mass crimes' (ibid., p. 32).

Robert Fisk opposes crusading journalism but thinks:

> that when a journalist sees something which is outrageous, to write as if it's just a road accident, or an earthquake or an act of God over which he has no opinions or no feelings as a human being, then there's not much point being a writer let alone a journalist.[21]

The radical Australian journalist Wilfred Burchett rejected 'the commonly enough held opinion that journalists should remain aloof from politics, not join parties or accept the discipline that membership implies. Journalists are members of human society with the same rights and duties and social responsibilities as everyone else, including those of political options' (Burchett, 1980, p. 328). For Burchett, journalism was about conscience and his obligations to his readers. He believed that he had in his working life achieved 'a sort of journalistic Nirvana', resistant to political, institutional or commercial pressure or interference:

Over the years, and in many countries, I had a circle of readers who did not buy papers for the stock market reports or strip cartoons, but for facts on vital issues affecting their lives and their consciences. In keeping both eyes and both ears open during my forty years reporting from the world's hotspots, I had become more and more conscious of my responsibilities to my readers. The point of departure is a great faith in ordinary human beings and the sane and decent way they behave when they have the true facts of the case. (Ibid., p. 328)

This is certainly pertinent to the problem of impartiality in coverage of the Israeli–Palestinian conflict, specifically the serial attacks by Israel on Gaza in the period 2006–14. And the question is this: how can the broadcast media presume to report with balance and impartiality the most asymmetrical conflict of recent times?

BALANCED ASYMMETRY: REPORTING ISRAEL AND GAZA

The journalism of attachment has usually only been possible in civil conflicts such as those in the Balkans in the 1990s, where western political and military involvement is peripheral or intermittent, and/ or where they involve a clearly definable enemy. The ongoing conflict in Syria and Islamic State's campaign against the Yazedi minority in northern Iraq have also been reported with a degree of attachment, especially where they involve a humanitarian angle. Yet the journalism of attachment would have been an unthinkable way of reporting the conflict in Northern Ireland (1968–94);[22] and it has been largely absent from coverage of the recent Israeli operations in the Gaza strip (2006, 2012 and 2014).

In my research to date into the media reporting of the Northern Ireland conflict, I have found no instance where a local, British or inter-national journalist has stood before the TV camera and pronounced himself or herself unable to be impartial in face of what was happening on the streets of Belfast or Derry (McLaughlin and Baker 2010 and 2015). Part of this was professional – especially for broadcast journalists who adhered to strictures of internal control such as producer's guidelines or the system of referral upwards (Schlesinger 1987; Miller 1994) – and part of it was a response to official British news management strategies (Miller 1994). Indeed, the very fact that 'both sides of the conflict' consistently complained that media reporting was biased against them was enough to convince journalists and editors that they were somehow getting the coverage right in very trying circumstances. Even more revealing than this piece of self-redeeming sophistry is the number of times journalists have asserted it without challenge. In Northern Ireland, the reporting narrative was simple and consistent, characterised by what David Butler (1995) has called 'balanced sectarianism'. The narrative here was of a sectarian war between two tribes divided by religion and national identity, with the British state acting as neutral arbiter, containing the conflict as best it could while fighting a war on another front against the paramilitaries affiliated to both sides. Put simply, every sectarian attack or outrage perpetrated by one side was invariably balanced with one from the other. As Butler and others such as Miller (1994) and McLaughlin and Baker (2010, 2015), have argued, however, this reporting framework was rather too simplistic as a starting point for understanding the conflict, its history and its underlying causes and effects. But it worked for the media as a routine rule-of-thumb, and even as a training template for young British reporters such as Mike Nicholson, Kate Adie and of course Martin Bell, all of whom went on to report the Balkan conflicts of the early 1990s.

The conflict in the Middle East between Israel and the Palestinians presents a different challenge again to western reporters and news organisations: how to explain the actions, motivations and attitudes of two of the most unequal protagonists in any recent conflict as if they were in fact equally balanced in military capability, political power and international sympathy. Allied to that problem are two others. How to report the diplomatic, peace-making gambits of the USA and the EU as neutral when in fact they arm and provide diplomatic legitimacy to Israel at the expense of the stateless Palestinians. And how to represent the countless resolutions of the UN Security Council and the General Assembly against Israel as anything other than empty gestures, routinely defused by US veto, Israeli pressure or diplomatic power play.

Before questioning the assumption of balance in media coverage of this conflict, particularly as it applies to Israel's periodic assaults on Gaza, it is important to consider in outline the extent of the imbalance of power between the protagonists. According to Jane's *The Military Balance 2014*, the Israel Defence Forces (IDF) comprises 133,000 soldiers, 9,500 navy personnel and 34,000 air force personnel – a total of 176, 500. It also has a reserve force of 465,000 (mostly army) personnel. In Gaza, Hamas has 20,000 personnel in active service, 10,000 of which normally serve in a police role but who can be called up for a military role in wartime. The other principal militia, Islamic Jihad, has up to 3,000 personnel.

The imbalance of arms and munitions is even more striking. Jane's *Defence Weekly*[23] estimates that the IDF have at their disposal: 3,500 tanks, 456 artillery guns, 620 self-propelled guns, 138 multiple rocket systems, 750 mortars, 900 anti-tank weapons, 200 anti aircraft guns, 7,684 logistical vehicles, 64 navy ships including 3 destroyers and 3 submarines; an air force equipped with 490 combat aircraft and 80 attack helicopters;[24] an indeterminate arsenal of long range conventional missiles; the Iron Dome missile defence system and, last but not least, 200 nuclear warheads, the existence of which Israel has refused to confirm or deny.

It is difficult to quantify the weapons capability of the Gaza-based al-Qassam Brigades (allied to Hamas) or Islamic Jihad because they do not publish such information; but various estimates sourced online suggest that al-Qassam have an arsenal of between 5,000–10,000 missiles of varying ranges (20 km, 75 km and 150 km). During the IDF's latest attack on Gaza, Operation Protective Edge in 2014, Hamas released pictures to the international media of what it claimed to be one of two drone aircraft in its possession but the fog of the wider propaganda war made it impossible to confirm the authenticity or provenance of the images. Whatever the difficulties in establishing the true extent of even the combined military capacity of Hamas and Islamic Jihad, it would seem safe to conclude that it is minuscule in comparison with that of Israel, the Middle East's dominant military power. Sadly for thousands of Palestinian civilians, this has been demonstrated time and again with devastating results. But the remarkable aspect of all this is that the international media rarely if ever emphasise such a gross imbalance of forces when reporting the latest flare-up in the conflict.

Between 2006 and 2014, the IDF carried out four major military operations against Gaza, a tiny, densely populated strip of land cut off from the world by an Israeli blockade. They have pounded it with hundreds of tonnes of munitions including, in 2006, illegal phosphorous shells; razed hundreds of houses using military bulldozers; shot unarmed and innocent civilians on sight; and imposed other repressive, on-the-ground security measures such as arbitrary arrest and internment without trial. Israel consistently claims that such operations are carried out in 'self-defence', in response to 'terrorist' activities by paramilitary militia such as the al-Qassam Brigades and Islamic Jihad, specifically arms smuggling via tunnels across the border with Egypt and the firing of rockets into Israeli towns and settlements. These four operations alone (there have been many smaller ones in between) left over 3,000 Palestinians dead, included hundreds of children, thousands injured and over half a million civilians displaced; the Israeli toll is much lower and more difficult to quantify but civilian deaths total less than 100.

All this information is in the public domain yet the mainstream media seem strangely impervious to it. The official Israeli version of what happens and why, is reproduced by large sections of the news media with little deviation or question. Even in the few instances where reporters stray from it, Israel's propaganda machine is quick to respond with rebuttals, corrections and threats, the cumulative effect of which has been to create a culture of fear and inhibition. As a BBC news producer put it: 'We wait in fear for the telephone call from the Israelis' (Philo and Berry, 2011). Journalists such as Alex Thomson, who reported on two of the Israeli operations in Gaza, is scornful of this kind of timidity:

> If anyone finds that a pressure, they're in the wrong job! I mean, that's what you expect. If you do stuff on the Israelis, you're going to get flak. I mean what do people expect? It's like saying I'm going to join the lifeboat but I'm a bit upset because I'm going to get wet and cold. This stuff is ridiculous! That comes absolutely with the turf. They should relish that, they should engage with that, they should be robust about what they're doing and defend what they're doing.[25]

It is difficult to find journalists willing to offer an independent critique of Israel's actions and operations in Gaza. In Britain, Robert Fisk and Patrick Cockburn of *The Independent* and John Pilger have been persistent and critical voices in the media wilderness. On the broadcast front, Channel 4 News and ITN have been most open in allowing access to critical or oppositional voices. Apart from these, Middle Eastern media outlets such as Al Jazeera and Abu Dhabi TV or the Israeli newspaper, *Haaretz*, give space to Palestinian perspectives, though these outlets would have very small audiences in the EU and the US. It is a situation that is no doubt replicable across the international media spectrum but what is curious is that this restrictive media narrative seems unresponsive to a growing cross-section of wider public opinion that opposes the IDF's increasingly punitive and disproportionate military operations against Gaza. It is a constituency that is turning to alternative sources via the Internet (e.g. The Electronic Intifada, Media Lens and Democracy Now!) and/or social media such as Twitter for information and discussion that is largely absent from mainstream media coverage.

So what are the contours of mainstream media coverage of what Israeli journalist, Gideon Levy (2010), calls 'the punishment of Gaza'? Greg Philo and Mike Berry (2004) provide an in-depth analysis of British TV news coverage of the Al-Aqsa or Second Intifada that began in 2000; and, more recently, Israel's Operation Cast Lead in Gaza in 2008/09 (Philo and Berry, 2011). This reveals persistent patterns of reporting that: absent or obscure historical explanation of the conflict; represent Palestinians as provocateurs and the Israelis as defenders; emphasise Israeli casualties and underestimate Palestinian casualties; obscure the military imbalance between the IDF and organisations in the occupied Territories such as Hamas, Fatah and the Popular Front for the Liberation of Palestine (PFLP); and that accept the peacemaking *bona fides* of Israel's western allies even though these allies continue to arm Israel with the latest hi-tech weaponry. Philo and Berry consider a number of factors that might explain these patterns of coverage, such as organised propaganda and flak campaigns that shape or restrict the limits of how the media report and explain the conflict. They also demonstrate a direct link between this and public understanding. Using audience focus group research, they have found a significant level of public ignorance of the Israeli–Palestinian conflict, its causes and consequences, with many of the focus group respondents admitting that their main source of knowledge of the conflict had been one or more of the main TV news networks in the UK.

But this problem is more than one of intimidation, flak and propaganda on the part of the Israeli state. It depends on a certain cultural and ideological disposition among western journalists – a ready receptiveness to the propaganda messages and images that make it apparently easy to internalise them as natural and incontrovertible realities. Thus can the BBC's Middle East correspondent Jeremy Bowen remark in his memoirs that the bitterness between the protagonists is deepened by 'the obduracy of the Palestinians and the stamina, determination and strategic vision of the Israelis' (2006, p. 238) – hardly a statement that wishes a plague on both houses. And as Alex Thomson sees it:

Hamas fires a rocket into Israel, it's a war crime, in the sense that they're just firing at a country. They're not interested in what they hit and what they don't. Almost all the ordnance fired by Israel into Gaza is not a war crime. It's the legitimate use of munitions but the margin outside of that is going to kill a lot of people when perhaps the right care isn't taken, when perhaps the right target selection isn't gone through and so forth. But (it's) very simple to report an asymmetrical conflict. I mean [...] the Americans, the greatest force the planet has ever seen, has just been defeated [....] by a bunch of guys with improvised explosive devices (IEDs) and Kalashnikovs in Afghanistan. So the reporting of the essential truth that a conflict may be asymmetrical does not mean to say that...the heavy side of those scales is necessarily going to win.[26]

Studies such as Philo and Berry's go some way towards an evidence-based critique of news coverage of the conflict as opposed to the kinds of tit-for-tat, partisan debates that are often played out in the media themselves. Yet even they tread carefully when they conclude in their original study (2004) that: 'The dust-storms of propaganda, which are created by those seeking to defend their "own side", will in the end do nothing more than prolong the conflict and the agony that the people of the Middle East are having to endure' (p. 260). This appears to contradict the evidence of their own analysis, that in propaganda and media coverage, as much as in the war itself, the conflict between Israel and the Palestinians is deeply asymmetrical and the fact that most sections of the mainstream media report it as otherwise is an indication one would think of the success of Israel's well-funded propaganda and public relations machinery over the poorly resourced efforts of the Palestinians. In fairness, Philo is less circumspect elsewhere when he argues that western media accounts offer us 'a one-sided account of the causes and origins of the conflict, which can then have profound impacts on audience beliefs to the detriment of any rational public debate on how this crisis may be resolved' (Philo, 2012, p. 163). Alas, rational public debate in the UK or anywhere else in the West will not solve the crisis. Only two states can solve the crisis: Israel and the United States of America. So far, both have shown themselves unmoved by international criticism, democratic protest and media dissent.

The argument here is not that reporters should shed their impartiality in an asymmetrical conflict and overtly take one side against another. Rather it is that the reporting of the latest Israeli military operation in Gaza or the latest rocket attack on an Israeli settlement must surely signal, even if only occasionally, that this is a deeply unequal conflict – militarily, politically and diplomatically.

CONCLUDING REMARKS

Looking back on his idea of the journalism of attachment and the debate it provoked, Martin Bell stands by it in principle but insists it was 'widely misunderstood'. The 'journalism of attachment' he says, 'is not a license for campaigning journalism, to which I am opposed.'

> I'm very suspicious, and I've seen it happen, when people go into foreign countries, and war zones...knowing what they're going to find and lo and behold they find it. I never belonged to that. I would in retrospect wish I had emphasised more the part of my doctrine which says that the facts are sacred. It's just that I don't believe that journalists should act as if they had no influence because they do. They affect the events that they are reflecting; there's no question of that. They do have a moral responsibility, which I think is increasingly accepted. And I wasn't so much prescribing a new journalism as describing a changed journalism; it changed in the 30 something years I was doing it and I was describing what I believed to be best practice at the time I was leaving it in 1997.[27]

Bell tells an anecdote from Bosnia that he believes to be apocryphal, but a neat illustration nonetheless, of the kind of dilemmas journalists confront in the war zone. A reporter visits a sniper position in or around Sarajevo: possibly Serb, possibly Muslim, possibly Croat. The sniper tells him he has two civilians in his sights. 'Which of them do you want me to shoot?' he asks. The journalist turns to leave and the sniper fires twice. 'That is a pity!' the sniper calls after him. 'You could have saved one of their lives!' (1997, p. 9).

While Bell may not have deserved the opprobrium that was heaped upon his head in the wake of his heresy, it is clear that he touched a nerve in the debate about the proper role of the journalist in the war zone.

The problem for critics of the journalism of attachment is that reporters are not accountable for the words they speak in the same way as democratically elected politicians or international organisations such as the United Nations. It is not simply an issue of conscience, they argue, but the wider consequences of the decision to get emotionally or morally involved in the story. John Burns argues that journalists cannot lay claim to 'providing the highest standards of objective and balanced reporting while still presenting themselves as impartial arbiters pressing for action' (1996, p. 98). Phil Davison of The Independent has said that too many journalists in Bosnia took sides in the war on a purely emotional level, a reaction he thought was wholly unjustified.[28] To do so with little or no objective knowledge of the conflict, its root causes and history, argued Misha Glenny, was tantamount to 'fanning the flames of conflict in the Balkans.'[29] In a three-sided civil war like Bosnia, each protagonist is acutely sensitive to the value of the international media and of harnessing world opinion in favour of their cause. Peter Arnett tells how he made contact with Chechen rebels in the first Russian–Chechen war and found their morale buoyant in spite of their isolation and their hopeless military position. 'We have the support of the government of the international media', they told him, 'and you are one of its ambassadors' (1996). The problem with diplomatic immunity, of course, is that it can always be cancelled. Arnett's anecdote should serve as a reminder to reporters everywhere of the delicate balancing act they must walk between 'caring as well as knowing' and becoming 'ambassadors' for the next big cause. War correspondents are not diplomats or politicians and they are certainly not part of any government yet some forget this in their reporting of 'humanitarian crises' and call for 'something to be done.'[30]

In the high-octane, high-risk space that is the modern war zone, reporters are susceptible to a host of physical risks and ethical dilemmas around the practice of objectivity and impartiality. But they also face the pressures and challenges of the very media technologies that help make their job possible. There is the pressure to submit to the tyranny of the satellite uplink and the demands of the 24-hour, 'real-time' news agenda. And there is the double edged sword of the new social media that offer journalists the opportunity to report breaking news of war in an instant, raw and exciting style; yet present to journalists a challenge to their authority and professionalism as reporters and writers.

4

From Luckless Tribe to Wireless Tribe: The Impact of Media Technologies on War Reporting

The Egyptian revolution was planned on Facebook, organised on Twitter and broadcast to the world via YouTube. The global news channels, above all Al Jazeera, became a massive amplifier for the amateur reports and videos, spreading the revolution's impact across the world.

Paul Mason, Channel 4 News[1]

One of the features of conflicts in the post-Cold War era of the late 1980s/early 1990s was their live-ness, their status as instant television news. CNN became famous for its habit of being on the spot at the latest global crisis to report events live as they happened: the Tiananmen Square massacre in Beijing, the fall of the Berlin Wall and the East European revolutions, the Gulf War, and the August coup in the Soviet Union. It was this live-ness that concentrated the minds of policy makers and analysts, military strategists and media professionals alike. They identified something called the 'CNN effect', or 'CNN curve', by which live instant news of conflict and crisis appeared to lead to instant decision making by the world's most powerful countries (Neuman, 1995). Yet something radical appears to have happened in the few decades since then: television news seems to have been short-circuited in its importance by the rapid emergence of the new social media – Internet blogs, Facebook, Twitter and Instagram, to name the most prevalent. Now it seems that the 'mass' in mass media is no more – we are all individuals with our smart phones, tablets and data clouds. Recent research from organisations such as Ofcom in Britain or the Pew Centre in the US suggests that such talk may be exaggerated.[2] But the use of social media by all sides in the recent Arab uprisings, 'the Arab Spring' as they were rather hastily described, not to mention various western militaries, authoritarian regimes, militia and terrorist groups, adds an important new dimension to the study of media and war.

Yet it is not a simple case of there being a direct line of technological advance from the mid nineteenth century to the early twenty-first century because even a brief history of the technologies of war reporting throws up some surprising parallels. The telegraph is a medium that is barely thought about today in the age of Twitter yet it revolutionised journalism as a written form in the nineteenth century. Suddenly, reporters had to write to limits of space, punctuation and character. Photography and the moving image played a major role in reporting and visually representing the great conflicts of the twentieth century yet the authenticity of even the greatest and most iconic war photographs has been questioned. Radio was a medium that came into its own in the Second World War and for the first time allowed people to hear the sounds of battle, to experience something of war at first hand. Even today, in the era of digital sound recordings, the magnetic sound recordings from the BBC's coverage of the Second World War still hold a certain excitement and fascination as authentic records of 'history in the making'. Television emerged in the 1950s as a new and apparently potent medium, bringing news of war into the living room, making it more personal yet more objective and impartial than any other form that preceded it; yet today, its authority and impartiality as a news source have been consistently challenged and debated. Each of these media forms had its day in the war zone and each in its own way appeared to bring new qualities of immediacy and drama to the reporting of war. In reviewing their various impacts and influences, this chapter assesses whether the advent of social media marks just another advance in the possibilities of war reporting – making it now ever faster, ever more immediate and impactful, and ever more personal – or a radical break in the paradigm? Is this the advent of the citizen war reporter – truly individual and independent of political or institutional restraints? And do social media have implications for the military and their need to control and restrict the reporting of what from whatever source?

THE TELEGRAPH

The telegraph was invented in 1843 and was initially greeted with a mixture of scepticism, resistance and anxiety among politicians and the press. In 1889, London's *The Spectator* lamented the impact of the telegraph on diplomacy and journalism, complaining in an editorial that, 'The world is for purpose of intelligence reduced to a village. All men are compelled to think of all things, at the same time, on imperfect information, and with too little interval for reflection.' The telegraph, it went on, encouraged rumour, speculation and emotionalism in the conduct of international relations: 'The constant diffusion of statements in snippets, the constant excitements of feeling unjustified by fact, the constant formation of hasty or erroneous opinions, must in the end, one would think, deteriorate the intelligence of all to whom the telegraph appeals' (Neuman, 1995, p. 19). The armies of the great European powers, on the other hand, viewed it as a communications technology they could deploy to considerable tactical advantage. Diplomats also saw the advantages, although they were concerned that it was too instantaneous, that it would cut valuable negotiating time and rob them of their power and their sense of indispensability (ibid, p. 30).

The status of the American Civil War as the first major conflict to receive comprehensive press coverage was helped by the telegraph. Its use coincided with other developments in transport and technology that speeded up the time it took a dispatch to reach the newsroom from the front line onto the front page. It lent immediacy to reports and therefore made them more valuable in the eyes of newspapers and their readers alike. The importance proprietors attached to coverage of the war was underlined by the level of investment they put in to it, ensuring that their reporters were at the front to describe the major battles and strategic developments. About 500 correspondents reported on the war on the Union side alone (Knightley, 2004, p. 19). The Confederate states were less well served – their press was much poorer in terms of resources and about 30 years behind the North in terms of technology. This situation was worsened as the South lost ground to the advancing Union armies. Only a few Southern newspapers, such as the *Memphis Appeal* and the *The Chattanooga Daily Rebel*, were able to up sticks and retreat with Confederate forces. Some were closed and dissolved by the North but most were forced into increasingly desperate measures to publish; the *Pictorial Democrat* and the *Stars and Stripes* were reduced to publishing on the blank side of wallpaper (ibid, p. 25).

Yet as Knightley, Neuman and many others note, all this new technology had little effect in improving the quality of what journalists reported. Wilbur F. Storey, editor of the *Chicago Times*, ordered his reporter at the front to 'telegraph fully all news you can get and when there is no news, send rumours' (Knightley, 2004, p. 23). Neuman shows how the telegraph's use during the Civil War gave rise to two famous bylines in the history of the press. The first was 'By telegraph', signalling immediacy and freshness, if not accuracy. The other was the personal byline, 'From our own correspondent', which meant that the correspondent and the newspaper had to take direct responsibility for the story in matters of libel, slander, and inaccuracy. As a result, journalists at the front became much more cautious and less direct in their reporting and that to a certain extent suited the military.

William Howard Russell found reporting the Civil War for *The Times* a bitter experience, and part of his problem was an inability to adapt to this new technology. The telegraph speeded up communication from the front but shortened reporting deadlines that put more pressure on the journalist to write concise copy and write it at speed. It therefore encouraged the development of a new style of journalism that did not suit Russell and his elaborate narrative style. As press coverage of the American Civil war showed, there was little room in the telegraph age for detailed analysis of military strategy, descriptions of military technology, or careful, blow-by-blow accounts of the major battles. Alan Hankinson (1982) shows that even when Russell went to report the Franco–Prussian war in 1870, he was still as detailed as ever even though he was being scooped by rival correspondents, especially those that came over from America in numbers. Thanks to the transatlantic cable – an account of the battle of Metz on 19 August appeared only two days later in the *New-York Tribune*. Such a commitment cost the *Tribune* some $5,000, but it was a sound investment: it boosted circulation and thus profits in an era of intense competition to be first with the news. The press in London was quick to learn these lessons. The new style of commercial reporting was cut to suit the demands of the telegraph and the pressures of time and space (p. 216). It was an affront to everything Russell had stood for. To the new breed of journalist, 'reporting was a job and a glorious game rather than a vocation.' Accuracy and information were secondary on their scale of news values to being first and being entertaining. They bragged about their 'courage and cunning' and would think nothing of cheating to scoop their rivals (ibid, p. 217).

Indeed, the instantaneous nature of telegraph communication sometimes meant that the press could scoop even governments on news of a particular battle or war. In 1847, the US went to war with Mexico over the disputed territories of New Mexico and California. The fall of the key Mexican stronghold of Vera Cruz was a critical moment in the war but the first President Polk heard about it, says Neuman, was not through the War Department, as was the convention, but via telegram from the *Baltimore Sun* – and only then after the newspaper published the story (1995, p. 36). This probably exalts the role of the telegraph and the press somewhat. Information-wise, the Polk administration was prone to excessive leakiness and details of peace feelers and draft treaties were already in public circulation (Blanchard, 1992, p. 7ff). The Spanish–American War of 1898 was a conflict that saw the worst excesses of the popular yellow press – the coverage was sensationalised and inaccurate and reporters had an inflated sense of self-importance, of their influence on policy and power. Most controversial, for example, was the role of William Randolph Hearst, owner of the *New York Journal-American* and mythologised by Orson Welles in the movie *Citizen Kane*. Much like Rupert Murdoch in the 1980s, Hearst attempted to monopolise the available technologies of telegraph and industrial printing for competitive advantage; truth and accuracy seldom got in the way. For example, he sent his chief illustrator to Havana to capture some of the action with dramatic images. Days later, he received a telegraph from him saying: 'Everything is quiet. There is no trouble here. There will be no war. I wish to return.' Hearst telegraphed back: 'Please remain. You furnish the pictures. I'll furnish the war.' At one stage in the war, the *Journal* appeared on the streets with the front page emblazoned with the headline, 'How Do You Like the Journal's War?' (Neuman, 1995, p. 43). In fact, the war transformed the *Journal*'s reputation and circulation figures. In 1896, the paper was selling 150,000 copies per day; by the time the Spanish–American War began in 1898, it was selling 800,000 copies (ibid, p. 45).

The growth and speed of communication via telegraph, and of mass literacy, fuelled increasing demand for newspapers. War correspondents gained eminence because they provided sellable copy – reports of battles and heroism, most of the time inflated or invented, were immensely popular (Knightley, 2004, p. 44). The Franco–Prussian war of 1870 saw the first organised use of the telegraph by journalists to report action from the front. At the instigation of George Smalley, of the *New-York Tribune*, they formed a news pool in which they shared the right to use each other's dispatches and helped each other circulate them to the widest possible readership. The scheme worked well and enabled dispatches to be telegraphed to America and published within a day or two of the reported event, a tremendous advance on the previous standard of a week (ibid, p. 48).

The Spanish–American War also became known as 'the journalist's war' because of their tremendous freedom to report and to move, even in the midst of naval battles. The writing style that had emerged out of coverage of the American Civil War continued to change and develop during this period in a way that, as Neuman puts it, 'made metaphors of facts and heroes of correspondents' (1995, p. 52). But there was in its aftermath a sense of unease that the press had played an undue influence over the course of the war and, in eerie prefigurement of today's anxieties about the impact of social media, even the swashbuckling Richard Harding Davis worried about the speed and seductive power of the new technology. 'The fall of the war correspondent', he said, 'came about through the ease and quickness with which today's news leaps from one end of the earth to the other' via the rapidly expanding telegraph network (ibid, p. 53). In the Crimean War, the reporter's dispatches took much longer to reach the front page, usually long after any information it contained could be of benefit to the enemy. In the Spanish–American War, the speed of the telegraph ended all that and threatened military security. The military responded by tightening censorship. Dispatches from Havana to New York, for example, were in some cases relayed to Madrid, ostensibly for military clearance, but actually as an effective delaying tactic. By the time Harding Davis went to Europe to report on the First World War in 1914, these techniques and devices had been developed and perfected to such an extent that he declared the end of the war correspondent (ibid).

The telegraph, then, speeded up communication and lent reports immediacy and freshness. It increased the popularity of the war correspondent as hero, but also fuelled the growth of the popular press and yellow journalism, encouraging a style of journalism that favoured the drama and sensation of war over truth and accuracy. The new technology improved the means of reporting war, but not the quality and reliability of the journalism.

PHOTOGRAPHY

The invention of photography and its development into a commercially viable technology of representation brought with it the possibility of bringing to the public a more 'realistic' or even 'objective' image of war. Without entering into a detailed history here, there are two aspects worth considering: photographic representation of war, and the potential for manipulation and propaganda; and the impact of war photography on public opinion.

As William Howard Russell is recognised as the first war correspondent, Roger Fenton is widely regarded as the first photographer of war, if not a war photojournalist. His photographs from the Crimean front in 1855 show a war in which everything is in good order, in which the troops are well fed, and in which officers and infantry mix freely in harmony. They also show the aftermath of battle minus the dead and wounded. After the Charge of the Light Brigade, Fenton wrote how he surveyed the carnage on the battleground and decided not to take any photos of it. He packed up and returned home, satisfied he had done his job. What his work demonstrates, says Philip Knightley, is that 'while the camera does not lie directly, it can lie brilliantly by omission' (Knightley, 2004, p. 14). However, it must also be noted that Fenton was limited by the technology; photographic hardware in 1854 was still bulky and unwieldy, and limited exposure times made it impossible to capture movement and action within a single frame. Fenton's shots of the Valley of Death in the aftermath of the Charge of the Light Brigade showed a largely empty terrain, clusters of spent cannonballs the only visual evidence of what had passed.

Images of the casualties of war have always presented a problem for the military censors. Vietnam is often called the first living room war for the terrible images of death and bloodshed that television brought nightly into people's homes. But Vicki Goldberg argues that the 'first living-room war' was not Vietnam but the American Civil War because it was brought home to a mass public through the photographic image (Neuman, 1995, p. 78). This, as Neuman argues, overstates the case. Photography was not a mass medium at the onset of the Civil War and even when it developed into the twentieth century, it never really achieved the same audience reach or impact as television did in the 1960s. Nonetheless, the work of Matthew Brady and other photographers added a dimension to the visual depiction of war that Roger Fenton could not or did not explore on his Crimean assignment. The Battle of Antietam saw 20,000 dead and wounded in a single day, 17 September 1862. There was nothing in the photographs of its aftermath to suggest the glory and heroism of war conveyed in the semi-fictional accounts of so many reporters. The carnage was recorded in explicit detail, showing, as Johanna Neuman puts it, 'bloated, gouged, twisted, grotesque figures in painful demise' (1995, p. 78). Yet the photos of Antietam, and of the war in general, did not turn public opinion; there were no public protests, no political backlash. Neuman guesses that perhaps too few people had seen them as they appeared in the newspapers or in a public exhibition in New York in 1862, for them to have had any real impact. She suggests the possibility that 'photography had to instruct before it could shock [and that] perhaps the emotional content of pictures was a learned response' (ibid, p. 79). Such photos did not lead public opinion but followed it; they were viewed in a political context – the public will or lack of it to fight a war. Furthermore, the memory and experience of the viewer frame the photograph as much as the photographer. Sometime between Antietam and the Second World War 'the public had learned to decipher horror, had been trained to focus on grief' (ibid, p. 82). Nonetheless, Susan Moeller acknowledges the historical significance of the Civil War photographs as 'the first systematic attempt to document a conflict in its entirety' (1990, p. 24).

In the two world wars, the military censored war photographers more severely than their reporter colleagues, and the penalties for breach of restrictions was much more severe. The fear was that photographs packed an emotional punch that would weaken public support for the war effort. For example in the First World War, printed publication of material deemed by the military as helpful to the enemy incurred a 20-year prison term. For taking photos at the front, in the initial stages of the conflict at least, the penalty was death (ibid, p. 81).

Photography has always been seen as a medium that is especially prone to simulation and manipulation. One of the most famous but now controversial war photographs is Robert Capa's 'Death of a Republican Soldier', taken during the Spanish Civil War, 1936–39. It appears to show a Republican militiaman falling to the ground at the instant of being shot. It made Capa famous as a war photographer and has since become an icon of the Spanish Civil War, reprinted countless times in historical accounts of that conflict. However, Philip Knightley (2004) has challenged its authenticity. What is significant about this photo for him, as it appeared first in *Life* magazine, was its dependency on the caption. On its own, the photo is ambiguous. It could easily be a photo of a soldier who had just tripped and fallen in training. It is blurred and unclear so we are unable to see if he really has been wounded. Only the caption fixes its memory: 'Robert Capa's camera catches a Spanish soldier the instant he is dropped by a bullet through the head in front of Cordoba' (p. 227). Knightley set out to investigate the exact circumstances in which the photo was taken and discovered conflicting versions. One was that Capa took the photo by sheer luck during a Republican assault on a Nationalist machine gun position. Sheltering behind a parapet, he lifted the camera up at full stretch and snapped blindly in the hope of capturing some of the action. This would hardly be extraordinary or controversial since much of the great action photography is taken by photographers who are good enough to make their own luck. As Capa said, 'If your pictures aren't good enough, you're not close enough!' (Moeller, 1990, p. 209). Other versions of what happened are much more controversial. One has suggested that the photo was not Capa's at all but that of another photographer on the scene, while the *Daily Express* reporter in Spain with Capa at the time, O. D. Gallagher, claimed that it was a posed photo, set up for the photographers when they complained to Republican officers about the lack of good photo opportunities. Capa apparently bragged to Gallagher that the photo was even out of focus, making it look all the more genuine. However, the late Martha Gellhorn, who reported the Civil War in Spain and knew Capa well, insisted to Knightley that the photo was genuine, that it was indeed a photo taken at 'the moment of death' for a republican soldier (Knightley 2004, pp. 227–30; Brothers, 1997, p. 178ff).

War photography can be used to good effect to represent war in all its horror but it can also be used to select certain truths and omit others, to 're-present' reality in a way likely to change or manipulate our responses to what is being done in our name, to perhaps even influence our opinion. Caroline Brothers looks at the photography of the Vietnam War, the Falklands War and the Persian Gulf War and makes key distinctions between each. The photography of the Vietnam War was characterised by its 'surfeit of realism', the notion that its stark representation of war helped, like TV images, to turn public opinion against the war. In fact, many of the most celebrated photos from the war were not originally taken as antiwar statements. The photo by Eddie Adams of a South Vietnamese army colonel executing a Vietcong suspect (1968) appeared in newspapers around the world, 'firmly embedded in the rhetoric of American resoluteness' and support for its South Vietnamese client against a ruthless enemy. But as the dominant consensus about the war collapsed, the image was appropriated by anti-war protesters as evidence of the horror of war (1997, p. 204).

Compared with Vietnam, the Falklands War of 1982 was characterised by the relative absence of photographic record. The British naval task force set sail for the South Atlantic in April that year to retake the Falklands islands from Argentina, which had occupied them and claimed them as its own territory. It took with it a small, exclusively British media pool that included only two photographers. The navy and the military were determined not to make the same mistakes they thought the Americans had in Vietnam and sought to impose strict controls on media reporting. They made the job of taking, developing and transmitting photographs especially difficult. For a good part of the Falklands war, remarked Robert Harris, 'the camera might as well have not been invented' (ibid, p. 206). Only 202 photographs were transmitted, most of these contrived by the military for propaganda use. One of the most famous and deliberate propaganda photographs from the Falklands appeared in the *Sunday Mirror* as British forces retook the islands. Captioned, 'Cuppa for a Brave Para', it showed the residents of San Carlos welcome British troops onto the island and appeared to symbolise everything that was British about these distant islands. A soldier stands by a very English-looking, white, picket fence drinking a very English 'cuppa tea'; the image provides an instant connection between the Falklands and home, communicating even to the doubters what the war was about (ibid, 208). Most images of battle action came courtesy of war artists but, like the war artistry of the American Civil War, this was very much comic book depiction. It promoted the heroism of British forces and their liberation of British territory from enemy occupation; and it did this by recalling all the old myths of the Second World War – of the Blitz and the Battle of Britain – that were sure to bolster domestic public opinion in support of the war (ibid, p. 207).

The Persian Gulf War in 1991 is now thought of as the perfect 'television war' and a case study in what Jean Baudrillard (1995) calls the 'hyperreal'; in other words a conflict defined by the manufacture of suitable images, not of what actually happened but what the allies wanted us to believe happened. For that reason, Baudrillard and others have argued that the Gulf war did not take place. What we witnessed was a virtual war, a Hollywood spectacle. We were not allowed to see or know about the death of up to 200,000 people or the untold economic and environmental devastation wrought on Iraq and Kuwait. Throughout the war, technology that made possible almost instantaneous transmission of photographic images was of little use when the US military ground rules for the media explicitly banned 'Information, photography or imagery that would reveal the specific location of military forces or show the level of security at military bases or encampments' (see US military regulations, Appendix 4). Photographers were reduced to taking photographs from approved television footage at the media centre in Riyadh. Only occasionally did we get a glimpse of the reality. In the closing stages of what was euphemistically called the 'land war', a large column of Iraqi soldiers in military and civilian vehicles, most of them conscripts, fled in panic from Kuwait City and up the road home to Basra. It was cut off by the Americans at a place near the border called Mutlah Ridge and wiped out by Apache helicopter gunships in what they called 'the turkey shoot'. There is little photographic evidence of the carnage that ensued except for a gruesome photograph of the charred skeleton of an Iraqi soldier at the wheel of a burned-out army truck. Taken by Kenneth Jarecke, it was rejected by most of the international press, appearing only in the *Observer* in Britain, under the headline, 'The True Face of War' (3 March 1991), and *Libération* in France (4 March).[3] Other major newspapers, such as *The New York Times*, claimed that it was too indecent to publish but there was a suspicion that it simply did not fit the sanitised story of the Gulf War that the media had been peddling throughout. There was, however, military video footage of the slaughter at Mutlah Ridge, eventually broadcast on television after the war, not on the news but on a programme in Channel 4's now defunct science and technology series *Equinox* (May 1991). The footage was taken from the cockpits of Apache helicopters and its pictures of helpless Iraqi soldiers being destroyed by missiles and machine gun fire makes for chilling viewing. Relating back to the point Brothers makes about the photographs of the Vietnam War, one cannot help wonder if the release of such pictures during the war would have made much difference given the level of public support that had been already achieved by anti-Iraqi propaganda? Indeed, the demonisation of Saddam Hussein and his army was so effective that it persisted in western public consciousness even as the regime collapsed and yielded to invasion in 2003.

NEWS REEL FILM AND WAR

Of course we cannot talk about photography here without reference to film and its role and impact in representing the realities of war. The Boer War is said by many to have been the 'first media war', certainly the first major conflict covered by what we now call the mass media: press, photography, and a new medium: film. William Dixon of the Biograph and Mutoscope Company arrived in South Africa to capture the action in motion pictures (Foden, 1999a and 1999b). These prototype movie cameras were large, cumbersome and static in operation. In *Ladysmith*, Giles Foden's semi-fictional novel about the Boer War, Dixon is depicted as a character called 'The Biographer', a man who thinks himself defined by the uniqueness of this wonderful new medium; as if the specialist skills required to handle it set him apart from journalists such as Winston Churchill (*The Morning Post*) and John Black Atkins (*Manchester Guardian*), men he spent time with socially as well as professionally:

> The Biographer wished he was elsewhere. These people, these colonels and aides-de-camp, ...these civil servants and silver-tongued correspondents...they were like another breed. Even the way they held their bodies was different. Look at Churchill now, for instance, listening as another one of them blathered on. Even when he wasn't centre of attention, he had a patronizing air, a way of holding his head that said, 'I'm cock of the walk'. The Biographer never felt like that. He wished he had his big camera with him; with its armour in front of him – its huge elm-wood box, glass plate and hood – he felt protected, in control, unassailable. (Foden, 1999b, p. 34)

There was no doubt that, in the Boer War, film's time had come as a medium of news and information, but Johanna Neuman questions film's 'intersection with diplomacy and war, whether film mirrors truth or illusion, whether filmed propaganda should be sugarcoated or force-fed, whether leadership in an age of film can compete with its power to cast spells' (1995, p. 121). In the Boer War, the illusory qualities of the new form were more decisive than its potential for authenticity. For the British, one of the problems of fighting the Boers was their invisibility – it was a bush war fought not in the open battlefield but by guerrilla methods of ambush and hit and run. The film cameramen who wanted to shoot pictures of soldiers shooting each other faced the same problem – the lack of battle action to film – so they made it up for themselves. For the still unsophisticated audiences at home, any film footage of the war was viewed as real just because it was film and it made an enormous impact.[4] For the first time, people were gathering as a public audience to 'watch the news' about a distant war rather than find out about it as individual newspaper readers. It was a new, immediate, and collective experience that signalled the advent of the mass media age.

On the whole, journalists were divided about film's potential as a tool of news or an instrument of illusion and propaganda. In America, the newsreels brought home to people images of two world wars and are credited with helping to bring about American intervention in each case but they were confections – part news, part entertainment or 'info-tain-ment' as it is called today. Most newsreel battles were reconstructions, sometimes pure inventions, and they were cut with footage of natural disasters and human interest stories. American humorist, Oscar Levant, called the newsreel, 'a series of catastrophes followed by a fashion show' (Neuman, 1995, p. 123). Photography and film supplemented war reporting with images that lent some authenticity and realism, some emotional impact, to the printed word. But military leaders have realised their potential for propaganda and persuasion because of the ease to which the photographic image, still or moving, can be manipulated.

RADIO

Radio was just becoming established as a mass medium when the Second World War broke out in 1939, but throughout the 1930s the BBC had been developing methods of outside broadcasting that involved heavy, cumbersome equipment such as the Blattnerphone in 1931 that recorded sound magnetically onto a large reel of steel tape at three feet per second. In 1935, the Corporation experimented with gramophone-like machines that cut grooves on magnetic aluminium discs, instantly ready for playback. This was unreliable technology but it relieved radio broadcasting of the pressure to present every programme live (Hickman, 1995). With further streamlining, they would come into their own during the war when reporters had to relay their reports from remote frontlines like the deserts of Northern Africa. Just months before the outbreak of war, saloon cars were converted into mobile recording studios, featuring a single turntable called the 'Mighty Midget', capable of four minutes recording time. The equipment did not require very much power and the recordings could be played back over telephone lines or even the less reliable short wave radio transmitter. These studios were in effect the first ever BBC radio cars and they were used to report major events like the Battle of Britain from Dover on the south coast of England. For a major reporting operation such as coverage of the 8th Army's North African campaign, the BBC fitted out a large van, nicknamed Belinda, which enabled multiple recordings to be made, transmitted, and broadcast within days. Developments like these helped reporters bring the realities of battle right into the living room with an immediacy and apparent authenticity which the printed word or photograph could never hope to match. Reporters had to match their style of address to the technology they were using. Just as the telegraph forced the reporter to describe the various battles, and the conditions of war, in a sharper, more economical style, radio forced the reporter to describe what was going on with a new intimacy, to communicate with the mass audience and the audience of one at the same time. The CBS journalist Ed Murrow understood this; so did Richard Dimbleby of the BBC. Murrow reported from Britain on the Second World War and was acutely aware that he was being used in a campaign to bring America into the conflict. He took advantage of the relative leniency shown to American journalists by the censor to consistently remind listeners of the fact and to complain about the quality of available information about controversial or difficult events such as the Battle of the Atlantic or the allied retreat from Dunkirk (Knightley, 2004, pp. 248–49).

The BBC's War Reporting Unit made the Corporation's reputation as a serious news provider. Its regular War Report programme became essential listening for people with access to a radio and among its most famous correspondents was Richard Dimbleby. Dimbleby was present to witness the liberation of Belsen, one of the Nazi death camps, and his first dispatch was deemed so shocking that his bosses back home at the BBC refused to believe it was true at first (Dimbleby, 1975, pp. 188–94; Hickman, 1995, p. 189–91). Former BBC radio journalist,

Robert Fox, has argued that the medium never lost that quality and that even by the late 1980s it was still 'the cleanest and quickest medium of serious journalism', a point he says was vindicated by radio coverage of the Falklands War but lost on the politicians and broadcast executives (1988, p. 15).

The broadcast potential of radio that made Murrow and Dimbleby famous also made it an ideal, seemingly instant and direct instrument of propaganda. 'Germany calling! Germany calling!' was the call signal of William Joyce or 'Lord Haw Haw', who broadcast crude German propaganda to whoever would listen in Britain. It had limited impact because it was broadcasting to a largely hostile and resistant audience. Fifty years later, in Rwanda (1994), radio propaganda of a more sinister nature played a significant part in genocide. The privately owned *Radio-Television Libre des Milles Collines* (RTLM) was controlled by the Hutu extremists who carried out the slaughter of between 500,000 and one million people in a matter of a few weeks in April 1994. Its basic message was that 'Tutsis need to be killed' but it targeted anyone deemed a threat to 'Hutu power', including many Hutu people (Keane, 1995, p. 10). Another of its murderous slogans, 'One Belgian Each', went out just days before the torture and murder of 6 Belgian civilians and 10 Belgian paratroopers by the Rwandan Presidential Guard. It also issued detailed instructions on handling weapons and a methods class in effective killing (Misser and Jumain, 1994, p. 74). RTLM was dubbed 'Radio Television La Mort' as its true role became clear, although an *Article 19* report has suggested that it did not so much incite genocide as actively organise it; the killing would have gone ahead with or without the help of RTLM (McNulty, 1999, p. 274ff). In his powerful account of the genocide in Rwanda, Philip Gourevitch (1998) writes that the station's propaganda may have been crude and inflammatory but it acted as an accurate weather forecast of political developments in the country. It predicted the fate of President Juvenal Habyarimana days before he was killed on 6 April in a mysterious plane crash, hinting to listeners that 'there will be a little something here in Kigali and also on April 7 and 8 you will hear the sound of bullets or grenades exploding' (p. 110). So when Thomas Kamilindi, a reporter for Radio Rwanda, wanted to know what was going to happen in the wake of the assassination, he tuned his radio to RTLM and kept it tuned:

The radio normally went off the air at 10pm, but that night it stayed on. When the bulletins ceased, music began to play, and to Thomas the music, which continued through his sleepless night, confirmed that the worst had been let loose in Rwanda. Early the next morning RTLM began blaming [the] assassination on the Rwandan Patriotic Front and members of UNAMIR [United Nations Aid Mission In Rwanda]. But if Thomas believed that, he would have been at the microphone, not the receiver. (Ibid, p. 111)

TELEVISION

It has long been assumed in official quarters that pictures of dead or wounded American troops going out on television screens night after night took their toll on public opinion and turned it against the Vietnam War. As one critic put it, 'for the first time in modern history, the outcome of a war was determined not on the battlefield, but...on the television screen', while the US commander in Vietnam, General William Westmoreland, complained that 'television's unique requirements contributed to a distorted view of the war...The news had to be compressed and visually dramatic' As a result, 'the war Americans saw was almost exclusively violent, miserable, or controversial' (MacArthur, 1992, p. 132).

Those who pushed this view at the time pointed to the anti-war protests on the streets of American cities, even though those protests accounted for a tiny proportion of the population. President Richard Nixon remarked that TV coverage of the war resulted in 'a serious demoralisation of the home front, raising the question whether America would ever again be able to fight an enemy abroad with unity and strength of purpose at home' (Cumings, 1992, p. 84). However, there is evidence to suggest that critical television coverage was minimal and the majority of the population disagreed with the administration's war policy, not the morality of the fighting the war in the first place. Lawrence Lichty shows that although half of all TV reports filed from Vietnam were about military operations, 'most showed very little fighting'. In a five-year period, from August 1970 to August 1975, about 3 per cent of all evening news reports from the war showed what Lichty calls 'heavy battle' footage of incoming fire and images of US casualties: a total of 76 out of 2,300 reports on the war (MacArthur, 1992, pp. 133–34). Daniel Hallin uses a much broader definition of combat footage than Lichty but reaches similar conclusions. In the period 1965–68, 22 per cent of all film reports from South East Asia included combat footage, and even then it was often shots of troops under fire from a sniper or a mortar position. Hallin also shows that 24 per cent of reports showed images of casualties; in the period 1965–68, 16 out of 167 stories showed a picture of a dead or wounded soldier (ibid; see also Hallin, 1989, for a full and extensive analysis of the Vietnam war as seen on TV).

The sort of coverage the American news viewer was actually exposed to is summed up well by Michael Arlen when he describes it as a 'nightly stylised, generally distanced overview of a disjointed conflict' that featured little or no serious combat footage' (MacArthur, p. 134). One reason for this was technological: instant satellite links were theoretically possible but far too expensive for even the big American news networks to afford. Journalists in Vietnam had to make do with canning their film reports and flying them back to their newsroom – a procedure that took two or three days. By that time, they were only good for background pieces and if the viewer ever did see battle scenes or war casualties, it was out of context, bearing little or no relation to current events. Public opinion turned against the war Vietnam because the pro-war consensus among the political elites in Washington broke down. If there was any media effect, it was not the sight of dead and wounded night after night but of politicians appearing on the news debating the war. According to Lichty's analysis, in the period immediately following the Tet Offensive, three TV networks featured a rough balance of pro- and anti-war guests and that by 1970 the number of critics exceeded the number of supporters. He concludes that, 'This opinion trend paralleled the trend in the publicly expressed opinions of many senators and congressmen, perhaps because senators and congressmen were so often those interviewed' (ibid, p. 136). Hallin argues that editorial commentaries on TV shifted after Tet from 4:1 for the war to 2:1 against. These shifts in media orientation away from a pro-war perspective are encapsulated in this recollection from Max Frenkel, executive director of *The New York Times*: 'As protest moved from the left groups, the antiwar groups, into the pulpit, into the Senate... as it became majority opinion, it naturally picked up coverage' (ibid).

Satellite, cable and the digital information age

By the 1990s, advances in satellite and cable television technology had changed the nature of TV news again. From being a novelty or special feature for the big set-piece event, the live broadcast from 'our own cor-respondent' on the spot quickly became an essential guarantor of the news organisation's credibility and status in a hi-tech, competitive media market. The reputation of CNN was made in the late 1980s on its apparent knack of being in the right place at the right time with live, uninterrupted coverage of the most important world events of the period. The quality of its coverage at the time was derided by the major American network news programmes but these criticisms belied a certain nervousness, an attempt to distract from a crucial fact: CNN was there and they were not. The organisation was quick to shed its image as 'Chicken Noodle News' and build on the plaudits it received for its coverage of the Gulf War. It continued to beat its rivals to the big stories of the 1990s. Contrast that with the British news channel ITN, which suffered in the late 1980s when it missed some of those big international stories, including the August coup in Moscow in 1991 and the assassination of India's president Indira Ghandi (McNair, 1994, p. 93). Taking live feeds from CNN and television news agencies was not good enough.

For some, the quality of broadcast journalism suffered as a result of this competition for instant-fix news. In the early days of television coverage in Vietnam, there was the news crew of journalist, cameraman and sound-recordist, all 'tied' to each other with electric cables. In the present satellite and digital age, there is just the journalist and the satellite uplink – no cables – yet the journalist is still tied to the demands of the technology. Brent MacGregor calls this 'palm tree journalism' in which all that is needed is a stand-up journalist and a suitable backdrop or prop to authenticate location and convey immediacy (1997, p. 184). Maggie O'Kane of the *Guardian* tells the story of staying in a hotel in Srebrenica, Bosnia, during the Serb siege of the city, and watching an American reporter in the next room spend his entire working day standing on the balcony doing live, stand-up reports, telling the same story and giving the same information over and over again. But while he was doing all that, she wondered, where was he getting the time to be a real journalist, to go out into the city and see for himself what was happening?[5] She is not the only journalist to understand the restrictions of the satellite uplink. Evan Wright (2004), who reported the Iraq War 2003 for *Rolling Stone* magazine, describes the frustrations of colleagues who kept faith with the technology:

I have observed other reporters in combat areas. They have so much equipment. Even wire service guys who are beaming up stories from their laptops. They have to get in line of sight with the satellite. That takes time. Even if you have solar panels, they never work. So you have to worry about recharging your battery. It becomes this big technical problem. You're tethered to it. So in my situation, I would not have been allowed to go with the actual front-line troops had I carried equipment...I know some print guys who did have satphones and who did go close to the front. But most of the people covering the war were not magazine people. So it's a technical advantage being low tech. (p. 332)

Alex Thomson of Channel 4 News says that routine television news tends to select a leading story and structure everything around that. Foreign news is no different. 'It's the headline story everyday', he says and sometimes that is led by technology. He presents the following scenario to illustrate the reporter's predicament:

You're in Pristina and something's going on and you've got...maybe a hour, hour and a half to do a bit of filming; smash and grab something, put it together, come back because they want you live at the [satellite] dish for the lunchtime news. Smash and grab! Edit! Smell of burning rubber! Get it over the bird [satellite link]! Fine! Up to the stand-upper [to-camera piece]! Is the hair straight? Tie straight? Great! Mic working? Fine! Fire away! Out again in the afternoon! Maybe you've got an hour, two hours if you're really lucky. Same thing! Smash! Grab! Live spot...for the 5.40! And then in the evening, fine! There may be nothing going on or there might be, so you can to some extent recut more leisurely, and they want another live [spot]. How do you do it?[6]

Lindsey Hilsum thinks that ultimately this can only impair the ability of reporters to make proper judgements in complex crises:

Obviously...if you are under constant time pressure...there is a danger of forming the wrong conclusion and there is a danger of making judgements too quickly because you have to get the story on the air... So you have two dangers. One is making a wrong call, making a wrong judgement, misinterpreting because you haven't enough time to do enough research. And the second one is lowest common denominator journalism: 'On the one hand this, on the other hand that, I can't quite conclude because I haven't had time to find out. Lindsey Hilsum, Channel 4 News in the middle of nowhere'. So you have to be very careful about that.[7]

Other journalists were more optimistic about the impact of technological change in the 1990s. Nik Gowing was an enthusiastic advocate of the liberating potential of the new technologies and how they would compress still further the time and space it takes the correspondent to report fast moving events across the world and to do that on a self-sufficient basis:

> To me it's actually the fascination with the dynamic of how information flows...The technology has arrived. It's cheaper [and] you've got the compression of the time line between gathering and transmitting the news and you've got the removal of filtering processes. [...] It's got to be *now* because the technology lets you do that. You can sit in a hotel room, somewhere, with a tiny edit pack and a satellite uplink called *Livewire* or one of the new systems, which means you can put that stuff out...close to real time. You don't have to rush back...to a feed point or a hotel. You do it *now*! [...] So you've got this compression there but at the same time you've got the broadening. No longer have you just got ITN, BBC, Sky. [...] You've now got a fantastic broadening right across there and this enormous tree includes email, the internet, websites.[8]

Gowing recognises the danger of fetishising technology as an end in itself, of blinding oneself to its potential for manipulation. He is interested in the inherent contradictions of the information age between 'low-cost, high-penetration, highly mobile hardware and the quality of what we put out'. Does the technology help improve the quality of the end product, the actual reporting? There is in his business 'the temptation and the pressure...to get it out now and to get it out right but [these are] not necessarily the same thing'. He worries that 'a lot of people in this [news] environment haven't yet worked out the dynamic and the pitfalls of this wonderful new technology. [...] You may have someone on a satellite dish in the middle of a jungle but does that mean they're telling you good things which are accurate, enlightening you even more?'[9] David

Halberstam writes that 'immediacy doesn't necessarily mean better, more thoughtful reporting' and wonders whether 'the lack of satellites and comparative slowness of the transmission process in the old days permitted the news desks...to act less as prisoners of technology than they do today'. He argues that improvements in the technology of news have seen an inverse decline of 'the editing function, the cumulative sense of judgement – the capacity...to blend the visual and non-visual' (1991, pp. 385–86). For Philip Knightley, in this respect, print journalism still has an edge in the television age: 'A good picture to illustrate a thoughtful report is still a bonus in quality print journalism, not an imperative' (1988, p. 13). Bob Woofinden believes that these fears are unfounded. The major television news organisations put their editorial priorities and resourcing issues first and that in this respect 'the technology can only be a huge advantage' (1988, p. 15).

The instantaneousness of news that these technologies make possible can be used *against* journalism as much as *by* journalism, what Gowing (1998) calls 'the information boomerang'. He draws examples from his own research on the media and the Great Lakes crises in Africa:

> [You are] sitting in the desert or the jungle broadcasting the horrors up on your [satellite uplink] and it's broadcast on BBC World and the people who are committing this are sitting in their villas nearby and thinking, 'Those people, they're spies!', whereas in fact all they are doing is good journalism...That's a part of the downside of technology. So you've got the accuracy and credibility problem and the other one is the impact, which can actually be more profound than many people feel comfortable with.[10]

The BBC's John Simpson appreciates,

> the standing danger that because you can report 24 hours a day from anywhere in the world that people will try to get you to do that and that...it leaves less time for finding out what's really happening...but I think everybody now understands that so fully that that's been pretty much counteracted.[11]

During the NATO bombing of Yugoslavia from March to June, 1999, Simpson made hundreds of hours of broadcasts from Belgrade without feeling confined to the spot for the next satellite link. If he needed to go out he would simply put it off until he was ready. He dismisses the idea that reporters are burdened by the tyranny of technology: 'We're able to do what we pretty much need to do. Otherwise, the advances in technology are purely advantageous...We're in charge rather than the machine I think.'[12]

The degree to which reporters are in charge of the machine is a moot point but it is clear that most if not all journalists are aware of the impact of new technologies and the opportunities and dangers that they present. Perhaps the most fatalistic view comes from Pete Williams, National Broadcasting Company (NBC) correspondent and ex-Pentagon spokesman (during the Gulf War): 'I suppose there are purists who argue that sending back a live picture isn't journalism...It may not be journalism, but it is television, and that is a fact of life' (Dunsmore, 1996, p. 4). Neuman argues that what is new today is not technological change so much as the sheer speed of that change, with some startling advances in brief periods of time (1995, p. 7).

There is also a political angle to this low-tech versus hi-tech debate, which I set out in more detail in the first edition of this book (McLaughlin, 2002a, pp. 182–98). Suffice to say here, arguments about the quality and reach of television coverage extended logically to its impact on foreign policy and military interventions in civil or humanitarian conflicts, most especially in the 1990s. Television pictures of thousands of Kurdish refugees stranded on a wet, windswept hillside in northern Iraq, in April 1991, for example, became emblematic of the Gulf War. Just as the images of 'smart weapons' seemed to say something about the superiority of military technology in the west – war it seems at the flick of a switch – images of these stranded people seemed to bring home to people the contradictions of the war and undermine the purity of western *real politik*. Martin Shaw (1996a) sees the Kurdish crisis as possibly the clearest cut example of how intense media pressure can in some way affect foreign policy. It was, he says, 'TV's finest hour. The same media that had been so thoroughly managed in the Gulf campaign were gloriously liberated in its aftermath.'[13] Daniel Schorr (1995) is just as fulsome in his celebration of the US media's role in apparently forcing a complete foreign policy U-turn on the crisis:

Score one for the power of the media, especially television, as a policy-making force. Coverage of the massacre and exodus of the Kurds generated public pressures that were instrumental in slowing the hasty American military withdrawal from Iraq and forcing a return to help guard and care for the victims of Saddam Hussein's vengeance. (p. 53)

Yet, in the case of the Kurds at any rate, the western alliance was simply put on the spot: it had encouraged the revolt in the first place only to then stand back and allow Saddam Hussein to crush it. It was now being held accountable and responsible for the terrible consequences. 'The Allies', argues Nik Gowing, 'had thought about only fighting a war to get the Iraqis out of Kuwait, not what happened next. They didn't envisage the Kurds spilling over from Northern Iraq to southern Turkey and so that's why there was no policy; there was a policy vacuum, policy panic'.[14]

It is less clear whether that set a precedent for subsequent crises such as Bosnia, Rwanda or Somalia. These featured some of the vital components determining decisive media influence. In Bosnia (1992–95) and Rwanda (1994), there were plenty of pictures of atrocities and human suffering on a wide scale but they provoked limited international action. The massacre in Rwanda in 1994, mainly of the Tutu population, was truly horrific and much reported and written about. However, other waves of mass killings of Hutus by Tutus in Burundi in 1993 and again in 1996 in the former Zaire barely made the international news agenda (Gourevitch, 1998; Gowing, 1998). None of these crises reached the critical mass that would invoke concerted international intervention. In Somalia in 1993, by contrast, pictures of dead US Rangers being dragged through the streets of the capital, Mogadishu, provoked public outrage in America and, apparently, the subsequent withdrawal of US troops from the United Nations Aid Mission in Mogadishu. However, Gowing suggests that a policy reversal was already underway and that those video pictures simply hastened the inevitable.[15]

WAR, 'CITIZEN JOURNALISM' AND SOCIAL MEDIA

In the second decade of the twenty first century, these important debates of the 1990s – about television news, its technological advances and its impact – already seem rather distant. The agenda has moved on and has been dominated by debates about the emergence and growth of the new social media – weblogs, Facebook, Twitter, Instagram among many others – that seem to have closed the gap between audience and news stories even further and faster than any predecessor technology. Indeed, their potential to bypass or short circuit traditional forms and spaces of journalism, to usurp the apparent authority and objectivity of the tightly packaged article or broadcast report and empower the private citizen to make his or her own news, presents a serious challenge to the future of traditional journalism. In the context of this book, we may now have to reconsider the future of war reporting and our image of what a war reporter is or should be.

Even by the close of the twentieth century, commentators were highlighting the potential of the Internet and e-mail for offering a diversity of sources of latest news about conflicts such as that in Kosovo to a new public of internet users (Fleming, 2001). It would mean greater choice of content and create hundreds of fragmented, niche audiences whose value to advertisers would be determined by differentiated incomes and lifestyles rather than narrowly fixed social categories. Caryn James, of *The New York Times,* argued that the diversity of news sources available to the American public in the aftermath of 9/11 and the new 'war against terrorism' rattled the major television networks, which expressed unease at the threat these new media sources represented to their monopoly yet at the same time were happy to use web-based content to fill an information vacuum.[16] One of the most high-profile examples of this at the time was 'the Baghdad blogger' Salam Abdulmunem, or Salam Pax as he was also known. His daily blog posts about life in Iraq before and after the US invasion of 2003 were syndicated by major newspapers around the world and quickly published in book form (Pax, 2003; see also Carruthers, 2011, pp. 209–52).

Other commentators have pointed to the propaganda potential of the new social media. Ariel Peled argues that the use of social media during Operation Pillar of Defence, Israel's assault on Gaza in 2012, bypassed not just traditional media outlets but traditional propaganda sources as well. For the first time in this long-running conflict, civilians on both sides were actively involved in the propaganda war, not just passively subject to it:

Civilians from both sides of the conflict and interested citizens worldwide shared news reports, blogs, stories, links, pictures and videos that supported their point of view or refuted others' claims or mainstream media reports. Beyond the physical war, a high-intensity virtual war on the hearts and minds of all netizens was being waged.[17]

Yet Paul Mason points to the 'networked consciousness' of the social media user and its power to resist spin and propaganda:

Sure, you can try and insert spin or propaganda but the instantly networked consciousness of millions of people will set it right: they act as white blood cells against infection so that ultimately the truth, or something close to it, persists much longer than disinformation. (2013, p. 77)

In an updated interview for this book, Alex Thomson remembers reporting the bombing attacks on London in July 2005, for Channel 4 News. He recalls the novelty of getting instant footage from inside King's Cross tunnel via someone's mobile phone and reflects on how quickly and so expected that has become since then, even in the most routine news bulletins. 'Now, when anything goes wrong', he says, 'when there's a war, a revolution…or some attack like that in London or somewhere else, the first thing you expect…is that someone, somewhere, would have filmed [it] on their mobile phone or would have got something.' Whether that constitutes citizen journalism or not is, for him, another question:

I mean we can get all highfalutin about everyone is a citizen journalist or everyone's a paparazzo. No! Everyone's got a means to film stuff and everyone's got a means to take pictures of it. That is not the same actually as being a paparazzo. At the end of the day, clearly people value the need for someone who's been around the block a bit to have a look at events and put them into some kind of context and I think that's very important.

Thomson offers Channel 4 News's coverage of the tenth anniversary of the bombings as an example of where the difference between the professional and amateur journalist really matters:

There's a world of difference between a tourist outside St Paul's cathedral today, standing there with an i-Phone filming what's going on with people arriving at the church and perhaps someone like myself standing there saying, you know, the state and the media need an occasion like this but actually the pain is there for everybody who lost people *and* there are families, don't you know, across Iraq and across Afghanistan *today*, just as innocent, who are feeling exactly the same pain and they deserve our thoughts also. And I can say that because I've seen those people and I know that's true and that tells you a rather difficult fact about 7/7 and why that happened and that's the difference between one and the other, you know. I think if you conflate both of those as journalism, you've got a problem. (Original emphasis)[18]

Peter Preston of the *Guardian* is also convinced that in the confusion and uncertainty of civil wars such as in Libya in 2011, where citizen journalism, not the mainstream media, provided the first draft of history, 'war reporters are still absolutely essential.' Events there, he argues, 'only got clearer when actual reporters...got over the border and near to the heart of the action. Then we actually had an information revolution: facts we could more or less rely on.'[19] On the other hand, his phrase 'actual reporters' belies a rejection of the very notion of 'citizen journalism' yet what is so often missed by critics is that the concept of the citizen journalist or even the citizen war reporter is rarely if ever self-ascribed. Of all the background reading I carried out for this topic, I did not come across a single example where someone using social media to communicate the latest events of the Arab uprisings called themselves a journalist of any description. The closest historical precedent for this phenomenon might be the English radical press of the eighteenth and nineteenth centuries – challenging the status quo of establishment rule, mobilising the emerging working classes on a mass scale around causes and protests, yet surviving by necessity on an ethos of voluntarism and contingency. The citizen journalists of the radical press may not have seen themselves as such; they certainly were not seen as such by their professional counterparts in the elite press; but that did not mean that they were not.

CONCLUDING REMARKS

These debates highlight the problems of theorising the role of social media in the reporting of conflict. Social media content is so ephemeral, provisional and anonymous that we can only speak definitively of its significance in the moment: as instant communication, as immediate source of raw information, as channel for the mobilisation of protest or resistance. Demonstrating its long-term outcomes is a different matter. What cannot be denied, however, is the challenge that social media and citizen journalism present not just to state repression or authoritarianism, but to the authority and primacy of the international mainstream media and official discourse. As Paul Mason (2013) argues:

> Slowly, quietly, the mainstream media have become, for many involved in activism, politics and journalism itself, a secondary source of information, while social networks have become the primary source. This, in turn, speaks to the emergence of an undeclared dual power between the world of ideas and the world of official politics. (p. 269)

If the argument here about social media and their role and impact in conflict reporting seems speculative and loosely formed, then that is because it is so. This chapter has traced the journey from luckless tribe to wireless tribe but it is too soon yet to identify an obvious transition from traditional war reporting to a definably new form of correspondence, a move away from the professional to the amateur, from the careerist to the citizen. But from being a sceptic and even a cynic about the significance of social media in the reporting of conflict, this author has moved from a rejectionist position to, at the very least, the contemplation of radically different technologies, forms and spaces by and through which we may come to understand the next major conflicts of this century.

Part I of this book has looked at the risks, motivations and traditions of the contemporary war correspondent, the problem of reporting the horrors of war in an objective or impartial way, and the opportunities and challenges presented by media technologies. It is the war correspondent as sovereign individual, making choices and justifying them. But as we shall see in Part II, there is another dimension to the story – the relationship between journalist and soldier. With its history of conflict, control and collusion, it appears to leave little or no room for the individual agency of the journalist.

Part II

The War Correspondent
and the Military

5

Getting to Know Each Other: From Crimea to Vietnam

One of the deadliest weapons wielded by the ruling classes of all countries is their power to censor the press for thereby they are able to create under the pretext of military necessity an artificial public opinion with the object of hiding their fell designs.

Morgan Philips Price, 'The Truth About the Allied Intervention in Russia', 1918[1]

The relationship between the war correspondent and the military is often portrayed in media journalism as a power struggle in which the correspondents do their best to get the right stories and the right pictures, while the military do their best to stop them. Indeed, the relationship was one of the biggest stories of media coverage of recent major conflicts such as Afghanistan in 2001 and Iraq in 2003. The pros and cons of the embed system of reporting and the military briefings; the treatment of independent reporters, or 'unilaterals' as the military call them; and the deaths of reporters at the hands of the US military, were reported and debated in feature articles and television documentaries as if they were new and shocking realities of the modern warzone. However, in this section of the book, I want to show that the military–media relationship has a long history and that it is defined by one persistent truth. This is the fact that from the Crimean War, 1854–56, to the Iraq War in 2003, the various militaries involved have learned valuable lessons from previous wars in how to manage the demands of the media, while the media it seems have not learnt anything at all. Indeed, the ability of governments and armies to censor and control journalists in the warzone, to create this 'artificial public opinion' as Morgan Philips Price put it, is as much down to the passive acquiescence of the international media as any other factor.

This chapter begins with the Crimean War and traces the early development of military media management up until the aftermath of the

Vietnam War, an historical turning point when the military's relatively
ad hoc approaches to previous conflicts was replaced by something more
evolutionary and above all systematic.

THE CRIMEAN WAR, 1854–56

While William Howard Russell and Edwin Godkin were quite different
in journalistic style and approach, both of them were appalled by the
inadequacies in British military leadership in the Crimea – Godkin
described the officer class as a 'slutten aristocracy' – and the terrible
conditions suffered by the troops (Knightley, 2004, pp. 10–17). Russell
wrote to his editor that a once proud army had been reduced to a sorry
collection of 'miserable, washed-out, worn-out spiritless wretches'. And
while he agonised over his criticisms of the military leadership, his editor
John Delane encouraged him to, 'Continue as you have done, to tell the
truth and as much of it as you can, and leave such comment as may be
dangerous to us who are out of danger' (ibid., p. 11).

  Russell's criticisms of the military in the Crimea attracted vehement
protest among the officers at the front and the authorities in England.
They objected to his reports revealing troop and artillery deployments,
arguing that once these found their way into the pages of *The Times*
they would be picked up in Moscow and lend the Russian army much
valuable intelligence. Delane agreed and ordered Russell to confine
his reporting to past events even though the Russians learned about
British military tactics and movements on the battlefield, or through its
spy-network, not from the pages of *The Times* (Knightley, 2004; p. 11;
Hankinson, 1982, p. 58). Britain's ally, France, imposed strict censorship
on the French press, and tried to make a case with Britain for excluding
journalists altogether once their armies went into action; though, as
Hankinson argues, this would have been impossible to enforce (1982,
p. 57). Public opinion at home had expanded due to the increases in the
electoral franchise and the growth of literacy and, since newspapers were
powerful organs for amplifying such opinion, there would have been
uproar had there been any attempt to exclude the correspondents. The
alternative option, of direct censorship, would have been problematic,
too, for the same reasons, but it could have been achieved through a
workable system agreeable to military and journalists alike. In the end,
the Commander of British forces, Lord Raglan, froze journalists out,

offering them no information or assistance at all. As Hankinson remarks, 'It was the policy of the ostrich and it was to cost [Raglan] dearly' (ibid., p. 55). The military's experience of this new breed of journalist influenced the introduction of formal military censorship commonplace in most wars since. Sir William Codrington, the new Commander-in-Chief at the Crimean front, issued a general order in February 1856 prohibiting correspondents from reporting military details of value to the enemy on pain of removal from the front. Although the war ended before the order came into effect, it was to make its impact on the reporting of subsequent conflicts (Knightley, 2004, pp. 15–17).

THE AMERICAN CIVIL WAR, 1861–65

In spite of the opportunities it offered journalists to shine, the American Civil War marked for many critics a low-point in the history of war reporting. Philip Knightley writes that most were 'ignorant, dishonest, and unethical' and filed some of the most 'inaccurate...partisan and inflammatory' copy of the war (ibid., p. 21). Battles were reported that had not taken place, towns were invaded by armies that had not reached them, journalists were praised for reports they had simply invented, and war artists indulged in a high degree of artistic license to sketch non-existent battle action. One journalist tried to interview a mortally wounded soldier, begging him not to die until the interview was finished and promising him that his last dying words would be published in 'the widely-circulated and highly influential journal I represent' (ibid., p. 26). The story was no different among Southern correspondents. In general, journalists refrained from reporting negative news about the war such as dissension in the ranks, the punishment of deserters, racism in the army, rivalries between eastern and western regiments in the northern armies, inadequate medical facilities at the front, and civil resistance to conscription. Knightley mentions some honourable exceptions: Ned Spencer of the *The Cincinnati Times* and Samuel Wilkinson of *The New York Times* reported the war with integrity and sensitivity to its horror and brutality (ibid., pp. 33–34).

A contributory factor in the poor coverage was the antagonistic relationship between reporter and soldier. General Sherman hated the press and saw their presence at the front and on the move with the army as a burden and an unwarranted interference in the conduct of the war (ibid., pp. 28–29). A correspondent for the *New York Tribune* wrote in April 1865 that 'a cat in hell without claws is nothing [compared] to a reporter in General Sherman's army' (Hammond, 1991, p. 5). Sherman saw journalists among other things as 'dirty newspaper scribblers who have the impudence of Satan', as 'spies and defamers' and 'infamous lying dogs.' The day would come, he was sure, 'when the press might surrender some portion of its freedom to save the rest or else it too will perish in the general wreck' (Ewing, 1991, p. 19). Just before Christmas of 1862, he issued an order, directed mainly at war correspondents, that 'Any person whatever...found making reports for publications which might reach the enemy giving them information and comfort, will be arrested and treated as spies' (Lande, 1996, p. 110). His colleague, General George Meade, was quick to show the way when he had reporter, Edward Crapsey of the *Philadelphia Inquirer*, put backwards on a horse with a sign round his neck, 'Libeler of the Press', and chased out of camp to the tune of *The Rogue's March*. However, on that occasion, reporter solidarity was such that Meade's name was left out of future dispatches, a factor said to have done some damage to his career ambitions (Knightley, 2004, p. 28). Another commanding officer, General Burnside, would have had William Swinton of *The New York Times* shot for espionage had it not been for the intervention of General Grant (Roth, 1997, p. 6).

Some of this flak was aimed at newspapers as well as individual reporters. The Union government prosecuted those that publicised information likely to aid and abet the enemy or compromise military security; and closed down those that printed material harmful to the Union war effort. The *Chicago Times* was closed down temporarily for criticising President Lincoln (ibid.). By 1864, the Union Secretary of War, Edward Stanton, was so concerned about the state of public morale that he took on the role of propagandist, 'dispatching' his own reports 'from the front' complete with favourable embellishments, strategic omissions, and downsized casualty figures (ibid.). Southern papers were allowed a greater degree of freedom of reporting and of opinion. The Confederate President, Jefferson Davis, promised freedom of the press in his inaugural address and, unlike President Lincoln in the north, he never closed down a newspaper during the war. This was perhaps more by default than enlightened military policy; the authorities simply did not have the resources to police and censor journalists. By 1862, the Confederate Army at the Potomac tightened existing reporting restrictions. All reports had to be dispatched through the military censors and correspondents were banned from the front; the breach of these restrictions would be treated and dealt with as a criminal act (ibid.).

Looking back at his many angry, bitter clashes with journalists during the war, General Sherman came to recognise the need to find some compromise between the military and the press. 'So greedy are the people at large for war news that is doubtful', he conceded, 'whether any army commander can exclude all reporters without bringing down on himself a clamor that may imperil his own safety. Time and moderation must bring a just solution to this modern difficulty' (Ewing, 1991, p. 29). Ironically, some 40 years after the war, journalist Henry Villard found himself in sympathy with Sherman's original hard line; the presence of the press on the frontline, he thought, 'must lead any unprejudiced mind to the conclusion that the harm certain to be done by war correspondents far outweighs any good they can possibly do. If I were a commanding general I would not tolerate any of the tribe within my army lines' (ibid.). These conflicting requirements for secrecy and publicity continued to influence the relationship between military and journalists in subsequent conflicts during the final decades of the 19th century, a period known, ironically enough, as 'the Golden Age' of the war correspondent.

FROM THE 'GOLDEN AGE' TO THE FIRST WORLD WAR, 1865–1914

The disillusionment and cynicism that infected journalism during the American Civil War were not symptoms of some new malaise. They were endemic to the evolution of a commercial and fiercely competitive press in the nineteenth century. The decades that followed the American Civil War, up until the first world war, are commonly regarded as the 'golden age' of the war correspondent but reporting in this period had more impact on the circulation figures of major newspapers, and in feeding into the popular myths of war as glamourous adventure, than it had in influencing people's opinion against war (Knightley, 2004, p. 43–66). When it came to the development of modern military censorship, however, the blueprint was the Japanese model during the Russo–Japanese War of 1904. Japanese reporting restrictions effectively kept western journalists well away from the front but, as Michael Sweeney argues, the way in which Japan dealt with foreign war correspondents was not uniquely eastern but learned from historical precedent, from the way in which other militaries had dealt with journalists in previous wars; not so much their restriction of movement as the denial of factual information, censorship by omission (1998, p. 555).

Thus, from the onset of the First World War in 1914, Britain and France similarly learned from the past, their concerns about the press fed by decades of experience going back as far as the Anglo Zulu War of 1879. The commander of British forces in that campaign, Lieutenant General Lord Chelmsford, complained in a bitter letter to the Secretary of War that it was 'more probable with such a large number of newspaper correspondents in camp, that many false impressions may be circulated and sent home regarding our present operations either intentionally or ignorantly.' He resented the journalists whom he felt were 'always ready without insufficient data for their guidance to express opinions on every conceivable military subject *ex cathedra*' (Laband and Knight, 1996, p. *v*). One of Chelmsford's officers, Sir Garnet Wolsely, saw the correspondents as a 'race of drones [and a] newly-invented curse to armies' (Hankinson, 1982, p. 243). Nonetheless, the correspondents themselves, people such as F. R. MacKenzie of the *London Standard* and Francis Francis of *The Times*, identified closely with the might and right of the imperial cause and if they were ever critical it was of issues of leadership and strategy. They saw the officer class as primary sources and saw little benefit in alienating them with undue criticism. Conversely, the officers appreciated the benefits of a 'good press' for their reputations and careers so they tended for the most part to cultivate good relationships with the correspondents. The only significant exception to this cosy relationship was the antipathy felt by Chelmsford towards Archibald Forbes, whose persistent criticisms of his leadership damaged his standing in military and political circles back home in Britain (Laband and Knight, 1996, p. *viii*). The British commander, Lord Kitchener, was especially hostile to war correspondents and tried to impede their movements and obstruct their work in every possible way (Knightley, 2004, p. 56). 'Out of my way, you drunken swabs!' was his dismissal of correspondents in Sudan, setting the tone for his approach to press relations in the Boer War and the First World War. Still, his antipathy to journalists did not blind him to their uses and he was never beneath the occasional letter to the press to advance his career ambitions (Royle, 1989, p. 46).

It was no surprise to the press in the First World War that Kitchener should adopt a policy of the strictest censorship and control. Correspondents were refused official accreditation in the first year of the war and they had no choice but to submit to an official drip of information from the newly formed Press Bureau, which censored British Army information before passing it on to the British and international press. The Bureau's communiqués were usually old news that the newspapers already knew about because it was published elsewhere (Farrar, 1998, p. 5). The aim essentially was to do or say anything but not mention the war, an objective clearly on the mind of Winston Churchill, himself a former war correspondent, when he talked about the 'fog of war'. In the first few months of war Britain and France treated all journalists the same, wherever they came from: they were free to report anything they wanted except what the war was really like. Lloyd George told C. P. Scott, editor of the *Manchester Guardian*, that if people really knew what was going on in the war, it would be stopped immediately: 'But of course', he said, 'they don't know and can't know' (Knightley, 2004, pp. 116–17). The British discouraged neutral correspondents from moving between fronts with the threat that if they were caught, they would be shot as German spies. The Germans subsequently introduced this ruling, too, so that most neutral journalists decided to stick with one side or the other for the duration and became fully immersed in the propaganda war (ibid., p. 122). It was a situation that provoked Philip Gibbs of the *Daily Telegraph* to conclude that 'By one swift stroke of military censorship, journalism was throttled' (Farrar, 1998, p. 9). The picture was hardly any better with the Russian army on the Eastern front; indeed, it was probably worse. The few western reporters to make it there were very much on their own, enjoyed little or no privileges, access or facilities, and were rarely allowed to visit the frontline (Washburn, 1982).

There were early instances of voluntary censorship in which the press chose not to report significant events such as the mobilisation of the BEF (British Expeditionary Force) to France. How such mass movement of troops could be kept secret was not considered but there was a vain hope that the War Office would reward the press for playing a responsible and patriotic role. The official argument was that censorship had to be imposed blanket fashion since it was impossible to predict or anticipate what information would or would not be useful to the enemy (Farrar, 1998, p. 11). The attitude to journalists who tried to operate outside of these restrictions was unforgiving. Any reporters found in the field of combat would be arrested, stripped of passport and deported back to England; they were 'outlaw correspondents'. The official daily briefings and press releases so common in war reportage today were unknown then so journalists depended on a high degree of mobility and flexibility to gather information and build credible reports and stories (ibid., p. 12). But how could they do this if they were treated as potential spies or have their reports so severely delayed or heavily censored as to render them useless as news? As Farrar shows, the ultimate effect of the War Office policy on the press in this early phase of the war was to create an information gap that bred uncertainty at home and lent tawdry respect to rumour. Philip Gibbs wrote how the press became so desperate for information that they would report 'any scrap of description, any glimmer of truth, any wild statement, rumour, fairy tale, or deliberate lie' if it would fill the vacuum (ibid., p. 14).

However, the *un*accredited 'outlaw' correspondents in France were sending back dispatches that undermined official censorship. Gibbs and also Arthur Moore of *The Times* moved around France, relying on fortitude and luck to avoid arrest and get real information on events at the front, especially strategically important battles such as that of the first battle of Marne (5–12 September 1914) and the first battle of Ypres (October–November 1914). Their accounts presented a very different picture of the situation than provided by the military, particularly the change of strategy from fighting along mobile fronts to the static trench warfare for which the First World War became notorious (ibid., p. 25ff). The War Office publicly denied their very existence but was careful at the same time to place restrictions on their dispatches: 'No correspondents are at the front', it said in a press release, 'and their information, however honestly sent, is therefore derived at second or third hand from persons who are in no position to tell coherent stories and who are certain to be without the perspective which is necessary to construct or understand the general situation.'(ibid., p. 22). The government eventually made some concession to the rising public clamour for news from France but it was, to use Farrar's term, 'renovation' rather than complete overhaul. An official army correspondent, Colonel Ernest Swinton, was assigned to General Headquarters (GHQ) in France, in September 1914, and charged with the job of writing articles on military operations (also subject to censorship) with the byline 'Eyewitness' (ibid., p. 23). Swinton however was not a journalist and his 'dispatches' were written in turgid military-speak unfit for public consumption. Crucially, though, it was never intended as an alternative source of public knowledge about the war; it was simply a cover for continuing the policy of non-information (ibid., p. 24).

The real breakthrough in this situation came in March 1915 amid continued public debate about the role of correspondents at the front. Four journalists were invited to visit British GHQ during the battle of Neuve Chapelle; others joined the Admiralty Fleet on its way to the Dardanelles where plans were afoot to open up another front and put pressure on German forces. As a result, news from Neuve Chapelle reached the front pages back home within days rather than weeks (ibid., p. 47ff). Furthermore, in May 1915, the military finally granted permanent, pooled accreditation to five war correspondents under strict censorship and control: the hitherto 'outlaw correspondent' Philip Gibbs (*Daily Telegraph, Daily Chronicle*), as well as Herbert Russell (Reuters), William Beach Thomas (*The Daily Mail, Daily Mirror*), Perry Robinson (*Daily News, The Times*) and Percival Philips (*Daily Express, Morning Post*). Their reporting from and movement in the war zone was governed by the War Office's 'Regulations for Press Correspondents Accompanying a Force in the Field'. There was also an official register of accredited reporters who could be trusted to comply with regulations and not betray military information to the enemy by accident or design (ibid., p. 4). Correspondents were to be accompanied at all times by military minders, invariably officers who despised journalists and made it their business to obstruct them as much as possible. They had the power to read and censor not only journalists' dispatches but also their private mail. Once reporters typed up their dispatch, it was given to their minder who vetted it before sending it onwards to GHQ where it was telephoned to the war office and from there by hand to the newspapers. Neither the War Office nor the newspapers could edit or alter a dispatch once it was passed by GHQ. There was little or no resistance to any of this from the five, pooled correspondents or their newspapers (Knightley, 2004, p. 102). Farrar passes severe verdict on their performance. 'The introduction of journalists to the Western Front could have helped the Home Front in their search for the truth', he says. 'What was created, however, was a group of correspondents who conformed to the great conspiracy, the deliberate lies and the suppression of truth.' These correspondents, with their honorary officer ranking and uniforms became part of the establishment and their primary job, to report news of the war as truthfully and accurately as possible, became an inconvenience (1998, p. 73).

As the First World War went on, public opinion in Britain became more apathetic. The government tried desperate measures to renew their propaganda campaign against the Germans, including the revival of false atrocity stories like that of the factory that boiled the corpses of German soldiers to produce glycerine for munitions. The knock-on effect of wide public skepticism about news reporting was a reluctance to believe true stories such as the Turkish atrocities against Armenians (Knightley, 2004, p. 111). If the journalists in the First World War had not become propaganda tools and if censorship had not been so rigid, what stories should or could they have filed? The real stories, the stories not fit for public consumption included: the stalemate at the front that turned the war into one of attrition with millions of dead and injured; the shortage of arms and ammunition at the front; the use of black soldiers from the colonies to save the lives of white soldiers; and the hostility between officers and troops (ibid., p. 115).

A look at the work of journalists from neutral countries in the early stages of the first world war provides some useful comparisons with those from the combatant countries. All parties to the conflict had an interest in good public relations when it came to handling such journalists, especially Americans. Britain and France wanted the United States to enter the war, while Germany wanted it to stay neutral. This meant that in the early stages of the war, American correspondents were able to report stories that were officially censored or embargoed, like the German army's first use of gas at the front, which Britain wanted to keep secret unless it should undermine public support for the war effort. While America remained neutral (up until 1917), its newspapers were so starved of information that they would send over amateur correspondents in the vain hope they might get accredited; over 20 had made the journey to neutral Austria by mid-October 1914. They were to say the least naive adventurers and the type of correspondent lampooned in the Evelyn Waugh novel, *Scoop*. One identified himself as a 'special correspondent' of the Transcript Press, a Boston publisher. He had bet his friend a box of cigars that he would make it to the front and return home for Christmas: 'Hence my determination to smell the smoke of battle in order to puff the cheroot of peace' (Crozier, 1959, p. 39).

Accredited journalists were none too keen on these new arrivals and accused them of being too ready to believe everything they were told about German atrocity stories, without interference from the censor. The reality was rather different. Knightley argues that American correspondents were less gullible when it came to atrocity stories and some of them expressed concern about the nature and reach of official censorship. Westbrook Pegler, of the United Press news agency was censored when he reported, during the winter of 1917–18, on the high incidence of fatal pneumonia among American troops at the front; and that this was being covered up by the authorities. He was soon recalled when the US army persuaded United Press that he was too young and inexperienced for war reporting. He wrote that 'Censorship is developing more in the news interests of the military than in that of the American reader' (Knightley, 2004, p. 140). A leading American journalist in London wrote that: 'The news hungry public was often misled in that period...News, lies, local color, human interest, fakes: all went down the public gullet in gargantuan gulps' (Crozier, 1959, p. 41). The American correspondents resisted the censorship and the intimidation and some of the best even went home rather than compromise their professional integrity, a principled stand that was very rare then and almost unheard of now (Knightley, 2004, p. 123). For the initial period of the First World War, while America remained neutral, American press coverage was better, more comprehensive, and certainly more impartial than anything available in the pages of the British, French or German newspapers. A poll asked 367 proprietors which side had their sympathy – two thirds expressed no particular preference. Editors, too, were careful to preserve neutrality in their selection of war news (ibid., p. 127). However, once America entered the war in 1917, the situation for American correspondents predictably changed. US Army censorship was managed by a committee of ex-journalists and ex-army officers and, in its short life, its job was bolstered by the Espionage Act of 1917 and the Sedition Act of 1918, which respectively legislated against aiding and abetting the enemy and criticising the conduct of government or military (Kirtley, 1992, p. 475). In effect, these Acts were catch-all legislation deployed to control the press with impunity.

According to Knightley, the key characteristics of most reportage from the front in this period were the exaggeration of military success, underestimation of casualties, and little or no sense of the true reality of trench warfare. When the hard questions were asked on the Home front, the truth of what was happening came as a shock to all (2004, p. 103). Farrar takes issue with Knightley about the degree to which journalists became propaganda mouthpieces, but they largely agree on the basic outcome of the censorship regime: subservience among reporters to the military and, as a result, public ignorance at the home front. They and many other writers agree that the 'Golden Age' of the war correspondent came to a close during the First World War; reporters were no longer the free booting adventurers of the Spanish American War or the Boer War. Not everyone thought such an age ever existed. An article in *The Daily Mail* defended the First World War correspondents against critics who hearkened back to reporters like Archibald Forbes whom, it was thought, would have done a much better job. 'There is a great deal of nonsense spoken about the old school of war correspondents', said the writer. 'The truth is, they were not supermen at all' (Farrar, 1998, p. 206). In the latter stages of the First World War, argues Farrar, they 'yielded to military pressure and became a propaganda tool. They betrayed the trust of their readership' (ibid., p. 226). Reporters came to accept the idea of systemised restrictions on both their reporting and their movement; it seemed to them that being near the front, bivouaced in some chateau under strict military supervision was better than sitting at home relying on second hand news. It was to prove a costly compromise. Henry Nevinson, described how correspondents 'lived chirping together like little birds in a nest', wholly dependent on the military to feed them news (ibid., p. 227). As Knightley puts it, 'What it came down to in the end was that, in the eyes of GHQ, the ideal war correspondent would be one who wrote what he had been told was true, or even what he thought was true, but never what he knew to be true. Given these restrictions, the war correspondents might just as well have stayed in London' (2004, p. 101).

THE SECOND WORLD WAR, 1939–45

War correspondents during the Second World War were known in the armed services as 'warcos'. By 1944, as the allies pushed the Germans out of France and Belgium, there were 150 warcos from Britain and the

US all filing stories to 278 million readers worldwide 'like the script-writers of a long running soap opera' (Collier, 1989, p. 178). They were fitted out in officers' uniforms, including caps, Sam Browne belts and arm badges with the gold letter 'C' for correspondent. They were forbidden to carry arms, although if captured and held as prisoners of war they could assume the status of captain. However, an American press officer remarked that when at large the warcos 'assumed the rank of field marshal...and recognised no conventions' (ibid.). The warcos had come to expect good treatment from the military without considering the cost in terms of professional integrity and independence. Alan Moorehead, of the *Daily Express*, admitted that 'Like the children of very wealthy parents it seemed quite natural to us that we should occupy the best houses and hotels, that we should have at our command cars, motor launches, servants and the best food' (ibid.). The big question mark, of course, hung over the parents. What would their attitude be to their spoilt and unruly children? One of indulgence or discipline? It is instructive to compare the British approach to control of the media with that of Germany in the early stages of the Second World War and then to compare both these with the new, public relations approach taken by the United States army when it eventually entered the war in 1941.

In Germany, all agencies of communication were brought under the direct control of the state so that journalists were conscripted along with film and radio producers, printers, artists, writers, and photographers, into the ranks of the Propaganda Division of the Army. They were given basic military training and were sent to the front to fight when necessary. But their principal role was as propaganda shock troops: they were to help to keep up morale on all fronts, and to damage enemy morale (Knightley, 2004, pp. 240–41). The German approach to neutral correspondents, especially Americans before the US entered the war, was rather more seductive. Its Ministry of Propaganda under Goebbels facilitated neutral correspondents through its Foreign Press Department. They were given a range of perks and privileges (extra rations, petrol expenses and special exchange rates, among others) and a free hand to report what they wanted. However, in practice, all communications out of the German theatre of operations were carefully monitored and journalists who filed negative copy were intimidated or even arrested for spying. As Knightley suggests, this was an easy charge to make in wartime where the line between journalism and espionage is a rather fine one; its effect was to encourage self-censorship. Still, the conditions experienced by foreign correspondents in Berlin in the early stages of the war were much more favourable than those prevailing behind Allied lines and it was little wonder that over 100 journalists based themselves there (ibid., p. 240).

The British approach was just as effective but far from seductive or subtle. The government used the Emergency Powers Act to censor all public and private communication out of the country that was thought to be of use to the enemy. The media – which now included radio as well as the press – were subjected to the same reporting restrictions as in the First World War. A limited number of correspondents were allowed to the front under the watchful eye of a senior Ministry of Information minder, called 'Eyewitness' as in the First World War (ibid., p. 238). They were subjected to strict procedures of accreditation and essentially became part of the BEF. Furthermore, their dispatches from the front were censored so they would not undermine morale at home. Four British correspondents accompanied the BEF to the Maginot Line in France where they worked in a pool system. The system of media control in France was so stringent that by the time a correspondent's dispatch reached the newspaper it was barely news any more. Such was the dearth of hard news and skilful media management from the Ministry of Information, *The Daily Express* complained that Britain would need to launch a leaflet drop on itself to inform its citizens about the course of the war so far (ibid., p. 242). Its correspondent O. D. Gallagher suggested that British Army public relations was so ineffective that it would be better to adopt the German system instead. After pressure from the military, Gallagher was recalled from the front and sent around Britain to report on civil defence arrangements (ibid., p. 243).

The approach of American reporters to British censorship was to fight it. Ben Robertson, of the New York paper *PM*, was covering a dogfight between German and British planes mid-channel and reported the loss of three Spitfires to seven Messerschmitts. But one of the censors on duty in the Ministry of Information struck out the references to British losses. Robertson took exception and appealed upwards, eventually to the Minister himself, Alfred Duff Cooper, who agreed to let it through. For Robertson, the main obstacle was not so much the system in place as the individual censor, often lowly ranked and poorly paid, and quite unwilling to stray from the rules (Collier, 1989, p. 49ff).

Robertson and his compatriot colleagues were used to a different culture of information and expected openness and public relations skills from their military. The US army saw public relations and news management as a vital part of overall strategy; as General Dwight D. Eisenhower put it to a meeting of US newspaper editors, 'Public opinion wins war' (Knightley, 2004, p. 344). Considerable resources were afforded to the job of accommodating and controlling the burgeoning demands the media were making for information about the latest developments in the war. Military officers became adept at handling journalists and catering to their professional requirements. The concern was to strike a working balance between necessary censorship and good public relations: to bring reporters on side and accommodate their needs as much as possible; to give them good stories and pictures; and to be mindful of the impressions of the military journalists would bring back home after the war (Braestrup, 1985, p. 30).

Eisenhower told reporters that it was 'a matter of policy [that] accredited war correspondents should be accorded the greatest possible latitude in the gathering of legitimate news' and that 'Public Relations Officers and Conducting Officers give...war correspondents all reasonable assistance' (ibid., p. 31). Of course, the power to define what 'legitimate news' was rested with the military. American reporters were subjected to censorship but they were allowed easy access to the front, accompanied always by a public affairs officer. Reporters from other countries, including Britain, envied the facilities offered to the American press corps. American field commanders were more open with reporters, British commanders more suspicious. American reporters were treated as active officers and given room and equipment to do their job, including the services of a press officer; while British reporters were watched closely at all times by a duty escorting officer and were subject to a raft of reporting restrictions and censorship procedures (ibid., p. 41).

Braestrup notes that the US Army allowed journalists in on the planning of major operations such as the D-Day landings and both parties got to know each other quite well. 'The journalist had time to understand the problem and the plan – and hence gain some basis for later assessments of what actually took place' (ibid., p. 28). The amphibious landings by the US army in Europe and the Pacific were 'set-piece affairs', well planned in advance to include the accommodation of a select number of journalists. Just before the Normandy landings, reporters based at Army headquarters were assured that they would be well looked after by the Public Relations division, which would offer them 'the very best in information and communication.' They were encouraged to see the Public Relations Officer as 'true friends', some of whom were reporters themselves and who knew a good news angle (ibid., p. 36). The public relations strategy did not quite work in practice when the invasion finally went ahead. The contingent of reporters with US forces was small and severely stretched. Reporters found themselves isolated and unable to access communications facilities. John McVane of NBC remarked on 'All the vast public relations preparations and only a lieutenant there to help us' when he tried to report on the Omaha beach landing (ibid., p. 40).

The treatment of journalists at the Normandy landings was not flawless but it was a great improvement on earlier operations, such as the disastrous raid on Dieppe when reporters were largely kept in the dark, given little or no information and subjected to unreasonable censorship (ibid., p. 41). It was also true that improved military public relations translated into better or more extensive coverage of the war by the American news media. The Asian and Pacific theatres were not well covered at all simply because there were not enough reporters to cover every battle. Important battles such as the now famous 'Battle of the Bulge' at Bastogne in December 1944 went unreported by American correspondents (ibid., p. 27).

This was not to say that all sections of the British armed services were lacking in public relations skills. The British army in the North African theatre was taking a very different, more media friendly approach (Knightley, 2004, p. 332; Hickman, 1995, p. 155ff). For the British army, the North African campaign was a chance to shine against the enemy in apparently wide-open and empty spaces without having to worry too much about civilian casualties. Furthermore, it distracted from their own deficiencies in the European theatre of war where it was becoming apparent that defeat could only be averted by American intervention – both financial and military. The war in the desert also appealed to the warcos. When the offensive began, in December 1940, six reporters accompanied the British armoured brigades. Within a year and a half, there were 92 of them, and more arriving by the day (Knightley, 2004, p. 332). Field Marshal Montgomery was a charismatic and dynamic military leader and appreciated the value of a friendly and amenable press corps for self-promotion and propaganda in his personal duel with the German Field Marshal Rommel. He went so far as to regard journalists as elements of his staff (ibid., p. 333). BBC correspondent Frank Gillard remembers 'the kind of relationship which could develop in this war between a war correspondent and the commander-in-chief' and says that it was 'crucially important to a correspondent that he should be recognised and trusted as a member of the Army family, even though he could never allow the army to use or manipulate him. This delicate relationship was greatly strengthened if it was seen that the correspondent was approved of in the top ranks of command' (Hawkins, 1985, p. 12). Duly approved of, and some with egos greatly inflated, the warcos saw little problem with this and some even considered giving up the job to enlist. They reported the desert campaign as a romantic adventure in which the British triumphed and where even the enemy displayed chivalry and military greatness.

Yet for all the public relations, few journalists ever got close enough to the North African frontlines to witness a single tank battle. Alan Moorehead, of the *Daily Express*, recalls that they 'were simply conscious of a great deal of dust, noise and confusion' (Knightley, 2004, p. 337). Furthermore, the PR approach did not extend to the few women correspondents accredited in the second world war and who turned up to report the action in Northern Africa. Army command barred women reporters from working in active combat zones and were especially irked whenever they caused a fuss and made difficult demands for equality with their male colleagues. The head of the British Army's Press Division, Lieutenant Philip Astley, wondered why women reporters could not be content with special 'visitor status' and segregated facilities (Sebba, 1994, p. 153).

Although journalists soon realised the implications of censorship during the Second World War, few if any confronted the system. They accepted it because they thought the situation would change for the better or that the war would soon be over. The criticisms and reservations were saved or their post-war memoirs when it was too late to have any real effect. A Reuters correspondent admitted that journalists were simply propagandists for their governments, mere cheerleaders: 'It wasn't good journalism', he said. 'It wasn't journalism at all' (Knightley, 1995, p. 45).

THE KOREAN WAR 1950–53

In the Korean War, General MacArthur repeatedly refused to provide a formal system of censorship and regular briefings, which he thought was impossible. Subtly, he shifted the burden of censorship onto reporters themselves, trusting on their good sense not to compromise military security or undermine the authority of a field officer with 'unwarranted criticisms' or personal attacks (Braestrup, 1985, p. 50). Reporters felt a deep sense of unease about this and actually demanded from MacArthur direct censorship and 'uniform guidance' with reporting (ibid., p. 50; see also Adams, p. 27ff). According to Braestrup, journalists feared that McArthur's permissive policy would put increasing pressure on them to disclose more information than their rivals. They also thought the lines of transgression too vague. How was a reporter to judge what might compromise security or endanger lives? And when did a reporter cross the line to make 'unwarranted criticism' of army operations or damage the prestige and pride of American forces? Where were the definitions and ground rules? For all their fears and anxieties, the voluntary code remained in place until the end of 1950 during which time, said the US Eighth Army censor, 'the disclosure of security information by correspondents was virtually a daily occurrence' (Braestrup, 1985, p. 52).

The situation changed radically when the Chinese army turned the tide of the war against UN forces from mid-September 1950. Suddenly, the need for tighter security and secrecy of information became more pressing. On 20 December, the Far Eastern Command (FEC) imposed a system of censorship in which all media material relating to the war would be submitted first for clearance. A Press Advisory Division was set up and based at the FEC public information office in Tokyo for the purpose of censorship. Field censorship in Korea was handled by the Press Security Division of the US Eighth Army (ibid. p. 53). It was estimated that 90 per cent or more of reporters favoured this formal system of censorship because it lifted the burden of self-censorship and eased competition with rivals. Some however tried to get round the new restrictions through loopholes and subterfuge and, as a result, invited further tightening of restrictions. But Braestrup argues that despite the imposition of formal ground rules in December 1950, the FEC attitude was still relatively lax throughout the war compared with other conflicts, before or after Korea, and the army rarely took drastic action against errant reporters. Journalists were allowed considerable latitude to criticise and analyse military operations, and to portray the war in its full horror. During the peace talks, they spoke out against misleading or inadequate UN briefings. Notably, says Braestrup, the military did not blame 'the security lapses, mood swings, exaggerations, or forebodings' of journalists for the growing dissatisfaction at home with the war (ibid., p. 54).

The Australian correspondent, Wilfred Burchett, reported the Korean War from a radical perspective and he always thought that the real 'press war' in Korea was between journalists and their American press officers (1980, p. 174). The most interesting phase of the war, as far as the role of journalists is concerned, came as it drew to a close with the ceasefire talks in Kaesong. The UN was deeply divided over bringing the war to a close and Burchett, along with Chinese journalist, Chu Chi-p'ing, and Alan Winnington of the British *Daily Worker*, found themselves in the position of unofficial briefers for journalists attached to the UN command. This happened, said Burchett, because of the 'suppression, distortion, and untruthful accounts of conference proceedings given by the official UN spokesmen'. Other international media outlets covering the talks increasingly took to lifting the accounts of these journalists and publishing them alongside reports of news agencies because their reports were generally found to be more accurate than those using the UN as a principal source (ibid., p. 165).

A significant example of how this worked concerned a crucial battle of words over the final line of demarcation that would define the ceasefire settlement: the 38th parallel. Using the UN as diplomatic cover, the Americans tried to get the line pushed back 35 miles from the existing Chinese–Korean front. The Chinese and Koreans argued that the existing positions on either side of the 38th parallel more or less reflected the original balance of forces and seemed a fair enough compromise for a settlement. The UN command produced a map to support its identification of the line but western journalists found themselves cross-referencing the three reporters over the precise demarcation line in question because there was 'an obvious discrepancy between what they were *told* and what we *knew*' (ibid., p. 166; emphasis in the original). The UN map released to the western press was a fake, something the UN press officer, Brigadier General William P. Nuckols eventually admitted.

In response, the UN launched a propaganda counter-offensive in which it contrived a breakdown of negotiations, one provoked by the Chinese and Koreans and resulting in their banning of western journalists from Kaesong. Before Burchett and his two colleagues had a chance to offset the crisis, and point out that only one day of talks had been cancelled, it was too late. Contact between the press and both sides had broken down, with the UN chief liaison officer, Colonel Andrew J. Kinney (US Air Force) claiming it was all down to communist obstruction, and that the communists were the ones who banned the press (ibid., p. 166). The policy of disinformation by UN press officers, and the habit of accredited journalists of cross-checking with Burchett and his other two colleagues, continued throughout the ceasefire talks with frequent crises and breakdowns in the relationship with the UN command. It presaged a new phase of military–media relations that would define and be defined by future international wars and the invasions and interventions that marked the latter stages of the Cold War. And it started with the Vietnam War.

THE VIETNAM WAR, 1965–75

One of the most enduring myths in the recent history of war reporting is the 'Vietnam Syndrome', the widespread belief that the mainstream US media were opposed to the Vietnam War and openly hostile to the US military and its South Vietnamese clients; and that as a result of their critical coverage they lost the war for the US. This of course bears little or no relation to the media's actual coverage of the war, yet it has shaped and influenced political and military control of the media in subsequent conflicts from the Falklands War to the US invasions of Grenada and Panama and in the Gulf War in 1991 (Hallin, 1986; McArthur, 1992; Williams, 1993).

The following discussion of the American media's relations with the US military in the Vietnam War relates to the period between 1965–75 during which US military involvement was at its most direct; so-called US military advisers were in place long before this, helping the South Vietnamese regime put down the nationalist and communist insurgents, collectively labelled the Vietcong. The turning point during this period came in 1968 when the North Vietnamese army launched a surprise offensive against the South Vietnamese regime on the traditional Tet holiday. From then on, the consensus among Washington elites about the conduct of the war began to leak. Popular support also waned, apparently because of hostile media coverage and the nightly images of dead and injured American soldiers. By 1975, US resolve had finally collapsed; total withdrawal swiftly followed.

Both the Kennedy and Johnson administrations were extremely sensitive to 'negative' news from Vietnam and, by extension, negative domestic comment and analysis in the elite press. Negative news was essentially any news that contradicted the official line that the military was making progress in winning the war (Braestrup, 1985, p. 62). The White House and the Pentagon consistently tried to counter every piece of 'negative' news with optimistic assessments and projections and Johnson even went so far as to second military commanders in Vietnam, including General Westmoreland, to help sell the war at home, which Braestrup describes as 'an unprecedented use of the military to achieve domestic political objectives' (ibid., p. 63).

The history books offer numerous examples of the freewheeling journalist in Vietnam, undermining military security and public morale with daily reports of tactical blunders, strategic incompetence and the terrible rate of attrition suffered by US troops for vainglorious ends. The reality was quite different. Reporters like David Halberstam and Neil Sheehan cultivated good relationships with their military sources, most notably Lieutenant Colonel John Paul Vann. They also got on well with the rank and file and delighted in hitching rides on the combat helicopters, describing their experiences in the first person plural rather than singular (Halberstam, 1979; Sheehan, 1989). With few exceptions, the American press corps in Saigon was composed of ordinary journalists who knew where their sympathies lay (MacArthur, 1992, p. 118).

Halberstam, who reported for *The New York Times*, is still thought of by liberals in the west as an exemplary war reporter: bold and courageous in the pursuit of truth in spite of the criticisms ranged against him at home for his reporting of the Vietnam War. In late 1963, the CIA produced an analysis of his 'lugubrious and pessimistic' reporting, which although accurate with the facts, drew conclusions from those facts that apparently impugned his objectivity (ibid., p. 116). Some of the most conservative sections of the US media also took exception to his subversive journalism. He recalls how the *New York Journal-American* accused him of being 'soft on Communism', and 'paving the way for a bearded Vietnamese Fidel Castro' (ibid., p. 119). President Kennedy wondered aloud to *New York Times'* publisher Arthur O. Sulzberger if he was planning to move Halberstam somewhere else (ibid., p. 120). In fact, like almost all of his colleagues in the Saigon press corps, he was a patriotic journalist who questioned certain operational and strategic decision-making that undermined the war effort against the Vietnamese communist and nationalist insurgents. As Neil Sheehan wrote of him, Halberstam was an example of 'the genius of the Anglo Saxon society of the Northeast for co-opting the talents and loyalty of outsiders with its social democracy. A society that would give...the grandson of immigrant Jewish peddlers a Harvard education and a job at *The New York Times* was innately good, incapable of perpetrating evil in other lands'. Halberstam was 'full of gratitude to that society and wanted to spread its good' (1989, p. 321) and rarely questioned the morality of US involvement in Vietnam or indeed anywhere around the world. In his book, The *Making of a Quagmire*, he wrote of his belief that 'Vietnam is a legitimate part of [America's] global commitment...perhaps one of only five or six nations in the world that is truly vital to US interests. If it is this important it may be worth a larger commitment on our part but if so we should be told the truth, not spoon-fed clichés as in the past' (cited in Braestrup, 1983, p. 4).

Halberstam, Sheehan and others were pressured not so much because of what they believed or wrote but because of the ideological battles raging on the home front over what was happening on the ground in Vietnam. Anyone who questioned any aspect of official policy was at best 'a liberal', at worst a 'communist'. It all depended on the nature of the critique and the context of its presentation. The more vital the policy to the economic and political interests of the state, the further left the critiques were regarded. Mildly critical journalists became unpatriotic subversives who, as the famous war correspondent turned establishment columnist, Marguerite Higgins, complained, would love their country to lose the war so they could be proved right (MacArthur, 1992, p. 120). Peter Arnett writes that 'Caught between the truth of what we saw and the nation's sense of patriotism, the Vietnam reporters became something like outcasts, destined to defend their professionalism for the rest of their lives' (1996).

This sets in context the daily US military briefings in Saigon and explains why they quickly became known as 'The Five O' Clock Follies'.

These were simply designed to feed the news media with a daily 'hard news' story but were not taken seriously by most journalists because they were based on 'hasty, fragmentary, inevitably inaccurate field reports' of action in a theatre of war where there was no actual frontline, moving or stationary (Braestrup, 1985, p. 63; see also Braestrup, 1983, p. 17). Only the US aerial bombardment passed as 'hard news' despite the fact that it was entirely detailed in army press releases; journalists were not allowed to accompany the aircrews on bombing sorties. The myth of heated clashes between spokesmen and journalists was, Braestrup suspects, more about journalist giving vent to frustrations about the lack of real news than sharp, perceptive reporters holding out tenaciously for the 'truth'. Any such journalist knew the truth was not to be had in the briefings. And as Braestrup points out, official optimism had become such a devalued currency over the first few years of war that journalists in Saigon 'were inclined to discount all optimistic assessments by official spokesmen, even as they dutifully reported them' (1985, p. 64). John Pilger recalls from his own experience that reporters like himself regarded the Follies as 'a bit of theatre' in which some journalists amused themselves by tormenting the briefer:

In fact I went down there and filmed the briefer...and asked him A-B-C questions like, How many men were serving in Vietnam? How many people were killed by friendly fire? How many men were killed by accidents? How many helicopters fell out of the sky because they were badly serviced? They threw him into a panic. He couldn't even tell me how many men were in the country. So from my point of view they were useless.[2]

Jacques Leslie reported the war for the *Los Angeles Times* from 1972 until July 1973 when he was expelled from the country for his habit of reporting inconvenient exclusives: the torture of women prisoners, corruption and ceasefire violations, and even a conspiracy by South Vietnamese army generals to smuggle valuable used artillery shell canisters out of the country for very profitable return. These stories were possible because Leslie cultivated good official and unofficial sources. 'The result, of course, was that I was finally kicked out of the country in July, 1973, an act the U.S. Embassy heartily endorsed.'[3]

Drew Middleton of Associated Press reflects that in Vietnam, as in Korea, no one was quite sure what the ground rules were so the military were much more wary of talking openly and freely with journalists (Knightley, 2004, p. 465). There were about 40 US and foreign journalists in Saigon in 1964, increasing to more than 400 by summer 1965 when daily briefings were provided for 130 correspondents. By 1966, there were 419 journalists from 22 countries, 179 of which were American (Braestrup, 1985, p. 64). The most troubling aspect was that, with few exceptions, the Follies became for the majority of reporters the principal source of information about the war. Pilger reveals that out of 649 journalists accredited to the Saigon press corps from 1968, only about eight of them made regular forays into the field (2001, p. 263). Jacques Leslie remembers it differently. He says that 'most journalists, unless they were too frightened or concerned for their safety, got out of Saigon – the good stories weren't in Saigon'. He takes credit for being the first American correspondent to go into Viet Cong territory, 'only because of the arrival of the ceasefire in late January, 1973. Before that, it was impossible – anyone trying before that was likely to enjoy the fate of my friend Alex Shimkin, a *Newsweek* stringer, who blundered into Viet Cong territory in 1972 and was immediately killed.' He does not see his actions as particularly daring or heroic. It was about being sensible and about being a good journalist. He had simply nurtured good contacts and sources, in this case Viet Cong sources, who assured him that with the ceasefire in place he would be safe and that he would be treated well. As he points out, 'it wasn't laziness on the part of other journalists that kept them out – rather, it was a quite reasonable fear of being killed, and the dearth of sources like mine.' Once he set the example and showed it could be done, others followed his footsteps, some of them quite literally 'to the very village I'd visited, until the village chief told them they were taking up too much of his time, and to pass the word to stop going there.' The majority of journalists never considered meeting the Viet Cong because they had nothing to learn. The VC were the enemy, they were evil; end of story. Leslie's bureau chief, George McArthur, 'rarely left Saigon for any reason, relied on his CIA sources for many if not most of his stories, and probably figured anyone who pulled off the feat would be treated to nothing more than a Potemkin Village-like performance for his efforts.'[4]

CONCLUDING REMARKS

Pilger, Braestrup and many other critics discount the myth that the media lost the Vietnam War and firmly point to political divisions at home, and poor news management at the White House, as part of the problem.[5] Braestrup himself reported the war and, like so many of his American colleagues in the press corps, supported its fundamental justification. Thus, he argues, the real folly in Vietnam was Kennedy's and Johnsons' habit of accentuating the positive while doing little or nothing to progress the war on the ground, of which the briefings in Saigon were merely an extension. Nixon took firm and positive action on the ground first and then sold it to the media but there was still a significant credibility gap there that could not be closed. Braestrup argues that any administration sending troops to war must prepare a clear media strategy and 'a sturdy resolve...not to gloss over difficulties' (ibid., p. 75). As I will go on to show, the post Vietnam era would see the development of a media strategy that put the emphasis on censorship and control, whilst appreciating the usefulness of public relations spin and gloss.

6

Learning and Forgetting: From the Falklands to the Gulf

[The briefers in the Gulf] are making reporters look like fools, nitpickers, and egomaniacs; like dilettantes who spent exactly none of their lives on the end of a gun or even a shovel; dinner party commandos, slouching inquisitors, collegiate spitball artists – people who have never been in a fistfight much less combat; a whining, self-righteous, upper middle class mob.

Henry Allen, *Washington Post*, 1991[1]

The prevailing and erroneous myth of a hostile media in Vietnam quickly took root in US military thinking about how to manage the media in the field of operations; and they were to learn much from the successes and failures of British military and political information policy during the Falklands war (1982). American military planners were impressed with British information restrictions but not with their approach to public relations and sought to develop a more balanced media strategy when planning their own subsequent operations in Grenada (1986), Panama (1989) and the Gulf (1991). The deployment in those instances of a more formal and restrictive pooling system than that used in both World Wars (Chapter 5), coupled with tightly managed daily media briefings, suggests that the historical development of military media strategy has been evolutionary rather than revolutionary or new. It is an argument that sets the context for what follows in Chapter 7: a proper understanding of the embed system deployed to great effect during the early stages of the US invasion of Afghanistan in 2001 and Iraq in 2003.

THE FALKLANDS WAR, 1982

When the Falklands crisis moved onto a war footing in 1982, the British armed forces struggled to formulate an information policy and media strategy. They too fell victim to 'Vietnam Syndrome'. As far back as 1970, Air Vice Marshall Stewart Menaul bemoaned coverage of Vietnam, concluding that 'television had a lot to answer for in the collapse of American morale'. At the same time, the Ministry of Defence's (MoD's) Director of Defence Operations advised colleagues to ask themselves: 'Are we going to let television cameras loose on the battlefield?' (Glasgow University Media Group, 1985, p. 8). With thinking like this it was little wonder that their approach to media management in the Falklands was so problematic. A limited number of British journalists were allowed to accompany the fleet to the South Atlantic. Only 29 correspondents – all of them British – were assigned to various pools on board the Royal Navy ships and the amount of help and assistance given to them was minimal. The government and military line was a familiar one: that reporting restrictions were necessary and vital to safeguard operational security and the lives of the troops. However critics argued that it extended far beyond such terms of reference and was designed to ensure coverage that would convey a favourable impression of the war at home (Glasgow University Media Group, 1985; Harris, 1983; Morrison and Tumber, 1988; Mercer et al, 1987). Journalists such as Brian Hanrahan (BBC) and Michael Nicholson (ITN) complained bitterly of heavy-handed censorship; and when they took to prefixing their reports as having being censored, this word itself was censored (Glasgow University Media Group, 1985, p. 9).

In a report for the Home Office, Valerie Adams (1986) argues that many of the problems experienced between the military and media were down to oversight or to specific failures of planning by the MoD, which failed to think in advance about how the media should be handled. For their part, journalists failed to understand some very practical, operational limits prevailing aboard ship (p. 4). None of this, however, should detract from the reality of direct and deliberate censorship of the media during the Falklands War. It operated on three levels:

- direct censorship and control by the MoD in the South Atlantic
- restraints imposed by the lobby briefing system
- self-censorship by journalists in the name of military security, or in respect to public opinion, taste and decency.

Direct censorship and control of the news media
by the MoD in the South Atlantic

Unlike the army, with its media experience in Northern Ireland, the navy
was not accustomed to having journalists aboard their ships and had the
government not intervened there would have been no media presence in
the Falklands at all. Once on board and at sea, the media pools were at
the mercy of their military minders. They had no facilities of their own
for sending reports via satellite and were forced to rely on ship communications. In many cases this was made extremely difficult; phones
were mysteriously busy when a journalist wanted to send a report on a
dramatic development, especially when things were going badly. From
a naval point of view, journalists expected to dispatch copy via ships
communications when it suited them but it soon got to the point where
almost 30 percent of traffic was press copy, not a situation the Navy could
easily tolerate for obvious operational reasons (Adams, 1986, p. 14). The
effect of all this on the quantity and quality of coverage was serious. In
some instances, unfavourable reports or pictures took days to find their
way to the newsroom.

Restraints imposed by the lobby briefing system

Things were no better for journalists reporting from the home front. The
MoD's public relations department was headed by a civil servant, Ian
McDonald, whose attitude to media management was so negative that he
was quickly dubbed the 'Minister for No Information'. He would appear
before the assembled media and read out brief, perfunctory statements;
questions from reporters or off-record briefings were not allowed. The
MoD's PR officers were even less helpful. They were 'relatively junior
people, lacking the authority, the experience, or perhaps the ability to
negotiate successfully' (ibid., p. 14). Walter Rogers reported the briefings
for the American Broadcasting Company (ABC) and thought that the
British journalists were too passive. If they had stood up for themselves
and demanded better treatment, the MoD would have given in sooner
(Philo and McLaughlin, 1995, p. 155). The Canadian CBS correspondent, Morley Safer, thought that the major difference between the MoD
briefings and the Five O'Clock Follies in Vietnam was that in the former,
the journalists knew less than Ian McDonald; in Vietnam, the journalists

knew much more than the hapless briefer, 'at least those...who'd been out of Saigon at all' (Pilger, 2001, p. 261). But McDonald's approach was soon challenged from within the MoD itself, namely from PR professionals like Neville Taylor who believed that it could give the media what they wanted – news and pictures – but on its own terms. By the middle of May 1982, off-the-record briefings were restored.

Self-censorship by journalists

In many ways, the MoD had no need to adopt such heavy-handed information management. It could rest assured that in a spirit of patriotism and a general atmosphere of fear most British journalists and their editors, on public service television as well as the press, could be relied upon to practice a large degree of self-censorship. The principal and ultimate tool at the MoD's disposal was the D-Notice, which barred publication of information thought by the authorities to compromise military security. But Morrison and Tumber have shown that apart from a set of standing orders issued three weeks before the Argentine invasion, no D-Notice was ever imposed during the conflict itself. Instead, the MoD favoured a more ad hoc arrangement in which journalists would seek informal guidance by telephone or meeting about whether or not to include certain information. In effect, journalists were cooperating with a system that put the onus of censorship not on the authorities but on themselves. Three criteria influenced the selection of combat footage for primetime television news: military security, standards of taste and decency with respect to pictures of dead and wounded, and intrusion of privacy with respect to interviews with families of troops killed in action (Morrison and Tumber, 1988, p. 220ff). A Commons Defence Committee inquiry into military–media relations during the Falklands War, led by Lord Beech, heard evidence from media and government representatives and concluded, perhaps not surprisingly, that the basic goals of information policy had been successfully met, the war was won and no serious breaches of security had been committed by journalists. The Beech Report concluded that in war time disputes will always arise about what constitutes 'operational security', but, crucially, 'where there are conflicting views...the military view must prevail' (Adams, 1986, p. 161). The Beech inquiry also looked at two other policy issues: the public's right to know and the government's duty to withhold information for security reasons. It recognised that censorship and propaganda had a place in concealing information from the enemy and also deceiving the enemy. 'Propaganda in itself is not objectionable', it reported, 'and it certainly need not involve lying and deception' (ibid., p. 15).

Lessons from the Falklands

Valerie Adams argues that journalists are not always in a position to judge and determine the boundaries of operational security and therefore they differ about what justifies censorship (ibid., p. 161ff). Max Hastings saw his reporting as 'an extension of the war effort', giving help and succour to the troops when needed (ibid., p. 47), while David Fairhall, of the *Guardian*, remarks that 'Much of what suspicious journalists regarded as news management could probably be explained as a mixture of ignorance, wishful thinking and a natural desire to put the best light on things when seen from a particular point of view' (ibid., p. 53). Mike Nicholson accepts that 'sensible censorship' is inevitable and to be expected but he objects strongly to 'idiot censorship, total blanket censorship by men who are too cowardly or too arrogant to allow things to happen as they should.' He is also aware that there is disinformation, and that 'it's terribly, terribly hard to know when you're being lied to. It's not until afterwards that you realise you *have* been lied to...I mean we're always the puppets here and unless you say to them, "I'm not going to report anything you say because I think you're going to lie to me", what do you do? It's a Catch-22!' (Emphasis in the original).[2]

Mercer et al. (1987) identify a crucial difference between the British and American information culture. The American Department of Defense (DoD) advocates public openness and accountability in accordance with the constitutional principles. 'Propaganda', it says, 'has no place in [DoD] public affairs programmes' (p. 4). The British MoD public relations staff seek to inform the public of its activities, also, but in wartime its primary function is of propaganda, in other words to 'create a favourable climate in support of these activities by the use of the news media, films, exhibitions and literature' (ibid., p. 5). Journalists may see that as quite ironic given the MoD approach to briefings but the Ministry was nonetheless successful in 'creating a favourable climate' in support of the war against Argentina; indeed, its approach was noted by military planners in the USA. In a US Army journal, Commander

Arthur Humphries drew a vital lesson from news management during the Falklands. Criticising British heavy handedness in their dealings with the news media, he advised that the military must give regular and friendly media briefings, and cultivate a relationship with the media based on mutual trust. This, he believed, would ensure 'the flow of correct information' and prevent 'faulty speculation.' He also accused the British of failing to 'appreciate that news management was more than just information security censorship. It also means providing pictures.' The crucial lesson, however, was control: 'Control access to the fighting, invoke censorship, and rally aid in the form of patriotism at home and in the battle zone.' Whatever about the rhetoric of free speech and democracy, 'the Falklands War shows us how to make certain that government policy is not undermined by the way a war is reported.' Humphries recommended that 'to effect or to help assure "favourable objectivity" you must be able to exclude certain correspondents from the battle zone.' In sum, then, Humphries advised that military planning 'should include criteria for incorporating the news media into the organisation for war' (MacArthur, 1992, pp. 138–40).

Adams concludes that 'given the accessibility of many potential theatres of war and the immediacy of modern systems of communication, the problems raised by information-handling, and by the speculation and commentary surrounding operations in the South Atlantic in 1982, seem likely to pale into insignificance' in any future conflict (1986, p. 194). Only a year after the Falklands War, the USA invaded the tiny Caribbean island of Grenada on 25 October 1983. Retired US army general, John E. Murray, argued against media presence in the combat zone on the grounds that 'engaging the press while engaging the enemy is taking on one adversary too many' (Braestrup, 1985, p. 21). It also appeared from opinion polls that media protests notwithstanding, a majority of Americans supported the decision taken to exclude journalists from Grenada when it mattered (ibid.). It seemed from the way their media strategy unfolded that the military were learning lessons about control first before thinking about public relations.

THE US INVASION OF GRENADA, 1983

The aim of the invasion of Grenada, what the Americans called 'Operation Urgent Fury', was to overthrow the Grenadan government, itself imposed by military coup d'état days earlier, on the grounds that it had allowed Soviet and Cuban forces to build up a military base there. The unease that the coup had caused among Grenada's neighbouring islands, and the apparent threat to resident American students on the island, was adequate pretext for the Reagan administration to order an invasion. It was left to the US army and navy to decide how to manage the operation. A key feature of their approach was to keep the news media in the dark as much as possible (Braestrup, 1985, p. 86). The Secretary of Defence James Baker even excluded his spokesman, Larry Speakes, from National Security Council planning; although the spokesmen at the Pentagon and at the State Department were told of the plans just before the invasion began. The reason for excluding those who routinely dealt with press enquiries was the conviction among planners that spokesmen would be forced to lie to the press to keep the secret and therefore undermine their integrity as press officers (ibid., p. 88; Baker, 1996). The military convinced the administration that the need for absolute secrecy in advance of the invasion was paramount for maximum surprise of attack and the ultimate success of the invasion. In his report to the Joint Chiefs of Staff, in 1984, Admiral McDonald, insisted that: 'The absolute need to maintain the greatest element of surprise in executing the mission to ensure minimum danger to US hostages...and to the servicemen involved in the initial assault dictated that the press be restricted until the initial objectives had been secured' (ibid., p. 90).

Operation Urgent Fury was an improvised affair that pitted quite a small force against a rather noncommittal defence. The way the military dealt with the media at large during the initial phases also seemed improvised. Again, the Pentagon left it to the commanders closest to operations, Admirals McDonald and Metcalf (ibid., p. 92). Metcalf was the commander in the field and he devised a system of relaying information, most of it inaccurate and fragmentary, from the USS Guam to the Commander-in-Chief of the US Atlantic Fleet (CINCLANT) in Norfolk, Virginia, where it was used to form the basis of press releases. Looking back at his role in handling the media during the operation, Metcalf was unapologetic: 'I cannot duck the issue', he said, 'I had a great deal to do with keeping [the media] out. I think I did the right thing' (ibid., p. 93). Moves to accommodate the media were made only after the operation was carried out and its objectives secured. A Joint Information Bureau was quickly established at Grantley Adams Airport in Barbados. This had no direct link to Admiral Metcalf. To contact him, Joint Information Bureau officers had to go through the US Embassy, who rang CINCLANT in Virginia, who in turn contacted Metcalf, and back again (ibid., p. 94).

Even when Metcalf finally gave permission for a small press pool to come onto the island from Barbados, on 27 October, they allowed only 15 reporters and photographers: twelve from the major American media and three from Caribbean media (ibid.). ABC reporter Mark Scheerer recalled the mood of frustration among reporters in Barbados at being corralled away from the action and given inadequate facilities (four telephones between 300 reporters); and the heavy-handed, hostile approach of the US Air Force, whose officers routinely went 'bonkers' and confiscated film and audio tape. Press briefings were constantly cancelled and the pool list kept changing (ibid., p. 98). Thomas E. Ricks, of the *Wall Street Journal*, had a similar tale of woes: 'There are no press briefings, no press releases, no nothing. Some television cameramen have been sitting here in the airport for six days. They talk half-seriously of storming the barricades' (ibid., p. 99). Once in Grenada, journalists were restricted to guided tours of preselected locations – restrictions that were not lifted until 30 October. There was only a trickle of information available during that period to Americans keen enough to look for it: ham radio broadcasts at first, threadbare press releases from the Pentagon, US students 'rescued' from the island, and reports from various Caribbean media (ibid., p. 19). An ABC crew captured the first news pictures of US marine activity at Grantley Adams airport, but, to their dismay, their material was held back from broadcast when the station's Pentagon correspondent 'waved the story off' after a briefing from a 'trusted' DoD source (Hertsgaard, 1988, p. 206ff).

Braestrup (1985) puts the Grenada coverage into some historical perspective when he compares it with the Normandy landings in the Second World War, the US intervention in Dominican Republic in 1956 and several operations in Vietnam, when the US handled the media more or less well than might have been expected. Journalists were generally free to move round Vietnam but their reporting of several operations was restricted by news embargo, or they were banned from the battle zone altogether. The key and crucial difference in Grenada was, says Braestrup, 'both an attitude and a lack of planning by the Pentagon and the White House.' The lack of on-the-ground guidance, of well-informed and experienced press officers, or of proper press briefings and press releases in Barbados and in Grenada itself meant that reports that passed for news were based almost entirely on erroneous Pentagon briefings (ibid., p. 104). However, Braestrup blames the media for their lack of imagination and laziness in overcoming the restrictions. It was possible at the time to see from the contradictions between various official sources, between CINCLANT and the Pentagon and the White House, that there were inaccuracies and exaggerations and lies, and to ask some hard questions. 'Oddly enough', he argues, 'the [media] seem to have devoted more of their energy to agonising over why they were excluded than on redeploying their man power and seeking to piece together the full story during the weeks that followed Urgent Fury' (ibid., p. 109). However, Martin Hertsgaard points to a much more fundamental problem: the 'remarkable tendency' of the US media to accept government information as the 'basic truth' rather than think about its strategic value as propaganda as was clearly the case with the Grenada invasion (1987, p. 209). It was also evident that the restrictive media policy throughout the operation had been 'a major coup for the "bad cop" faction within the [Reagan] administration who favoured taking a hardline against the press' (ibid., p. 236).

The only formal legal challenge against the reporting restrictions came from an unlikely source: the pornography publisher, Larry Flynt. He filed suit against the Department of Defense in the Washington Federal District and sought an order preventing further government restrictions on the media in Grenada on the grounds that it was unconstitutional. The court did not decide on the case until the following June, 1984, when it granted the government motion to dismiss the complaint as 'moot': in other words, as being a unique situation that was unlikely to recur. The court also ruled, crucially, that reporting restrictions in the theatre of operations were up to the commander in the field (Kirtley, 1992, p. 478). The indignant media were more successful with their call for a public inquiry into the affair. Led by veteran US Army Major-General Winant Sidle, it finally reported in August 1984 with a number of recommendations aimed at improving military–media relations in the event of future conflicts. The Sidle Commission advised that:

- the media should cooperate voluntarily with security guidelines

- the military should pay more attention to its relations with the media
- the military should help the media with logistics wherever or however possible in coverage of military operations
- any pooling system should be as big as possible but kept in operation for the minimum time possible.

The military's response to Sidle was to create the official DoD media pool that was basically a formalised version of the ad hoc system deployed in Grenada. It was intended as a temporary, stopgap measure that would satisfy both the media's need for information and the military's need for security at the critical moment of an operation. A small, select group of journalists would be ready at a moment's notice to go with the first wave in a military offensive, with the rest of the media pack joining up when the situation allowed. The first test for the Sidle recommendations, and the DoD's new pooling system, came in December 1989 with 'Operation Just Cause', when US forces invaded Panama to overthrow President Manuel Noriega.

THE US INVASION OF PANAMA, 1989

Ostensibly, the invasion of Panama was launched to overthrow the dictator and paid CIA informant, Manuel Noriega, for corruption and drugs-related crimes. Its real purpose was to secure US interests in the crucial Panama Canal Zone, with its bases, installations and commercial interests, before the Panama Canal Treaty returned the area back to Panama in 1999. Martha Gellhorn was in Panama City to report the operation and she saw it as a clear message to the developing countries of central and south America: that with the Soviet Union in retreat, the US was the only superpower left in town. She tells the story of how she tried to cash some travelers' cheques in Panama City only to find most banks closed because of the upheaval wrought by the invasion. She eventually found the Swiss Bank open for business but it was an international bank dedicated to transferring large sums of US dollars around the world; it did not cash travelers' cheques. Gellhorn left the bank with the thought that, '24,000 armed men, attack helicopters, tanks and riotous disorder... had not interfered for an hour with international banking' (Gellhorn, 1994, p. 270).

It did however interfere with media reporting. Sandra Dickson (1994) convincingly shows that coverage of the invasion by the US press was ideologically skewed towards a narrow, status quo explanation of why the invasion was launched and what it hoped to achieve. She points to the dependence of the news media on institutional sources such as the US State Department and the Pentagon, which, she correctly argues, is linked to professional and institutional routines. However, she barely mentions the means by which those sources forged that dependency and restricted public understanding of the invasion's geopolitical and strategic impulses: the media pooling system (p. 809ff).

William Boot defines the Department of Defense media pool as 'A select group of combat journalists that is never permitted to see combat. Sometimes referred to as "the public's eyes and ears"' (1990).[3] Up until the latter half of the operation, journalists were corralled like cattle at isolated US bases, well away from the action. The US Army Southern Command only briefed journalists once during the four days of the pool's deployment, while its 'media centre' was beset with technical problems, causing serious delays for the transmission of copy and photographs (Hoffman, 1991, p. 92).

The International Centre on Censorship pointed out that during the invasion, the pool was 'activated' too late to be of any help to journalists (Philo and McLaughlin, 1995, fn. 8). However, this was exactly what the US Secretary of Defense, Dick Cheney, had intended. He made no apologies for it but mollified media outrage by commissioning an inquiry into what happened, led by Fred S. Hoffman. The resulting Hoffman Report (1990) criticised the Department for excessive secrecy and noted that the reports sent back from Panama by the news pool were of 'secondary value'. It made 17 recommendations for improving the situation in future operations, among which were that in advance of future operations, the Secretary of Defense should state his or her official sponsorship of the media pool, and that the DoD should monitor the development of a public affairs strategy that includes proper accommodation of the media. The pool should be briefed regularly by senior officers and coordinated by public affairs officers and escorts from the section of the armed services involved in the operation. For their part, the pool participants should share all 'pool products' – news pictures and copy – with the other participants. The report also recommended that proper channels of communication and accountability be kept open throughout all stages of an operation so that problems and difficulties are rectified on the spot or as soon as possible thereafter. As an adjunct to this, there should be regular liaison between media and military to discuss any problems and clarify rules and responsibilities in the event of future operations; the armed services might also consider incorporating the media pools into military exercises (Hoffman, 1991, p. 105). In response, Dick Cheney welcomed the report but said he '[did not] agree with all the facets of it in terms of recommendations'. He accepted responsibility for his policy of secrecy and explained that he was 'very concerned about the possibility of premature disclosure of the operation [which would have] created enormous problems for us, obviously, and put at risk the lives of the men conducting the operation' (ibid., p. 108). Effectively, it was 'thanks but no thanks' to Hoffman.

In both Grenada and Panama, the military control of the media was highly successful and effective but it was arguably let down by poor Public Relations. They kept the media away from the battle zone but not on side and 'on message'. In the next major offensive involving US forces, the Persian Gulf War, in 1991, they exercised some public relations with the help and cooperation of a good number of journalists present. The Pentagon was ecstatic with the result, what assistant Secretary of Defense, Pete Williams, celebrated as 'the best war coverage we've ever had' (Boot, 1991, p. 24).

THE GULF WAR, 1991

Williams was right to be pleased with the outcome of the media operation during the Gulf War. It fostered an acquiescent posture among the journalists based in Saudi Arabia, and a skeptical, critical response among their colleagues in Baghdad to Iraqi efforts at public relations. For critics, two aspects of the military's handling of the media in the Gulf stimulated considerable debate: the news pools and the daily media briefings.

The news pools

As seen in the previous chapter, there was nothing new historically about the concept of the news pool in wartime – it had been first deployed to control journalists in the First World War. What was new about its use in the Gulf War was its purpose in a system of information management planned well in advance of hostilities. In fact, as early as 13 August 1990, just nine days after Iraq's invasion of Kuwait, the overall coordinator for the military's media operation, Michael Sherman, and his team began work setting up the main military briefing room and TV studio in the International Hotel in Dhahran, in Saudi Arabia.[4] Over 1,500 media personnel from the US (Fialka, 1992) and around 160 from Britain (Thomson, 1992) were accredited to report the war from bases in Saudi Arabia. These were grouped into news pools or 'Media Response Teams' that would be allowed to accompany troops on certain operations; each pool was overseen by a military minder, or 'public affairs officer' as the US military called them (Thomson, 1992, pp. 39–82).

John Fialka (1992) argues that when the news media came to the Gulf, they expected a long, Vietnam-style war of attrition in which they could move around on different fronts. Instead, what they got was a short and remote aerial bombing campaign followed by a brief 'land war', a strategy that evidently could not accommodate large numbers of journalists. Media pressure for increased accreditation on the news pools overloaded and finally collapsed the system. It led to bitter competition between informal media cartels among the news pools and to pedantic squabbling among journalists over definitions, rules and privileges (ibid., p. 8). Some journalists came prepared for a particular type of war, often with surreal results. Robert Fisk of the *Independent* remembers them well:

> One guy turned up from a small town [American] newspaper...wearing camouflage costume and he had boots with leaves painted on – Saudi Arabia of course has no trees as you're aware. And some of them came along in desert camouflage would you believe, from the Gulf, and turned up in Kosovo where there are leaves and trees and grass. These guys! Who are these people? What possesses them to behave like this? It's definitely not journalism, not the kind I'm involved in anyway.[5]

As the Gulf War entered its final stages, Pete Williams told the US Senate Committee on Governmental Affairs that the pool system was a compromise and designed for three reasons: 'It gets reporters out to see the action, it guarantees that Americans at home get reports from the scene of the action, and it allows the military to accommodate a reasonable number of journalists without overwhelming the units that are fighting the enemy' (Williams, 1995, p. 334). This was a very positive spin on the pooling system that gave no clue to its function as an instrument of control. The control was inbuilt and depended on one crucial dynamic: the degree to which the media would play along with it and effectively police themselves. The system bred an overweening competitiveness among them and some went so far as to inform on other journalists such as Robert Fisk, who tried to operate independently of the system. As Fisk argues, the last thing a journalist needs in the difficult environment of a warzone is for his or her colleagues to report them to the authorities and try to have them removed.[6] Fialka remembers that in-fighting among the American news pools was ceaseless and they were organised and controlled from within according to different priorities. There were arguments over what exactly was being pooled: the information or the correspondents? The 'big three' American networks – NBC, ABC, and CBS – objected to their correspondents having to do stand ups on CNN. The photography pool was 'a plutocracy' run by the elite of three news magazines, *Time*, *Newsweek* and *US News and World Report*; as well as two press agencies, AP and Reuters (1992, p. 37). This cosy arrangement was blown apart just as the war started when the newspaper photographers appeared in force and demanded fairer play from the 'Big Five' in terms of shared use of materials and shared responsibility for running the pool. The stakes were high. John MacArthur mentions the freewheeling French photojournalists who dubbed themselves the 'Fuck the Pool pool' that, by operating out with the system, captured some of the best images of the war (1992, p. 155).

The pool system also nurtured a culture of grievance and encouraged poaching and plagiarism of pooled dispatches; there were even paranoid suspicions that 'foreign reporters' were looking for material from the US news pool attached to US military units (Fialka, 1992, p. 32). Fialka and the other journalists in his pool 'discovered that the military had also found ways to make working conditions there more difficult. We encountered multiple layers of control, at least one of which always seemed to be there. Barriers seemed to raise automatically to blur the reality; buffers were always at the ready to blunt the sharp edges of truth' (ibid., p. 55).[7]

Perhaps forgetting the recent precedents of Grenada and Panama, Margaret Blanchard sees the Gulf War as the 'first time in American history [that] reporters were essentially barred from accompanying the nation's troops into combat' (1992, p. 6). Thus, Pete Williams' argument, that the media pools would allow journalists to see the action, was quite disingenuous in one way, but oddly accurate in another. The news pools offered journalists very little in the way of first-hand action with the possible exception of the Iraqi incursion into the Saudi border town of Khafji, or the final skirmishes in Kuwait City as the Iraqis withdrew in disarray. They saw little or nothing of the brief and much vaunted 'land war'. Instead they found themselves watching planes taking off from and returning to air bases or cruise missiles being launched from ships in the Persian Gulf; or even worse still, watching CNN and NBC in their hotel rooms for the real action in Baghdad.

Some journalists questioned the pooling arrangement while others – such as Chris Hedges of the *New York Times* and Robert Fisk – refused to work in it altogether and were dubbed 'unilaterals' or 'freelancers' by the military. Fisk points out that such labels were pejorative; he was a full time staff journalist with a British newspaper, not a freelancer. The term was purely a military moniker too readily accepted by the pool journalists who perhaps felt threatened by what could be achieved by the independents.[8] Chris Hedges (1991) writes of his experiences with other independent journalists and how some US and Egyptian army units subverted the rules to allow them unofficial passage in their successful bid to reach to Kuwait City before its official liberation. Their success was 'due in part to an understanding by many soldiers and officers of what the role of a press is in a democracy. These men and women violated orders to allow us to do our job' (p. 27).

In spite of the obvious vagaries of the media pools, most journalists cooperated with the system in something of a Faustian bargain. Kate Adie says the media and the military must 'do a deal and they must do it publicly – that is the pool';[9] while Martin Bell sees the need for trust between journalists and their military minders:

It's essentially part of being a journalist, understanding people and seeing soldiers as human beings and not as numbers in an order of battle. It does help, if you're reporting on soldiers, to have been a soldier. They get alienated by daft questions from reporters who don't know the difference between a brigade and a battalion. And they'll simply tell you more if they trust you more. I never saw that as a hindrance to good journalism; it was a help to it.[10]

Indeed, British journalist, Mark Urban, suggests there is a key difference between the American and British approach:

The Americans will try to short-circuit the gap between reality and publishable reality by telling lies sometimes and it's very rare that you catch the Brits doing that. I mean when they said in the Gulf War that they were not targeting Saddam it was plainly rubbish...We know absolutely it was their intention to try and kill him if an opportunity presented itself...it was a patent lie. You get other occasions when they're flustered, like when the Iraqis went into Khafji, where they're not exactly lying but they're on the hind foot and they're talking rubbish. The Brits are more trustworthy in that respect.[11]

That may come as a surprise to journalists who have tried to report, independently, other more contentious conflicts in which the British have been directly involved such as Malaysia and Northern Ireland where disinformation and psychological operations were used to create a 'favourable climate' for effective propaganda (see Carruthers, 1995; Glasgow University Media Group, 1985; Miller, 1994). Michael Nicholson learned a bitter lesson in media–military trust from his reporting of the Falklands War:

[My] first instinct was to believe what the [British] military were telling me. But of course it transpired that they were telling lies. People you trusted or thought you trusted were lying to you for their own military purposes and sometimes for their own reputations...[When] you go to war with Brits, with your own people, there is this naive assumption you're on the same side and you all want that side to win and therefore they can be trusted. But they don't trust you. That's the whole point of the aggravation that happened out there and in the Gulf. The military do not trust the journalists which I think was unfair...It was constant hostility.[12]

The media briefings

If the pooling system brought out the worst in journalists, the picture was hardly any better when they assembled in the briefing rooms in Dhahran or Riyadh. While the pooling system kept reporters well away from the action, the briefings kept the information away from reporters. Yet they said or did nothing to escape the accusation that they let the military get away with it. According to John MacArthur, journalists were made to look 'so bumbling and informationless [...] contrasted as they were with the purposeful and self-assured military briefers' (1992, p. 151). Added to this are the charges that they failed to challenge the slick Pentagon videos of 'smart bombs' hitting their targets with questions about their real accuracy and the actual ratio of 'smart bombs' to conventional, 'dumb' munitions used. Had these questions been asked, had journalists investigated further, with some research, they may have been able to ascertain that only 7 per cent of all munitions used were smart weapons. Instead, the briefings were like video war games that played to the whoops, cheers and laughter of the assembled journalists, most of them seemingly oblivious of the reality that human beings were dying in their tens of thousands under some of the most lethal firepower ever deployed – 'smart' or 'dumb' (Philo and McLaughlin, 1995). Their amnesia was probably induced by a directive from General Schwarzkopf that the briefings were not going to turn into the 'Five O'Clock Follies' of the Vietnam War, when briefers offered daily body counts. There was to be no body count in the Gulf, only weekly bomb damage assessments. Journalists were given details of how many tanks or artillery pieces had been knocked out but nothing about estimated casualties amongst the soldiers who presumably manned them (Thomson, 1992, pp. 97–98). This was restricted information according to the extensive media ground rules at the military's disposal (see Appendices 3 and 4) but, as Massing argues, an experienced and resourceful journalist could easily extrapolate hard information from the welter of statistics the military *did* release on a daily basis as a kind of fodder for those happy to take what they were given (1991, p. 24). The most damning indictment of these journalists must surely be that they did not ask the right questions at the right time and recognise that the briefers were military officers with a war to spin and sell. As in all wars, there were honourable exceptions but not enough to make a real difference.

The impact of these briefings and the easily processed images they provided made for 'good television' and certainly filled many hours of saturation coverage during the first week of the war. In London, two senior BBC journalists, anchor David Dimbleby and defence correspondent David Shukman, played and replayed the first video images from the briefing rooms as if they were analysing a soccer match, using laser light pens to circle targets and bring home to the viewer that this was indeed a hi-tech, low-casualty war where bombs and missiles were so smart 'they are able to destroy [a military target], no doubt kill all the occupants of it, but without causing casualties amongst the civilian population around' (Philo and McLaughlin, 1995). Journalists might wonder in response what useful information could be obtained from briefers who responded to questions in terms such as 'We just don't discuss that...I can't tell you why we won't discuss it because then I'd be discussing it' (Thomson, 1992, p. 83). But blaming the military for the briefings is rather futile; the briefings and the information policy that supported them fitted into a successful and effective military public relations campaign from the very outset of the Gulf crisis in August 1990 when Iraq invaded Kuwait. Like entertaining a party of children, the briefers kept the journalists occupied and out of harm's way. The journalists for their part got their ringside seat at the circus and wanted to keep it. But British and American media coverage of the war was not confined to Saudi Arabia or in TV studios at the home front. Some journalists based themselves in Baghdad and the test would be to see if their response to Iraqi news management tactics would be as compliant.

Media responses to Iraqi propaganda in the Persian Gulf War

In the first few days of the Baghdad blitz, journalists such as Brent Sadler (ITN) and Peter Arnett (CNN) came under heavy political flak in Britain for acting as propaganda dupes for Saddam Hussein. As Walter Goodman put it, 'Much of the abuse was strictly political. The Scuds came mainly from the [political] right', from critics who worried about images of civilian casualties being beamed around the world (1991, p. 29).

Typical of the type of material the critics had in mind was an ITN report by Brent Sadler, in Baghdad, that showed cruise missiles flying overhead on their way, it was assumed, to preprogrammed targets; it was probably the first footage of these missiles being fired in anger. What enraged right-wing opinion at home was hearing Sadler report how 'simple gunfire' brought down at least one of the much vaunted, hi-tech missiles; and seeing pictures of a hospital filled with civilian casualties from missiles that missed their target. The journalist also interviewed a doctor and civilian eyewitnesses, including a woman in a UN tracksuit, shouting to camera: 'This is not a game! These are human lives!' (ITN, 22.00; 1 February 1991). Mark Urban thinks such reports expose the myth that the media helped to sanitise the war and explain why they attracted such opprobrium from conservative media critics:

> We saw that there was a wobble in public opinion after the Amiriyah shelter bombing and we can only speculate, for example when a British Tornado dropped a laser-guided bomb on the market in Falujah and killed it is believed 160 civilians, what would have been the effect in the UK if Jeremy Bowen or John Simpson had been allowed to go there and say, 'We did this. The Brits did this', with all the sort of gore and suffering and screaming, which comes about when something like that happens.[13]

Urban's reference to the Amiriyah shelter bombing is an interesting case in point. This was a civilian air-raid shelter in Baghdad that was packed with civilians when it was hit by a missile, killing all or most of the 400 or more occupants. As Urban would expect, many good western journalists filed harrowing dispatches but the problem was what happened to those when they reached the newsroom for broadcast. ITN withheld the most difficult footage on the grounds that it was 'too distressing', an extension one could say of media policy during the Falklands War. However, the BBC's treatment of a report from Jeremy Bowen, its correspondent in Baghdad, stands out for the way in which it was so effectively interrogated and then emasculated not by some military censor but by the news presenter, Peter Sissons. In a pre-recorded two-way, Sissons in London questioned Bowen within the strictures of the Pentagon claim that the bomb shelter was a military command and control bunker. He left no doubt whose account he believed:

> *Sissons*: A few moments ago I spoke with Jeremy Bowen in Baghdad and asked him whether he could be *absolutely sure* there was no military communications equipment in the shelter, which the allies believe was there?
> *Bowen*: Well, Peter, we looked very hard for it. I'm pretty confident, as confident as I can be, that I've seen all the main rooms.
> *Sissons*: Is it *conceivable* it could have been in military use and was converted recently to civilian use?

Bowen: Well, it would be a strange thing to do...

Sissons: Let me put it another way, Jeremy, is it possible to say *with certainty* that it was *never* a military facility? (Emphases in the original)

When Bowen replied that he could only report what he could see, Sissons closed the two-way with the caveat that the reporter was 'subject *of course* to Iraq's reporting restrictions' (BBC, 18:00, 14 February 1991; emphasis in the original).[14]

An important point to stress here is that negative media reporting from the Iraqi side was only *occasionally* a response to intense political pressure back home. In most instances, the media could be relied upon to provide the negative spin without cues or prompts. An example of this was an ITN report broadcast on 26 January 1991, six days before Sadler's cruise missile footage caused such a political storm. It surveyed what the allies called 'collateral damage', that is damage to the civilian population and infrastructure. Right away, the news anchor rouses the suspicions of the viewer in less than subtle terms. The footage, we are told, was taken by an ITN camera but 'operated by a *Jordanian* cameraman' (anchor's emphasis), the implication being that we could trust the camera because it was British but not the cameraman because he was Arab. The film goes on to show footage of children in hospitals, and images of bombed-out houses and churches. The sources of the pictures are variously labeled on screen as being from 'ITN', 'Iraqi TV' and the 'Iraqi Ministry of Information', while the journalist underscores his voice-over report with the heaviest qualifications. The pictures 'show extensive damage caused, *the Iraqis say*, by allied bombers...an image of life in Iraq that Saddam Hussein is anxious for the world to see and believe.' A sequence of images 'supplied by the Ministry of Information [which] as propaganda graphically illustrates the suffering [and is] being used as a weapon...as a means to influence world opinion.' The problem, the reporter says, is that 'Iraqi-supplied material draws natural suspicions about its authenticity.' For example, over images of civilian casualties, he comments that they are '*claimed by Iraq* to be recent victims of the bombing but they have not been *independently verified* as such' (ITN, 21.45, 26 January 1991; emphases added). Walter Goodman highlights similar attempts by American reporters in Iraq to signal images of civilian casualties as Iraqi propaganda (1991, p. 30). The Gulf War, then, was sanitised because the western news media played a key role in constructing it as such. Under fire from politicians at home, reporters were sensitive in the extreme to charges of being propaganda dupes. Western supplied material did not raise 'natural suspicions about its authenticity' because, presumably, any such suspicions that existed would have been classified as 'unnatural'.

Lessons from the Gulf War

There were some attempts after the Gulf War to create a meeting place between journalists, military, and academics to discuss issues of media censorship and the freedom of information. However, such encounters took place on a rather unequal footing, as Mike Nicholson recalls from personal experience:

> I was once asked at some dinner, by some admiral if this was a wonderful thing to do, wouldn't this make things easier in the future? And I said no, of course it won't make things easier in the future. Nothing will ever change. All you're doing is learning our tricks – that's what it's all about. You're spending money employing us to come and talk to you because you want to know how we work. But you'll never let us know how you work. And he shut up after that.[15]

A collection of essays edited by Lloyd J. Matthews, entitled, *Newsmen and National Defense: Is Conflict Inevitable?* (1991) highlights the gulf of misunderstanding between the military officer class and commercial mainstream news media in the USA. For example, journalist Richard Halloran surveyed a sample of army officers to discover their perceptions of the media. Chief among these were: that the media were an all powerful entity with a liberal agenda that was instinctively anti-military; that journalists were just in it for the money or to 'sell newspapers'; that journalists were not really professionals; that, unlike the military they reported, they were not accountable to the public; that they were usually inaccurate with the facts; that they only 'printed' bad news; that they relied on unnamed and unattributed sources; that they often published classified material and used unauthorised information without thought about the consequences; that war and defence correspondents often lacked military knowledge or experience; that they took up precious military time and resources; and, worst of all perhaps in the eyes of the US military, they lacked patriotism (pp. 39–59). Other individual contributions to the volume crystallise the inherently contradictory assumption that the media are staffed by liberal elites from top to bottom and are run by all powerful corporations, in some cases corporations such as General Electric and Westinghouse which are instinctively anti-liberal in their business practices and that arm the US military with missile and radar systems (Sarkesian, pp. 61–71). Yet as William Hammond argues in the same volume, the US military has developed an acute sense of public relations as a cure for all these ills in the media–military relationship. However, he warns that after the sales pitch and the ad campaign, 'sales still depend on whether the product itself fulfills...expectations' and on the fact that 'the truth has greater ultimate power than the most pleasing of bromides' (1991, p. 15).

But there are lessons from 'abroad', from journalists in parts of the world not known for their celebration of the freedom of the press such as Russia. In the first Chechnyan war, from 1994 to 1996, the Russian army was ruthless in its attempts to intimidate the Russian and international media from reporting the story of its brutal war with Chechen rebels. Public opinion in Russia suggested that the army had considerable popular support to do what it deemed necessary to win. A favourite tactic was to suspend accreditation procedures at critical moments in the conflict and to tell journalists that their safety could not be guaranteed. Yet Russian journalists simply sought out alternative sources in the age-old tradition of good reporting (Peters Talbot, 1996, p. 48). As a result, they were able to resist the twin pressures of government censorship and economic constraint to 'break Soviet traditions of passive reporting and provide Russian readers with a broad array of views' on the first Chechnyan war (ibid., p. 51). They were praised for 'the frankness of their coverage' and their criticisms of the government's conduct of the war, 'the first time in Russia's five year democratic experiment that [they] have played such a role' (Rutland, 1996). Russia's second, still more brutal campaign in Chechnya, 1999–2009, coupled with an unstable, political and economic climate at home, took its toll on the concepts of freedom of speech and media pluralism. Yet, the Russian media's experiment with independence has shown their western counterparts that there is always a space in which journalists can ask hard questions of their military and political leaders in a war situation; and a space in which they can be resourceful enough to access alternative sources of information.

CONCLUDING REMARKS

Military public relations over this period, then, became more effective than direct censorship of the type familiar in both world wars. Serious examination of the most critical phases of the Falklands War, the invasions of Grenada and Panama, and the Gulf War, shows that these operations were carried out with most journalists under the thumb and the public in the dark. In this regard, the pooling system was successfully 'activated' in every instance while journalists, on the other hand, were effectively *de*activated. As Martha Gellhorn wrote after the Gulf War:

In the Falklands, Grenada, Panama and the Gulf War, our governments have shown a fine skill in controlling and manipulating the press. The press is shown what the government thinks fit when the government ordains. The press is treated to military briefings instead of finding out for itself. An accompanying officer or minder is always at hand. The result of this press management...is that we have had no real press coverage. In the interests of 'national security' or any phrase they wish to use, our governments have decided to neuter the press in wartime. (1993, p. 340)

Yet the military approach to controlling the media in the Gulf War, with its mix of public relations carrot and authoritarian stick, showed that the problem is not so much the extent and nature of reporting restrictions; the focus on these alone excuses journalists and deflects the blame onto their military minders. The problem is how journalists responded to propaganda from what they might see as their 'own side' as well as a host of other failures: their unwillingness to challenge reporting restrictions; their readiness to betray their own colleagues for minor advantage; their enjoyment of the razzmatazz of the military briefings; their susceptibility to disinformation and dissemblage; and their failure to corroborate source information against alternative material. And while they complained or expressed regrets about all this after the war, the US military planners were already thinking ahead and planning the next stage of development: the embed system that they first tried out in Bosnia after the Dayton Accords in 1995 and fine tuned by the time it was rolled out for the invasion of Iraq in 2003. As the next chapter will show, it was a propaganda triumph.

7

Goodbye Vietnam Syndrome: The Embed System in Afghanistan and Iraq

We need to tell the factual story – good or bad – before others seed the media with disinformation and distortions.

Public Affairs Guidance, US Department of Defense[1]

The embedded reporter system did not originate, as some commentators think, in the planning stages of the war in Iraq in 2003; it was conceived in the final stages of the Bosnian War and international efforts to broker a peace deal via the Dayton Accords of 1995. In its leading role with the United Nations Protection Force in the Balkans, the US military had clear ideas about their objectives and of how the media might help meet them. The General commanding the American sector in Bosnia, William L. Nash, had three objectives in respect to dealing with the media: to gain public support in America for the conduct of the operation; to maintain the morale of the troops; and to use the media to promote compliance with the Dayton Accords among the former warring factions (Nash, 1998, pp. 132–33). To these ends, his military planners developed a system of 'embedded media', purportedly a less restrictive version of the pooling system that operated in the Gulf War. Reporters (about 40 of them) would accompany troops on the ground for two weeks and get 'a more nuanced picture of our activities by allowing them virtually free access to the soldiers and commanders.' This of course required a revamp of the Joint Information Bureau system to ensure tighter coordination between all levels of command and avoid embarrassing and unnecessary conflicts of interest (ibid, p. 132).

A significant component of the Nash approach, one not seen in the Gulf War, was the idea of allowing journalists to be present with the troops on the ground, which would demonstrate the 'transparency of our operations and the firmness of our purpose.' Offering the example of

Linda Patillo, of ABC News, who witnessed a confrontation between a US Army Colonel and a Bosnian Serb Commander in the Spring of 1996, Nash was delighted with the public relations derived from the story that Patillo sent back. He said that it portrayed,

> ...a 'real life situation' in which armed conflict could have broken out at any minute. [It] showed the preparedness of [our] forces, their resolve to do their duty, and the colonel's...professionalism and calm nature in the execution of his duty. What a great story to show the American people! (ibid, p. 133)

Nash concludes that,

> it is essential that the military and the media engage *before* they need to do so. It is something that requires a break from traditional thinking and a recognition that good policy and good execution usually result in good stories...Don't sweat the spin. Work the issues wisely. (ibid, p. 135)

Nash does not explain how this new approach would fit into a system of information management – censorship and propaganda – but the potential was certainly implied and it was to be tried and tested in earnest during the US military's next major operations, in Afghanistan in 2001 but most especially in Iraq in 2003. As Pentagon public affairs official, Bryan Whitman, later admitted, much advance thought and discussion went into its implementation in the Iraq War. 'We did public affairs planning like we would do for any other form of war planning' he writes, 'We war-gamed it' (Whitman, 2004, p. 207).

AFGHANISTAN AND IRAQ

What the Pentagon 'war-gamed' was a refinement of the embed system tried out in Bosnia, combined with the daily media briefings familiar during the Gulf War. In their introduction to a volume of interviews with embedded reporters in Iraq, from the US and abroad, Katovsky and Carlson (2004) argue that the system promised journalists 'the coziest lovefest with the military since World War II' (p. *viii*). The procedures and ground rules that governed embedded reporting in Afghanistan and

Iraq were not far removed from those that applied to the media pools in the Gulf War but the challenge they presented to independence and objectivity seemed to be much more focused and controversial. The role of media briefings, where the military offer 'context' and 'background' to ongoing operations, is also critical here because when embedded reporters shrug their shoulders and admit that, of course they only offer part of the picture of war, they seem to forget the briefings and how those operate to fill in the blanks on the propaganda canvas. In the sections that follow, therefore, I argue that the twin system of embedded reporting and media briefing used in Afghanistan and Iraq was a propaganda triumph for the US and its coalition partners and a professional humiliation for the journalists who opted into it.

The embed system: procedures and ground rules

Section 2 of the US Department of Defence's Public Affairs Guidance (PAG) states that embedded media personnel 'will live, work and travel as part of the units with which they are embedded to facilitate maximum in-depth coverage of US forces in combat and related operations' (See Appendix 5). In a similar vein, the British Ministry of Defence Green Book states that:

> The purpose of embedding correspondents with units and formation headquarters is to enable the media to gain a deeper understanding of the operation in which they are involved, particularly through access to personnel and commanders. They will be afforded all possible briefings and other facilities, including the opportunity to accompany British troops during war-fighting operations. Their individual requirements will be met wherever possible. In return, they are likely to be subject to some military orders and training, both for their own safety and that of the unit. (Paragraph 22; see Appendix 6)

These military orders, what the Pentagon's PAG refers to as 'ground rules' (Section 4, paragraphs F and G) include categories of releasable and restricted information. Releasable information relates to *approximations only* of such things as unit strength and the types of ordnance at its disposal; 'friendly casualty figures'; and participation in a given operation by allied forces. Information that is not releasable, because it may 'jeopardize operations or endanger lives', relates to *specifics*, in other words 'specific numbers' regarding troops and units below corps level; geographical location of units; names of unit installations; future operations; and 'photography showing level of security at military installations or encampments'. Breach of the ground rules of embedded reporting could result in loss of accreditation or, to put it in the rather more ominous language of Section 4 of the PAG, 'the immediate termination of the embed and removal from the AOR [Area of Responsibility].' It is interesting to note that the phrase used in the preceding Section 3 of the PAG ('Procedures') is 'termination of the embed opportunity'.

The PAG rules and procedures are expressed largely in functional, military jargon but the very last line in the last section of the guidelines, Section 7 dealing with 'Miscellaneous/Coordinating Instructions', hints at the hidden public relations/propaganda agenda behind the embed system: 'Use of lipstick and helmet-mounted cameras on combat sorties is approved and encouraged to the greatest extent possible' (Paragraph 7C). The impulse to have the war depicted in soft focus was not a whim of the military planners. It fitted into a broader propaganda strategy, played out on TV networks at home in the US, to 'Hollywoodize' the personal experience of the ordinary US soldier in 'war on terror' wars like Afghanistan and Iraq.[2]

Reporters who declined to sign up to the embed system were accredited as 'unilaterals' to use the military jargon or, as they called themselves, 'independent journalists'. Without the relative protection of a military unit, their job could be a good deal more difficult and dangerous. Some journalists and media personnel, like ITN's Terry Lloyd and his interpreter Hussein Osman, lost their lives going it alone as independent reporters; others risked arrest and loss of accreditation. Luis Castro of Radiotelevision Portuguesa and his colleagues were arrested, detained and suffered physical abuse and intimidation at the hands of an American military unit for 2 days before being released and ordered out of Iraq. 'My men are trained like dogs!' the officer commanding told Castro by way of an explanation. 'They know only to attack!'[3]

The embed system and objectivity

The most obvious question to ask of a system that brings the journalist into such close encounters with the military is: how can he or she be really objective or even impartial, especially when viewing an operation from the single vantage point of a military position or, as happened, when the military unit fired on and killed unarmed civilians, or carried out abuses against civilians? Alex Thomson (2010) readily admits that embedded reporting only produces a partial picture of the wider conflict: 'Of course it is biased. And so are filming trips with the Taliban for that matter. It is the nature of the beast' (p. 21). He does, however, concede that some journalists take their 'embed opportunity' too far:

> You're always embedded with people to a lesser or greater extent. The difficult thing is how far it lets your brain get embedded...and how far you become a [public relations officer] for what's going on, which is essentially a game that the Pentagon and perhaps even more so the MoD clearly want people to play and it's depressing the number of journalists who are willing to go along with that.[4]

As seen from this and the following examples, responses from journalists who reported as embeds from Afghanistan and Iraq were divided between those who protested loudly their integrity and objectivity and those who admitted openly that although they were only able to offer a partial view of the conflict it was either that or not bother reporting at all.

There is no doubt that the intimacy and immediacy of the system blinded many journalists to its vices. Jim Axelrod, of CBS Evening News, confessed that covering the Iraq War as an embedded reporter was 'the great, pure, authentic experience of my career. I suspect it may be the purest thing I'll ever do. I was in the enchanted forest' (Katovsky and Carlson, p. 23). Stuart Ramsey, who reported from Afghanistan as an embed for Sky News, thinks that 'you can embed but you must remain honest and impartial. To do that, you must draw on your knowledge and deal with the rules of the embed' (2010, p. 30). However, John Burns of the *New York Times* draws a distinction between neutrality and fairness when reporting as an embed:

> In this profession, we are not paid to be neutral. We are paid to be fair, and they are completely different things. [...] Yes, we should be absolutely ruthless as to fact. We should not approach a story with some sort of ideological template that we impose on it. We should let the facts lead us to conclusions, but if the conclusions seem clear then

we should not avoid those on the basis of an idea we are supposed to be neutral. Because if that were the case, they might as well hire a stenographer, and a stenographer would be a lot cheaper than I am. (Katovksy and Carlson, p. 161)

One of the least discussed issues in this debate is the potential for the embedded journalist to participate in military operations. 'I was a non-combatant', said Chantal Escoto, 'military reporter' for the *Leaf Chronicle* in the US, 'but I told [the troops] I'd be ready to pick up a gun if I had to' (Katovsky and Carlson, 2004, p. 131). That would be in breach of the Geneva Conventions and although Section 4, Paragraph C of the Pentagon's ground rules prohibits reporters from carrying firearms of their own, there were incidents in Iraq when journalists found themselves aiding troops in combat situations. The BBC's Clive Myrie, attached to a British Army unit in Iraq, told a BBC documentary how he found himself passing flares from soldier to soldier during a firefight with Iraqi troops before stopping to think about what he was doing.[5]

The military briefings

As in the Gulf War, daily military briefings were a defining feature of media coverage of operations in Afghanistan and Iraq – and just as controversial. These were designed by military planners to provide context for embedded reporting on the ground or, to put it in more critical terms, to shape the daily news agenda, restrict information and release disinformation in the interests of propaganda or Psyops, psychological operations (see, for example, Miller, 2004b; Paterson 2014).

Conducted from a purpose-built media centre in Doha, Qatar, the so-called 'Freedom Briefings' offered the 700 journalists what the military described as 'information' but what a BBC documentary, 'War Spin', called 'maximum imagery, minimum insight'.[6] The official spokesmen, General Vincent Brooks for the US military and Group Captain Al Lockwood for the British Army, were the front men charged with providing the information and controlling the questions at the briefings as well as granting interviews. It was very clear from the start of the war that regardless of the coalition, the media briefings were being run by the American military for consumption on the major US TV networks such as CNN and NBC. Journalists with these networks were given the front row seats and first call on asking questions. The media of the coalition partners, including Britain, were second and so on down the hierarchy to media organisations from non-aligned and neutral countries. Journalists with Middle East outlets such as Al Jazeera and Abu Dhabi TV, were given short shrift by Brooks and other briefing officers whenever they asked awkward and difficult questions, which was most of the time. However, there were ground rules that applied to all the journalists who attended the briefings: questions were rationed out, follow-ups were discouraged and the briefers rarely provided full answers to questions.[7] Journalist and media critic, Michael Wolff, interrupted a briefing by Brooks to express the disquiet felt by many of the 700 journalists there about the amount and quality of information. 'My final question after which I was not allowed to ask anymore questions', he told the BBC, 'was the question every reporter was asking, not just every day but literally every minute, which was why should we stay? What's the value to us for what we learn at this million-dollar press centre?' Brooks replied that it was Wolff's choice whether he wanted to be there or not. For the military's part, 'We want to provide information that's truthful from the operational headquarters that is running this war'. Wolff was then barred from asking any further questions and, in a heated confrontation afterwards with Pentagon advisor, Jim Wilkinson, he was advised to 'fuck off and go home.'[8] Thinking back on his experience of the briefings, Wolff thought that,

> The profoundly interesting thing about Doha is that nothing happened [and that] even when you're not getting information from the guy who has the information to give, you're still getting information by the very fact that he's not giving it to you. (Katovksy and Carlson, 2004, pp. 41–42)

On the British side, Al Lockwood and his colleagues worked off a list of daily official lines that usually accentuated the positive or worked to disarm difficult questions. They even posted in their office a list of topics to be avoided or handled with extreme care, what they termed 'poo traps'; these included the use of depleted uranium, bombing accuracy and civilian casualties. When difficult incidents could not be avoided, such as the Coalition bombing of a civilian area in Baghdad on 28 March 2003, that killed 36 innocent people, the strategy was to first deny responsibility and then deflect the blame onto the enemy. In this instance, Brooks told reporters that it may have been a faulty Iraqi air defence missile or it could have been a deliberate act by the Iraqis to undermine public support for the Coalition internationally.[9] Both possibilities were thought by experts to be highly unlikely but they were effective as spin to manage the controversy until the story slipped down the news agenda.

However, the big stick of media control and manipulation in this operation was wielded behind the scenes by the 'special advisers', not least Jim Wilkinson for the US government and Home Office civil servant, Simon Wren, for 10 Downing Street. For most of the war, they worked well together to coordinate the official line from day to day, providing consistent background or off-the-record information. However, in the early stages the British were critical of how the American military was dealing with the non-American media and with their manipulation of stories such as the rescue of American soldier, Jessica Lynch, into something akin to a Hollywood action movie courtesy of Pentagon-supplied footage. According to the BBC, Simon Wren went so far as to pen a confidential memo to Tony Blair, expressing his misgivings about the situation and the need to put it right.[10] These tensions aside, the 'good cop/bad cop' approach to the briefings worked effectively to co-opt the media in the wider propaganda war, whether the media liked to admit it or not.

The wider propaganda war

If the first casualty of war is truth, then the second is understanding. Oliver Boyd-Barrett (2004) goes beyond ground-level debates about the embed system to look at its long-term effect – a story of war that is almost exclusively that of the victors:

> Western reporting of the wars in Afghanistan (2001) and Iraq (2003) were stories told by Western correspondents reporting from Western positions speaking to (mainly approved) Western political and military sources, mainly about Western military personnel, strategies, successes and, less often, failures, and backed with comments from (often vetted) Western military 'experts'. (pp. 29–30)

The irony is that in their anxiety to filter out 'unreliable' or 'unverifiable' information from outside the system, journalists from the western, corporate media seemed blissfully unaware of their 'dependence on government or military sources of their own side for...*safe* information, disinformation or lies' (ibid, p. 32; emphasis in the original). For Vaughan Smith, this has far reaching consequences beyond professional and academic debates about ethics. 'News management or spin', he writes, 'creates cumulative damage to us all by undermining our trust in the institutions that engage in it and subverting the quality of our conduct more widely in society. We are paying for these wars with more than blood and treasure' (2010, p. 47).

Debates about the pros and cons of embedded reporting, therefore, should not hide the essential point of the system in the first place: the military's need to control the media and co-opt them into the propaganda campaign driving the war effort in Afghanistan or Iraq. Only a few journalists seemed to be aware of this or at least admit it publicly. Jeremy Bowen, for example, writes that the 'best way to get ahead in the media battle is to control access to the war [...] Winning the information war is no longer incidental; it is a top military priority' (2006, pp. 111–12); while Oliver Burkeman describes the embed system as 'an astounding PR success for the Pentagon' (Allen and Zelizer, 2004, p. 6).

Some of the academic literature also considers the implications of embedded reporting in the wider framework of military information management and propaganda (see, for example, Boyd-Barrett, 2004; Keeble, 2004; Miller 2004a & 2004b; Paterson, 2014; Tumber and Palmer, 2004); and even the dark arts of psychological operations (Miller 2004b and Paterson, 2014). For example, Chris Paterson reveals that during the 1990s, CNN and National Public Radio (NPR) in the US offered internships to PsyOps officers, who used them not merely to observe and get to know the media better as a public relations exercise ahead of a future conflict, but to learn how to disrupt news flows to strategic advantage; a determinedly more subversive objective (2014, pp. 36–37).

Once again, the system of control, censorship and propaganda that produced such a stunning success for the military in Iraq marked yet another milestone in the evolutionary road from the days of the Vietnam Syndrome and open hostility to the presence of the media in the war zone. To put this in some perspective, the chapter concludes with a look at NATO's media operation during the Kosovo crisis in 1999, when the mechanisms of control and spin went wrong in the first phase of the campaign because of institutional and political division.

BOMBING SERBIA, 1999[11]

The military intervention in the Kosovo conflict of 1999, when Serbia was seen to be carrying out a policy of ethnic cleansing as a means of denying Kosovan independence, was largely led by NATO from its headquarters in Brussels. In the early stages of the operation, involving air strikes against the Serbian military and political infrastructure, NATO planes committed up to thirteen so-called 'blunders'. These were accidental bombings of civilians, including a Serbian passenger train on 12 April and a convoy of Albanian refugees heading out of Kosovo to Albania two days later on 14 April. NATO's unconvincing presentation of these incidents, particularly the bombing of the refugee convoy, opened up an information vacuum and offered spaces in prime time television news where, away from the briefing rooms, journalists could ask awkward questions about what they were being told.

Much of the uncertainty in the immediate wake of the bombing lay in the fact that NATO in Brussels was taking its cue from the Pentagon in Washington, where NATO Commander Wesley Clarke briefed aggressively against the Serbs only to retract it when some facts began to emerge. The organisation took another five days to finally present a definitive account of the circumstances surrounding the convoy attack and during that time, and quite independently of the Brussels media pool, news presenters and correspondents assessed the contradictory evidence with the sort of scepticism and open-mindedness seriously lacking during the Gulf War in 1991 and in Operation Desert Fox, the bombing of Iraq in 1998. 'The question remains', said a Channel Four News reporter, 'what were NATO planes doing in the area and why did they decide to attack these convoys, which included tractors and cars?' (14 April 1999). Later that evening, BBC *Newsnight*'s probe opened with this cautionary gambit: 'You won't find any starker examples of Dr Johnson's adage that *truth is the first casualty of war* than today's deaths in Kosovo' (emphasis added). Correspondent, James Robbins, considered NATO's case but cautioned that '*NATO has missed military targets and hit civilians before* and tonight in Brussels the Alliance spokesman, Jamie Shea, was *much more guarded in his response*' (emphasis added).

The next day, 15 April, NATO admitted that in fact there had been two vehicle convoys hit in different locations in the Djackovice area and that one of those, a refugee convoy may have been hit by NATO planes. The NATO line was that if this was the case it was regrettable but that the bomb was dropped 'in good faith'. The ironic *Guardian* headline the next morning quoted the military briefer: 'When the pilot attacked, they were military vehicles. If they turned out to be tractors, that is a different issue' (16 April 1999). However, the trickle of information and lack of hard evidence only served to sow more confusion among the news media about what exactly happened and what NATO was doing. As BBC news anchor, Anna Ford, remarked: 'There's still a lot of information that doesn't add up here. It sounds rather fishy!' According to her correspondent in Serbia the blunder and its fall out constituted 'a serious blow to NATO. Its credibility and its effectiveness are being questioned' (18.00, 15 April 1999). Channel Four News reported that 'NATO is on the back foot tonight' and that 'NATO's line has changed repeatedly.' While 'the Serbs have allowed foreign cameras rare access to otherwise dark corners of Kosovo...NATO has so far chosen not to show military video of exactly what happened during its attack' (15 April 1999). So, why the absence of video evidence? That would surely vindicate NATO's claims that the Serbs bombed the convoys among other civilian targets in the area and that NATO planes only targeted and hit military vehicles and positions? In an interview on Channel Four News, James Foley, spokesman for the US State Department, accused the western media of not demanding access from the Serbs to Kosovo and the 'horrific images of the poor victims'. The news anchor Jon Snow responded: 'Well you see the thing which is perplexing us is that *the western alliance is not giving western media access to images either*' in spite of its much vaunted and sophisticated aerial surveillance technologies (15 April 1999; emphasis added).

Midway through the operation, in May, the Spanish newspaper. *El Mundo*, published what was purported to be an internal NATO report lamenting the poor state of NATO battle readiness when it came to launching its media and public relations campaign (Goff, 2000, p. 18). Shea claimed that the document was 'not without value' but nonetheless denied it was official or that its unauthorised release had anything to do with him or anyone in his office. He did however concede that there were problems. He explained, for example, that just as the operation got underway he had to send half his staff to Washington for NATO's 50th anniversary summit and so was 'really flying by the seat of my pants for the first four or six weeks'. The lesson, he said, was 'that we have to have a big [media] organisation, even if we don't need it, from day one. It's better to have it and not need it than not have it and be found wanting'.[12] NATO's press relations budget for the Serbia/Kosovo operation was between 50 and 60 million Belgian francs, at the very most about GB£882,252. Shea revealed that rather than bidding for a supplementary public relations budget he 'raided the existing budget'. Most of the money went towards equipping a centre adequate to the needs of the international media presence in Brussels for the duration of the air campaign. This was what he had been 'begging for years for [and] which had suddenly become instantaneously and miraculously available during the air operation. So necessity was the mother of procurement if not invention'.[13]

There was suspicion in some quarters that the NATO press office in Brussels laboured too much under the weight of media expectation in the 24-hour news cycle, a danger long recognised in other official quarters and by many journalists. As far back as 1996, William Perry, then US Secretary of Defense, spoke in the abstract about the pressure for the instant response to media queries:

The pressure...is to say something... . If you simply say, 'I don't know what the facts are. We're going to have to take a couple of days to find out,' that's not very satisfying. Therefore the continual pressure is, 'Well, what do you think it is, what do you believe has happened? If that's happened what do you think you ought to do?' You can resist those but you resist them with great difficulty. (1996, p. 125)

And looking back at the Kosovo conflict, Channel Four News correspondent, Alex Thomson, referred to 'a kind of culture of information intimidation' whereby NATO was 'caught up in this desperate need to furnish this media beast with information at top speed'. He suggested that, 'They don't have to give daily briefings if they don't want to – give a weekly briefing! I mean they make the rules!'[14] Jake Lynch of Sky News was aware of 'a lot of acrimony behind the scenes [due to] the fact that Jamie Shea was not given the information' about the exact circumstances of the convoy bombing. Yet even at that, and this is from a purely NATO perspective, Shea 'inadvertently gave us more information than he should have done'.[15] Shea saw it differently. Far from being denied information by the Pentagon at such a crucial juncture, he was the one who held it up in the first instance because he thought it inadequate and in the long run detrimental to NATO credibility:

> Either we put all the facts on the table and say everything we know and answer all the questions and tell the journalists that we have come clean or we don't say anything. But I didn't want this [situation] of giving one explanation on Day One and giving an alternative explanation on Day Two and looking silly. Partial explanations are often worse than nothing.[16]

He also revealed that Pentagon spokesman, Ken Bacon, stepped in behind him and added some punch to his position:

> I'm very grateful to Ken who said, 'Look, we've made this commitment to journalists to own up even if it is going to be embarrassing to us and we can't renege on that'. He used a phrase, which I've used often myself: 'If we are not honest in admitting our failures, they won't believe us when we claim successes.'[17]

The military, said Shea, were concerned with getting on with the campaign, not expending time and resources to an investigation for the media:

> But eventually...I think we got the message through that this was so important in terms of NATO's public image and credibility, it was as important explaining this as getting on with fighting the conflict itself. And towards the end that was understood. The trouble is that in any organisation you often need a failure to turn a situation around...And it woke people up to the reality of conflict...that this was a real conflict with real consequences and that therefore we had to adjust.[18]

The adjustment came during the PR crisis over the refugee convoy bombing. Alistair Campbell, press secretary to Prime Minister Blair, stepped in to urge a revamp of NATO's PR operation, an intervention Shea thought was decisive. 'There was a blockage there', he admitted, 'and sometimes in organisations you need people with clout to overcome those blockages. When prime ministers thump the tub they get things done much faster than when Jamie P. Shea, the NATO spokesman, thumps the tub'.[19] Any intervention by Campbell into controversial issues or events was bound to become a story in itself in the British media. Indeed, Jake Lynch noted that Campbell's influence extended much further and deeper than simply supporting Shea's efforts with human and material resources. It shaped the whole presentation of information and material, which was to 'sort of ration out small nuggets of information and wrap around that as much material as you can in order to project the kind of story you want to project'. In other words, 'It had been very effectively "New Labourised" in that they thought stories. They decided from day one to try and control the agenda and did a reasonable job of it'.[20]

It is true that a good majority of British and American journalists accepted the fundamental rationale for bombing Serbia and Kosovo in spite of the rather dubious legal grounds on which the bombing campaign was carried out. There was a liberal, humanitarian consensus abroad that squeezed out radical dissent (Chandler, 2000; Chomsky, 1999). It was also the case that most journalists at the briefings were too willing to be fed information and digest it as transparent accounts of events on the ground rather than as selective and self-serving presentations of those events. Mark Laity, however, who left his job with the BBC after the Kosovo conflict to work as a media adviser at NATO, took a clear and unapologetic stance on the dependence of journalists on military sources, the briefings and the information they released. 'If you don't trust the military', he said, 'and they're the ones dropping the bombs, who are you going to trust? Who are you going to talk to? What you want to do is you want to talk to the operators, the players, the doers, that's NATO. You don't go and speak to a bloody academic do you?' He rejected the criticisms of his performance during the briefings and on air, pointing out that he was one of the few journalists who badgered the briefers about the circumstances of the convoy incident – about whether there was not one but actually two separate attacks on two separate convoys. 'So in a sense it was me who tied them up into knots', he argued, 'not the hostile journalists who were committed. It was the uncommitted journalists who tied them up into knots by asking them knowledge-able questions and in fact it was the ones who actually knew what they were talking about that tied them up into knots, not the ones who were making tendentious political points'. He insisted that:

The challenge for journalists is not to get all worked up because somebody has spun you; the challenge is to spot the spin and take it out. And given the choice between no information which is to a degree what we were getting earlier on and spun information what we were getting later, give me spun information every time [...] I've got the facts and in there there's layers and layers of priorities and prejudices and I've got to take them apart and say that's the key fact. And if I don't spot it then more fool me and good luck to them. It's a game. So spun information: they spun a lot but to my way of thinking they did not lie in between. They got things wrong but they were not deliberately lying. Sure, individuals might have but corporately I do not believe NATO were.[21]

One of the 'committed' journalists Laity had in mind here was Robert Fisk whose dismissal of Laity and most of his colleagues at the NATO briefings was withering: 'Most of [them] were sheep. Baaaa Baaaaa! That's all it was.'[22] Jamie Shea was, perhaps not surprisingly, complimentary of the journalists in the NATO media pool whom he described as his 'customers' and defended them against critics such as Fisk:

[He] accuses the press at NATO of slavishly following the Shea line whereas in reverse the charge I would put to him is that in order to distance himself from that he's totally dismissive of everything we did. It's an opposite form of extremism. I've got more time for a lot of [journalists] who were basically in the middle, that listened to us but came to their own balanced, professional judgement on things. But Fisk seems to have an excess of moral perfectionism.[23]

This was an extraordinary slight on a journalist of such experience and knowledge but typical of the attacks made against him when he showed up on one occasion at the briefings to ask questions about the real extent of 'ethnic cleansing' in Kosovo; and, more specifically, the relationship between NATO bombing and the exodus of Kosovar-Albanians across the border into Albania. His attack on the majority of journalists present that day no doubt fed their resentment and ill-feeling but the crux for him was his integrity as a journalist and he would not see his reporting of Kosovo as 'extremist' or as a crusade for 'moral perfectionism'. He suggested, instead, that insults and intimidation from 'the bad guys' is the price the good journalist has to pay for telling the truth:

> [If] you cannot write with passion, if you cannot say, 'This was a civilian target, NATO said it was military, it is not, it is a hospital, I've been there, I've seen it', etcetera. If you can't do that, you go home. There's no point in being there. And if the price of that is to be abused by NATO or whatever then that's the price you have to pay. Then... you have to take on the bad guys, I'm afraid. You have to do it! If these people are going to intimidate you into writing like Reuters, which is their intention, then you must leave your job! You're finished![24]

And while 'uncommitted' and 'knowledgeable' journalists such as Mark Laity asked questions when NATO was on the back foot about the detail and circumstances of the refugee convoy incident, they were content to sit back and graze after the organisation got its act together and, as Jake Lynch puts it, got 'New Labourised'. Jamie Shea takes this as a compliment to the way in which NATO recovered the public relations initiative in its presentation of the bombing of Serbia:

> I'll never forget one of my final briefings...at the end of May when we had another one of these incidents, number 13, when Nato struck a block of flats in a little town on the Montenegran border. [...] I didn't wait for journalists to ask me for the information, I came straight out with it because I had all the information without having to wait for five days and no journalists asked me a question, not one! Whereas a couple of months earlier Djakovice had become the single dominant issue. It was almost by that time treated as what the French call a *fait divert*, a passing little story of no great significance. We made more of it than the press did at the end. It was almost a reversal of roles.[25]

The majority of journalists present at the briefings may have cringed to hear Shea say that and he very definitely got the measure of them in the latter stages of the media operation. And despite the initial tensions between the Pentagon and NATO, the late Richard Holbrooke, driver of the Dayton Accords in the Balkans, described American media coverage of Kosovo as 'extraordinary and exemplary' (*Palm Beach Post*, 9 May 1999).[26]

Richard Keeble (1999) and Philip Hammond (1999, 2000) were very critical of British media reporting of NATO's operation in Serbia and Kosovo. Hammond argued that the coverage was 'highly conformist' (1999, p. 63); and that 'one casualty of the Kosovo war was British journalism, although some sources maintain it was already long dead. In its place we have propaganda' (ibid, p. 67). Edward Herman and David Petersen (2000) have cast a similar, critical eye on the role of the US media, particularly CNN, in actively selling the conflict to the American public. In the first edition of this book and elsewhere I argued that in the case of the British news media at any rate, there was real media counterweight to NATO spin; not from the media pool in Brussels but from some of the journalists on the ground in Kosovo and more especially in the news rooms back in London. Indeed, I took issue with Keeble and Hammond's withering assessment and argued that while TV journalism in Britain might have been ailing, it certainly was not dead (McLaughlin, 2002a, pp. 121–22; see also McLaughlin 2002b). However, I would revise my argument here and suggest that the skeptical reporting in evidence during the Kosovo crisis was more a result of a poorly planned, *ad hoc* approach to media management on NATO's part. When considered in the context of the history of the relationship between the war correspondent and the military, from Crimea to Iraq, resistance to spin control during the crisis was at the very most anomalous rather than indicative of a new, critical disposition among the mainstream media.

CONCLUDING REMARKS

What the historical review in this section of the book tells us is how military thinking about the management and control of the media at wartime has evolved since the Crimean war. From an instinct to simply censor journalists and deny them access to the warzone, western militaries have learned over a century and a half of conflict that incorporating reporters into the war effort, relying on their professionalism and patriotism, and giving them the right information and the right pictures (on military terms of course) is a much more effective form of control than an attitude of outright hostility. And it is effective precisely because of the media's readiness in every instance to conform, to accept the restrictions and only ask questions, if at all, when it is too late. The system of embedded reporting and tightly controlled briefings used in the Iraq

War of 2003 marked a high point for the military and a low point for the war correspondent. Only the military appear to be learning lessons of the last conflict with their approach to media management constantly re-evaluated and revised. Britain's Ministry of Defence happily admits that its Green Book (2013) 'is the result of continuing dialogue between the MoD and media organisations and representatives and takes account of past and present operations.' Those organisations and representatives include the BBC, ITN, SKY News, the Press Association, the Newspaper Society and the National Union of Journalists. Yet after every major war since Crimea, journalists have spent considerable column inches and air time agonising over the way in which they were cowed and controlled by the military and the implications of this for freedom of the press and democracy: too late then of course to put things right and take a principled stand. Some observers may suggest that the reluctance to challenge the system is simply a matter of pragmatism on the part of the media, a conscious deal with the devil in order to get the story and the pictures of war as fast and as efficiently as possible. But for others it is nothing less than co-option into the propaganda war and it works because it is ideologically inscribed into the professional assumptions of the majority of embedded war reporters. To borrow from Slavoj Zizek (2012), their loud protests that they report objectively, independently and freely masks the very absence of freedom in the system.

This brings us to the next part of this book and another important factor that we need to assess when considering the role of the war correspondent today: the ideological frameworks that they use to explain international conflict. Chapter 8 looks at the Cold War framework that had its origins not in the post-Second World War era as dominant histories suggest but in the Russian revolution of 1917 and persisted as a dominant interpretation up until 1991, with the collapse of the Soviet Union. Chapter 9 goes on to propose that the reporting of 9/11 and America's declared 'war on terror', as well as, most recently, the increasingly hostile reporting of Vladimir Putin's Russia, represents not so much a paradigm shift as a paradigm repair. It is back to the Cold War, the most successful system of thought control and political repression in the name of freedom since the hegemony of the Roman Empire.

Part III

The War Correspondent and Ideological Frameworks

8

Reporting the Cold War and the New World Order

Propaganda is to a democracy what the bludgeon is to a totalitarian state.

Noam Chomsky[1]

From the Roman empires of ancient history to the European empires of the eighteenth and nineteenth centuries, through to the American and Soviet empires of the twentieth century, propaganda has been key to the manipulation of domestic public opinion and behaviour. The construction of the virtuous self and the projection of the enemy image, an abject other by which the virtuous self can be measured and amplified, is of course an ideological project that finds its origins in the institutions of the state; but its validation and its endless reproduction depend on a nexus of social and cultural institutions that include family, education, religion and the media – what Louis Althusser (1971) has described as 'ideological state apparatuses'. So far, this book has examined how the war correspondent as individual has negotiated his or her way around the vagaries of professional practice (risk, the requirements of objectivity, the speed and impact of media technologies) and institutional control (military censorship) to report modern warfare. This final section focuses on the role the war correspondent might play in the reproduction of dominant or pervasive propaganda frameworks, particularly where those amplify a set of deeply ingrained cultural assumptions and values that may seem entirely natural and given. This chapter examines the media's role in sustaining the Cold War framework of the twentieth century and the crisis they faced when that framework appeared to collapse with the East European Revolutions (1989) and the collapse of the Soviet Union (1991). The next chapter will go on to explore the rhetoric of the war on terror that followed the terrorist attacks on America in 2001, 9/11, and the growing western hostility towards Russia, and ask if they mark not a replacement of the Cold War framework but its gradual repair as an ideological paradigm for explaining international conflict.

THE COLD WAR AND THE ENEMY IMAGE

The certainty for journalism throughout the Cold war was the bipolar world of East and West, Communism and capitalism, because it provided a framework of interpretation – a way of seeing the world and of reporting international relations – that conformed to predictable patterns and narrative outcomes. Pierre Bourdieu's idea of 'master patterns' is useful here, by which he means 'an infinite number of individual patterns directly applicable to specific situations' (1971, p. 192). The problem, Bourdieu argues, is that while such master patterns help us to sustain thought, they may also take the place of thought. While they should help us to master reality with minimum effort, 'they may also encourage those who rely on them not to bother to refer to reality' at all (ibid.). This is a crucial point when we come to consider the role of the western media during the Cold War. They constructed their Cold War imagery both through *and* within one such 'master pattern' or interpretative framework. If we accept this, we have to make a distinction between the actual framework, the 'deep structures' of thought and action, and the instrumental 'enemy image' which served to rationalise it. It would be wrong to argue that they are one and the same. The Cold War was characterised by alternating periods of hostility and *détente* and these determined the functional utility of the enemy image. But periods of *détente* did not signify crisis in the fundamental ideological framework. That remained constant throughout the conflict.

The western news media presented the Cold war as a standoff between two superpowers with sole responsibility for danger or trouble lying squarely with the Soviet Union, 'the evil empire'. As George Gerbner argues, the enemy image, 'has deep institutional sources and broad social consequences. It projects the fears of a system by dramatising and exaggerating the dangers that seem to lurk around every corner. It works to unify its subjects and mobilises them for action' (1991, p. 31). At its worst, the framework restricted thought and action. It was as much part of what Edward Thompson (1982) called 'the deep structure of the Cold War' as the nuclear arms race, because it helped dehumanise the 'other side' out of existence. The sources of the Cold War enemy image are rooted in the West's response to the October Revolution in 1917. Walter Lippman and Charles Mertz carried out a content analysis of *The New York Times*' coverage of the revolution and found it hostile and propagandist. For *The New York Times*, they wrote, the Bolsheviks were 'both cadaver and world-wide menace' (Chomsky, 1989, p. 26). Most journalists, and their newspapers, were ignorant of the causes and circumstances of the revolution and revolutionary politics, and they failed to report developments with any depth of analysis or insight; some were compromised by their involvement in the subversive activities of western intelligence agencies. Whilst the majority of European and American newspapers were reporting, mostly from outside Russia, that the Bolsheviks were doomed to fail and were without popular support, Arthur Ransome of the London *Daily News* wrote that: 'It is folly to deny the actual fact that the Bolsheviks do hold a majority of the politically active population' (Knightley, 2004, p. 133). *The New York Times* was the worst offender. In a period of two years following the October revolution, the paper reported four times that Lenin and Trotsky had made plans to flee Russia, three times that they had actually fled the country; three times that Lenin had been imprisoned; once that he was about to retire; and once that he had been assassinated (ibid.).

The Revolution's first great test was the allied intervention 1918, known in mainstream, western historiography as the Russian Civil War. Western reporting of the intervention was heavily censored and only reports sympathetic to its aims were allowed. Most dispatches, whether about Bolshevik thinking and strategy, or the course of the intervention, relied on sources close to western governments or exiled Russian groups hostile to the revolution. Arthur Ransome eventually disowned such sources, especially the British secret services, to report on a much more objective level that the allied attitude to the revolution was wrong and that it only bred Bolshevik suspicions about the real intention of the allies (ibid., p. 135). With few exceptions, coverage relied on anti-Bolshevik hysteria based on rumours and black propaganda. Reporting fell into the same pattern of falsehood and exaggeration that emerged in coverage of the First World War and the Russian Revolution. Defeats of the western alliance were reported as victories while low morale and poor discipline in the allied armies were not reported at all. The Red Army on the other hand was reported to be near collapse and defeat even as it was in fact rolling back the allied intervention (ibid., p. 142). Only a few journalists such as the radical American reporter, John Reed, and Morgan Philips Price of the *Manchester Guardian*, distinguished themselves with comprehensive and intelligent coverage. Philips Price reported events at the centre of Bolshevik power, providing insights into how the Russian revolution was faring in face of the western intervention. His reports were structured not around rumour and propaganda but first hand observations and interviews with the leadership (ibid., p. 139). Both journalists served their readers with first hand, immediate and non-judgemental accounts of a revolution in the making (see Philips Price, 1997; Reed, 1926).

The enemy image extended beyond factual media forms. Popular fiction in books, on television and in the cinema promoted images of the superpowers in simplistic binary opposition of good and evil: Uncle Sam versus Ivan the Terrible, the Eagle versus the Bear (an image used in a Pentagon video on the arms race), the Promised Land versus the Evil Empire. In the Soviet Union the images were reversed. The West represented the kind of economic and social inequalities that the Revolution sought to overthrow. The shortcomings of the Revolution were minimised with persistent reference to capitalist exploitation and western imperialism. Throughout the New Cold War of the 1980s, each side was commonly depicted peering at the other over the Berlin Wall with fear and suspicion (McNair, 1988; Dennis et al., 1991). While such portrayals were prevalent throughout the Cold War, they had a universal utility that could be applied to any external threat for the containment of the domestic populace (Chomsky, 1989, p. 28; see also Gitlin, 1980; Parenti, 1993).

The most negative and virulent images prevailed over relatively short periods of crisis in US–Russian/Soviet relations. A longer, historical perspective on how each side defined the other points to a more dynamic process of political and cultural conflict and struggle on all fronts of the Cold War. While the New Cold War saw the picture at its blackest extreme, other periods of *détente* witnessed mixed images and shifting perceptions. The propaganda was successful in concealing a history of more 'normalised' relations between the US and Russia as competing 'great powers', periods when they engaged in much more open economic, political and cultural exchange. Everette Dennis et al. (1991) work within a broad historical and comparative framework to examine changes in how the US and Russia/Soviet Union saw each other from the nineteenth century. For example, while condemning the inequalities of American capitalism, Leninist journalism would also praise its productive forces, its technological advances and its great engineering feats (Zassoursky, 1991; Mickiewicz, 1991). Among the US media, images of stupid and violent Russians would mix with stories of Soviet–American cooperation and friendship, especially during the Second World War when the alliance with the Soviet Union was so crucial (Gerbner, 1991; Lukosiunas, 1991; Richter, 1991; Zassoursky, 1991). The next section shows how the enemy image informed media coverage of the most crucial and persistent theme of the Cold War: arms control and the nuclear debate.

Reporting nuclear disarmament and the peace movement

Several research studies show how it was possible to understand the nuclear debate in the media on a number of levels: as a propaganda battle between the superpowers (Glasgow University Media Group, 1985; McNair, 1988; Hallin and Mancini, 1989), or between Conservatives and Labour in the 1983 and 1987 general elections in Britain (McNair, 1988). We can also look at the contribution to the debate from the peace movement and how it was reported within the broad cold war propaganda framework (Aubrey et al., 1982; Glasgow University Media Group, 1985; McNair, 1988). To measure the parameters of the framework, it might be useful first to offer an example of how the nuclear debate was *not* reported.

At the height of the New Cold War and the anti-Cruise missile demonstrations in the West, the *New Left Review* published *Exterminism and Cold War*. Edited by historian Edward Thompson (1982), this international collection of essays set out a socialist critique of the nuclear arms race and addressed the problem from four points of enquiry.

1. 'the social nature and basis of [...] "exterminism" – the apparent drive of industrial civilisation towards its own self-destruction in the post-war arms race';
2. 'the respective roles and responsibilities of the two (superpowers)';
3. 'the relative importance of the distinct major theatres of the Cold War – the Far East, Europe, and the Third World';

4. and 'the whole nexus of problems posed by the quest for a realistic way out of the looming dangers of "Exterminism and Cold War"' (p. *xi*)

The mainstream media, by contrast, offered the narrowest possible interpretation. They reported that the nuclear weapon was a defensive deterrent against the Soviet threat of invasion, domination, or even nuclear annihilation. Andrew Wilson, defence correspondent with the *Observer*, noted the culture of fascination with nuclear weapons and weapons technology among defence correspondents in general. As with all lobby correspondents, journalists on the defence beat came into regular contact with officials in the 'defence community' and in many instances forged lasting friendships. They became immersed in a defence culture that, as Wilson argues, 'provided the essential framework within which to pursue peace-time planning for operations involving the death of millions' (1982, p. 37).

Coverage of the nuclear debate was underwritten by strict adherence to the rules of a crude numbers game (Glasgow University Media Group, 1985; McNair, 1988). The debate became so abstract and quantitative that it distracted from an underlying, qualitative concept of 'first use' or the 'preemptive strike'. This assumed that a limited nuclear war could be fought and won by such 'overwhelming force' that the enemy would never have a chance to retaliate. As long as the public understood that the goal of arms control was to ensure 'nuclear parity' between East and West – each side having a rough equivalence of nuclear weapons – they would not think too much about what the weapons were designed for or about the capability of a particular missile over and above its counterpart on the other side. Unless of course there was an alternative source of information and argument, such as the peace movement.

The peace movement in Britain was a broad umbrella grouping of intellectuals, politicians, the Greenham Common women, and the Campaign for Nuclear Disarmament (CND), most of whom were labelled as 'extremist' or 'unpatriotic'. Other religious or establishment figures were labelled 'naive' and 'idealistic', or 'hysterical' and 'mad' (Sabey, 1982, p. 55). A television news reporter described them as 'at best misguided, at worst dangerous and subversive' (McNair, 1988, p. 178). Ministry of Defence propaganda linked the peace movement to the extreme left and claimed that the CND was directly funded by the Soviet

Union with the aim of undermining western security policy. Indeed, to express any kind of opposition and dissent against the 'nuclear deterrent' was to go against the interests of 'national security'. For example, in order to discredit a big disarmament protest in October 1981, sections of the media framed it as a domestic security threat in that it would tie up scarce police resources and leave Britain vulnerable to attack not from the Soviet Union but the Irish Republican Army (IRA). As a *News of the World* columnist complained: ' at a time when the risk of IRA attack is high, why allow people like the CND to hold a massive demonstration? Yesterday's march tied up more than 1,000 policemen. No wonder the bombers keep getting away with it'. The *Sunday Telegraph* reported that, 'Thousands of police, including helicopter patrols, kept watch amid fears that the demonstration could provide cover for another IRA bomb outrage' (Sabey, 1982, p. 60). Similar labeling was applied to the much more narrowly based, middle-class, middle-aged nuclear freeze movement in the USA (Entman and Rojecki, 1993; Gitlin, 1980).

Another significant feature of coverage at this time was the prevailing structures of access in the media. These were such that voices supporting the official view were able to dominate media coverage and define the issues from their perspective. Although alternative viewpoints did filter through, these were usually framed negatively. Whereas spokespersons for the official perspective were interviewed at length and without serious inquiry, representatives of the peace movement were subjected to close scrutiny and repeated interruptions.

Official propaganda also extended to public relations stunts by senior politicians which attracted significant media coverage (Glasgow University Media Group, 1985; McNair, 1988) One notable example was Easter 1983 when the then Secretary of Defence Michael Heseltine staged a visit to the Berlin Wall as peace marches took place all over Britain. The intent was clear: to draw a counterpoint between the West's defence of freedom and the peace movement's attempt to undermine the means of maintaining that defence, the nuclear deterrent. At around the same period, Prime Minister Margaret Thatcher declared that the women holding hands around the military base in Greenham Common would be far better off holding hands around the Berlin Wall. McNair points to another tactic that the British government adopted with considerable success: that was to simply ignore the peace movement in the hope that the media would lose interest. A demonstration in 1984, against the Trident nuclear submarine system at Barrow-in-Furness, was attended by 20,000 people yet ITN only gave it a summary item lasting a few seconds; the BBC did not report it all (1988, p. 179). The Glasgow University Media Group concluded that the implicit, damning assumption underpinning news coverage of the peace movement was, 'It won't change anything' (Glasgow University Media Group, 1985, p. 234).

The next section examines what happened from 1985 when Mikhail Gorbachev came to power in the Soviet Union, heralding a new era of *perestroika* and *glasnost*, a programme of economic and social reform that began to impact upon the image of the enemy. The 'enemy' began to influence and shape its image to its own advantage by using western-style news management strategies such as timing stories for maximum media exposure or creating 'exclusive' or 'controversial' media events.

The impact of glasnost and perestroika on the enemy image

Perestroika, or 'reconstruction', referred to the idea that the problems with the Soviet economy, the gap for example between supply and demand, could only be solved by a radical rethink of economic policy. *Glasnost*, or 'openness', refers to a new period of liberalism in Soviet life and culture in which criticism and debate were allowed as long as they were constructive, and as long as people suggested better alternatives for making the revolution work for the betterment of all the people. *Glasnost* was the means by which the public could be mobilised into supporting the programme of reforms proposed under *perestroika*, and projecting a more positive image to the world was a vital part of the task. Not least among these changes was the transformation of the Soviet leader from Evil Emperor to Nice Guy. In the image-conscious West, Mikhail Gorbachev achieved 'superstar' status. Compared to his predecessors, he was young, photogenic, and charismatic. But, as he toured the capitals of the West to popular acclaim, he became a propaganda liability for the West. Take, for example, his performance vis à vis Ronald Reagan during the Moscow Superpower Summit in May 1988. One of the highlights of the summit in this respect was his joint walkabout with Ronald Reagan around Red Square. Here is how BBC News and ITN compared the two men:

Newscaster: 'Mr Gorbachev saw the chance to win a few hearts and grabbed it with both hands (TAKES A CHILD IN HIS ARMS). All

Mr Reagan managed was a handshake. Like before, and more so here in Moscow, Mr Gorbachev is tending to out-stage Mr Reagan. He's a lot quicker with the repartee although Mr Reagan still scores the odd point' (REAGAN PUTS AN ARM ROUND GORBACHEV'S SHOULDER). (*Newsnight*, 31 May 1988)

Reporter: 'For all the world it looked like the two superpower leaders were campaigning together on a joint ticket, Mr Gorbachev producing a small boy from the crowd and bearing him aloft for a handshake with the President in true American election style. Mr Reagan appeared so taken with the moment that he threw his arm around the Soviet leader's shoulders.' (ITN, 17.45, 31 May 1988)

On the last day of the Summit, Gorbachev held a long news conference, speaking to the western media on all issues, sometimes without notes; and even stopping to reorganise the seating arrangements in order to surmount problems with the simultaneous-translation facility. The event contrasted with a poorly attended news conference at the US Embassy, where Ronald Reagan appeared to struggle with the issues and was criticised for selecting favoured US journalists for questions. The comparison was highlighted in some sections of the British news media. In Gorbachev, the BBC observed 'a man in control: quick-witted, dynamic, formidable' (*Newsnight*, BBC2, 22.30, 1 June 1988). ITN described his performance as 'an extraordinary tour de force without a note' (ITN, 13.00, 1 June 1988). The *Guardian* reported that 'Gorbachev was masterful and...Reagan was genially feeble, even by his own modest standards'. The *Independent* judged Reagan's conference 'deeply embarrassing' and 'a flop', although a more sympathetic account in *The Times* concluded that his 'rambling answers, inconclusive sentences, hesitations, and apparent difficulty in grasping the point of many questions' were due to fatigue.[2] Gorbachev's popularity and credibility rating in Europe was rising as Reagan's was flagging: the US leadership role was under symbolic assault. This was especially significant at a time when NATO planners were arguing for 'modernisation' of the alliance's nuclear forces in western Europe to defend against the Soviet threat.

The Soviets also showed they had learned some useful lessons in western style news management. When in Moscow for the superpower summit, President Reagan was scheduled to meet dissidents at the US

Embassy. But the Kremlin announced a major news conference with the famous dissident, Andrei Sakharov, to take place a few days later, on 3 June 1988. At the same time, they set up an interview for the western news media with controversial Soviet politician, Boris Yeltsin. That evening, the main news bulletins were dominated by the dramatic attack Yeltsin made on conservative members of the Politburo. It was reported as an exciting, sensational departure from the normal conduct of Soviet politics, and as a story in its own right. Yeltsin, unknown to western publics at the time, came across as a colourful personality with an interesting story to tell. His 'struggle for the people against the system' engrossed journalists and 'experts' on the Soviet Union alike. In marked contrast, Reagan's meeting with Soviet dissidents was only mentioned in a general round-up of the main summit events of the day and seemed rather routine set against the dramatic news of Sakharov's press conference.

The west could legitimise its stance on nuclear weapons, and its response to the peace movement, as long as the Cold War prevailed but change to *détente* undermined the tactic considerably. The solution was to project 'evil' and 'instability' from unseen metaphysical forces to what was visible. Gorbachev was a 'nice guy', yes, and the Soviet people no doubt wanted peace and friendship with the West but the West had to be careful. The Soviet empire was not quite evil any longer but it had a long way to go before it could be trusted on western principles of human rights. It was also undergoing unprecedented social and economic reforms with *glasnost* and *perestroika*. That brought its own instabilities, hence the oft-quoted truism that an empire is at its most dangerous when it is reforming itself from within. Once again, the Moscow Summit provides an illustration of how this rhetoric worked. It was originally arranged to mark the ratification of the Intermediate Nuclear Forces Treaty, concluded in Washington the previous year to reduce and eventually eradicate their stocks of intermediate or medium-range nuclear forces. The next logical step was further progress in talks for a long-range, strategic arms treaty (START), which, if agreed, would have profound implications for superpower relations and the entire basis of the Cold War. However, talks in Geneva had ground to a halt over America's refusal to include its sea-launched missiles in the negotiations. For the US, talk about START was out. So what did the media report? At events like superpower summits, disputes over complex issues in arms control could be eclipsed by other distracting themes. For example, the *impasse* over START at the Moscow Summit was explained with wider reference to human rights, and to the future of Gorbachev and his reform proposals.

In advance of the Moscow summit, the US news management strategy was to tap into the powerful ideological connotations that the concept of human rights carried and which easily filtered through to routine Cold War news. Thus, Ronald Reagan set the US agenda for the meeting when he stopped over in Helsinki to give a speech commemorating the Helsinki Accords of 1975. Although human rights protocols formed only a part of the Accords, Reagan focused on them exclusively. He accused the Soviet Union of failing to live up to them since signing.

On the basis of his speech, and his plan for an unofficial meeting with Soviet dissidents in Moscow, the western news media dubbed the occasion, The *Human Rights Summit*, before it had even started. 'Human rights is his theme', said the BBC headline (BBC, 13.00, 27 May 1988); 'President Reagan...has put human rights at the top of the agenda', announced ITN (13.00, 27 May 1988). Reagan was successful in framing the human rights theme with wider issues. BBC reported his view that 'international security cannot be separated from human rights' (18.00, 27 May 1988). In contrast, the Soviet position was reported as a negative, ritual response to the preferred US agenda, not as an equally valid contending viewpoint. Channel 4 News reported that the Soviets could only 'respond predictably' with 'ritual denunciations of the speech' (Channel 4 News, 27 May 1988). Accounts of internal Soviet affairs were framed in a similar way. For example, some reports on *glasnost* and *perestroika* focused on their destabilising influence over Soviet politics and their impact on western assumptions about Soviet society. This in turn undermined the certainty and predictability of East–West relations and the Cold War system. As one reporter put it, 'It was simpler for NATO when the Bear was always growling. The question now is how should the West react?' (*Newsnight*, 31 May 1988).

Ever alert to deception from any quarter, western think tanks and media pundits fulfilled their designated role as watchdogs for national security. Zassoursky refers to timely publications like *The Soviet Propaganda Machine* and *Mesmerized By The Bear: The Soviet Strategy of Deception*. (Zassoursky, 1991, p. 18). Caspar Weinberger, a 'Cold Warrior' with regular access to British television news, told Channel 4

News that the Soviets were simply using new tactics, public relations, for their old strategy of 'world domination' and that it was important for the West to 'keep [its] guard up' (Channel 4 News, 2 June 1988); there was no suggestion here that the West might also use public relations for its own strategy of world domination. On a similar note, *The New York Times* columnist, A. M. Rosenthal, urged US leaders to be cautious about Gorbachev, 'a man who is still the dictator of the most powerful totalitarian nation in the world' (Chang, 1991, p. 70). These were the principal western justifications for its non-response to Soviet initiatives on arms control.

This very negative enemy image was not always down to the western media alone. In some cases, the Soviet Union was its 'own worst enemy' when it came to putting its case across to western publics. McNair (1998) considers some of the constraints faced by western correspondents when reporting *from* the Soviet Union during the New Cold War and, conversely, the failure or inability of the Soviet authorities to shape or influence western news coverage of Cold War issues. This helped shape 'enemy images' of the Soviet Union as much as the West's own political and cultural prejudices. The Korean Airlines incident in 1983 is a good example of this. Soviet fighter planes shot down a Korean civilian airliner over a sensitive and restricted area of Soviet airspace, believing it to be a US spy plane. Two hundred and sixty nine passengers and crew were killed provoking outrage in the West. According to the US, it was proof of Soviet policy to shoot down any aircraft that strayed into Soviet airspace without first asking questions. The Soviets stuck to their spy plane theory but in the early, crucial stages of the controversy, they played to the wrong audience in the wrong way. They seemed more concerned with presenting their version to their own people rather than competing with the US in persuading western publics that they had a credible defence. Thus, US propaganda played unopposed to more sceptical European opinion until it finally began to collapse under the weight of its own contradictions and in face of more convincing evidence from Soviet and independent sources. By then, however, it was of academic interest; the western media had lost interest in the story (McNair, 1988, p. 80ff & p. 95ff).

So despite the new insights into Soviet life and culture that the policy of *glasnost* offered the West, and despite the new spirit of East–West *détente*, the ideological fundamentals of the Cold War system and its interpretive framework remained firmly in place for most of the Gorbachev era.

What few anticipated, however, was that the relative liberalism that *glasnost* allowed in the Soviet Union created the conditions for popular protest in the countries of Eastern Europe. In 1989, the people of Poland, East Germany, Czechoslovakia and Hungary took to the streets to demand more freedom and more democracy, building an unstoppable momentum that climaxed on 9 November with the fall of the Berlin Wall, the most abiding, visual symbol of the Cold War. The British media were quick to celebrate these events as marking the end of the Cold War but were to take longer to realise the long-term implications of the crisis.

THE EAST EUROPEAN REVOLUTIONS 1989: A CRISIS IN JOURNALISTIC FRAMEWORK

1989: the year of revolution in Eastern Europe. At least, that was the story television told us. The emergence of a competitive democratic opposition was very newsworthy for countries so long governed by the one-party state. A month after the June elections in Poland, triumphant Solidarity deputies took their seats and, 'Suddenly there was an outburst of democracy!' (BBC1, 13.00, 13 November 1989). John Simpson reported from the Spartacus Cafe in Budapest: 'the information centre for the brand new opposition parties [where] "You can't afford to miss a single day's newspapers at the moment!" someone said, "It's like a new country every day!"' (BBC, 21.00, 10 July 1989).[3] When the East German government promised 'free, universal, and multiparty' elections, the news focused on the newly legalised opposition group, *New Forum*. This 'cutting-edge of democracy' was not so much a political party as a pressure group of politically interested professionals (Channel 4 News, 9 November 1989). Their chaotic, ad hoc news conferences provided a spectacle of western democracy, of 'normal politics' (BBC, 21.00, 9 November 1989).

The principal theme of the East European revolutions was 'people power', which echoed the fall of the Marcos regime in the Philippines and implied that 'the people' could achieve anything if they took to the streets *en masse* and in peaceful protest. The BBC reported the opening of the Berlin Wall as a government 'giving way to the parliament of the streets'. Even the security forces were 'forced to retreat in the face of people power' (BBC1, 21.00, 10 November 1989). On BBC's *Newsnight* programme, live from Berlin, newscaster Peter Snow welcomed his reporter 'who's walking into the studio with a large brick in her hand'. It was a piece of the Berlin Wall. After years of western neurosis about what it represented, Snow laid hands on it, priest-like, and exclaimed to his gathered studio guests, 'I don't think this Wall's going to last as long as Hadrian's Wall! It looks pretty flimsy, doesn't it?' (10 November 1989).

The first few scenes in the drama of the Romanian revolution at the end of that year seemed to fit the 'people power' theme with ease: the Romanian people filmed toppling Nicolai Ceaușescu, invading his palace and throwing its contents onto the streets. When they took over state television and formed a new government live on air, the images recalled the days of New Forum in East Berlin, or Civic Forum in Prague. Of all the scenes from the East European revolutions, this seemed the closest to anarchy, to real 'people power' as opposed to the media confection. But when that power was extended to the summary trial and execution of the Ceaușescus, the shaky black and white video images of their bodies suggested something much more sinister and calculated. Looking back on the 'revolutions' and the whole sweep of events in Eastern Europe throughout the 1990s, Alex Thomson accepts that themes of 'people power' and 'freedom and democracy' were less than adequate for explaining these fast moving events:

> Romania was the great lie there. What happened in Romania? Was it the fall of Ceaușescu? Was it the collapse of Communism? Well of course it was all of those things but in fact...what we're actually seeing wasn't a revolution, it wasn't an upsurge of the people like the Velvet Revolution in Czechoslovakia a few weeks before. It was actually more like an in-house coup. So the Romanian example is quite a good one to bring in, in the sense that the overall, rather glib, simple conclusion that yes it's the fall of Communism, yes it's the fall of Eastern Europe, yes it's the fall of the Warsaw Pact, may cover you but it won't fully explain what's going on.[4]

The events in East Germany and throughout Eastern Europe in 1989 apparently marked the collapse of the Cold War. Old certainties and assumptions – economic, political or military – became null and void. The question remained, then, whether western public discourse would meet the challenge of interpreting revolutionary change (Halliday et al, 1992; McLaughlin, 1993, 1999). John Simpson, one of the few reporters to cover all the East European revolutions, thought that this placed an onus of responsibility on the reporter when trying to make sense of such events:

(When) the Berlin Wall came down and then the revolution in Czechoslovakia and then...in Romania...it makes you look at it very carefully because you know that there'll be controversy about these things for the rest of your life, so therefore you want to be absolutely certain of what you think the truth is and the reality is because people will be arguing about it for a long time and asking about it. But I just knew that that was a time when you knew history was being made. [...] I'm just profoundly glad, grateful that I was able to be there.[5]

Admiral William Crowe, cold warrior and chair of the US Joint Chiefs of Staff, summed up the loss of Cold War certainty and its implications for US national security interests: 'This is a time of very uncertain strategic transition. The future's not what it used to be.'[6] Indeed, the West's response to the end of the Cold War was hardly revolutionary or epoch-making. Many of the institutions and organisations set up to manage the conflict are still in existence – the UN, NATO, the European Union – and they have come under considerable strain in the face of continuing economic problems and an array of global crises. The news presenter, Jeremy Paxman, remarked that it took 'something of a leap of imagination to realise that there are some people – politicians, industrialists and, above all, generals – who've been watching the scenes in Berlin with a feeling other than joy in their hearts because the events of the last few days raise enormous potential questions' (BBC2, Newsnight, 10 November 1989). He might have added western journalists to his list of suspects because it was clear that there was no persistent, ideological framework of inter-pretation to replace the Cold War paradigm for reporting world events. John Simpson has argued that even in the midst of uncertainty, the role of television journalism was simply to 'reflect reality':

1989, like 1956 and 1968, was a year when the entire world changed direction and we're still living through the consequences of that: wars, upheavals, the collapse of old systems and old certainties. And until new certainties replace them, the real world will be a place of violence and conflict and our television screens will have to reflect that.[7]

The east European ' revolutions' were, as Noam Chomsky might say, 'the right story' of freedom and democracy in 1989. There was also a 'wrong story' of freedom and democracy that year and the international news media ignored it: an outburst of 'people power' and democracy in Brazil and Chile in clear defiance of the USA just as it prepared to run roughshod over Panama. Elections in Chile on 14 December and in Brazil on 17 December 1989 confounded the legacy of fascism and totalitarianism that had plagued the countries of South America for over a century but which the USA fostered and supported in pursuit of its political and economic interests. There was no live media coverage of these events or media celebrations and ecstatic front-page headlines. As Lawrence Weschler argues, this had serious implications for our understanding of connected events on both continents:

> (Our) media's failure adequately to cover developments...in Chile and Brazil badly skews our understanding of what is happening in the world in general and in Eastern Europe in particular. This is true not only retrospectively – Eastern Europe is not the only place in the world these days trying to struggle out from under decades of often violent and terribly constricting superpower domination – but also prospectively: the sorts of economic dilemmas eastern Europeans seem likely to face in the decades ahead as they attempt the transition to a wide-open free market – an acute polarisation of wealth, the inescapable consequences of their crushing national debts, the surrender of their national sovereignty over key economic decisions to such monitoring organisations as the International Monetary Fund – are precisely the sort that Latin Americans have been struggling with for several decades. Indeed, these two sets of concerns...were very much at the forefront of the campaigns in Chile and Brazil the past several months, though, again, they went largely unreported in the American media (1990, p. 26).

Interpreting the significance of the revolutions

The attempt by journalists to interpret the significance of the East European revolutions, and the eventual collapse of the Soviet Union in 1991, should be put into the context of a wider intellectual debate, both on and between the right and left. On the right, Francis Fukuyama (1989,

1992) predicted even before the revolutions, in the summer of 1989, the 'end of history', that is the triumph of liberal democracy, 'the final form of human government (that) could not be improved on' (1992, p. *xi*). Even as the fall of the Berlin Wall seemed to vindicate his thesis, other commentators, even on the right, took it to be a flawed and premature analysis to say the least. The international relations analyst, Samuel P. Huntington (1993, 1996, 2011) proposed that while the apparent end of the Cold War may have marked the end of ideological conflict, this would be replaced by cultural conflict, what he called 'the clash of civilizations' that could only be contained by 'the remaking of world order' on a multipolar rather than a bipolar axis.

Perhaps unsurprisingly, the response on the left to events was somewhat more defensive or defeatist. In Britain, traditional Marxist intellectuals such as Eric Hobsbawm and Martin Jacques finally admitted the end of communism as a system of political-economic management. General Secretary of the Communist Party of Great Britain, Chris Myant, went even further to declare the Bolshevik Revolution 'a mistake of truly historic proportions', with disastrous consequences throughout the twentieth century, such as the second world war, the Holocaust and the Vietnam War (cited in Callinicos, 1991, p. 12). Other, less orthodox Marxist thinkers, such as Alex Callinicos (Trotskyism) and Noam Chomsky (anarchism), insisted on decoupling Marxism from the ideological baggage of Leninism and Stalinism and using it instead as an analytical tool for making sense of the end of communism. The East European revolutions and the collapse of the Soviet Union allowed free rein to western imperialist impulses, most immediately in the Middle East with the Gulf War. 'What was taking shape' argued Callinicos, 'was not a new world order but a more dangerous version of the old' (1991, p. 82; see also Chomsky, 1992b).

For journalists, the story of the east European Revolutions seemed at first to fit the thesis proposed by Fukuyama: people and nations breaking free from communist tyranny to embrace the freedom and democracy of the west. Yet in 1993, as Poland and Hungary voted in their general elections to preserve some form of socialism, the *Guardian* slipped back into Cold War hysteria with the headline: 'Red Tide Sweeps Eastern Europe' (21 September 1993); while the *Daily Telegraph* was to remark that 'the economic consequences of western victory in the Cold War have brought chaos, not a new order, to Eastern Europe' (*Sunday Telegraph*, 19 December 1993).

This concept of a new order, a 'New World Order' to be precise, was a convenient propaganda cover for global policing in the immediate aftermath of the Cold war and the western news media played an important role in its projection. Indeed, the dominant news framework was as much an ideological construct as the Cold War itself. So long as the conduct and pattern of international relations and international crises seemed to conform to the dominant assumptions underpinning the Cold war – on all fronts and in all battlegrounds – then the Cold War news paradigm was a successful means of puzzle-solving, of making sense of international conflict. And while images of the Soviet Union altered according to the intensity of hostilities, or in response to the propaganda strategies of either side, the Cold War framework remained intact. Even during *détente*, the superpowers were still perceived as no more than 'Friendly Enemies' (Hallin and Mancini, 1989). Once the Cold war system slid into crisis and collapsed, then so did its explanatory framework. It was no longer adequate for intellectual analysis or for journalistic reportage but academics, politicians and journalists seemed to find if only for a brief spell an ideal replacement: 'The New World Order'.

NEWS IN THE POST-COLD WAR ERA

The 'New World Order' signified a conceptual world-view in the post-Cold War era. Yet it was a highly problematical intellectual framework and journalists who adopted it found that it failed to explain the global crises and conflicts that took place in the 1990s. In a special feature for the *Independent on Sunday*, Cal McCrystal argued that, 'Despite the end of the Cold War and promises of a "New World Order", we are continually reminded that war remains a bad habit' with around 30 'substantial' conflicts around the globe.[8] In fact, only a few years after the Wall, journalists were already thinking in terms of a 'New World Disorder' that, as Hugo Young wrote, 'touches its presumptive masters as well as its undoubted victims'.[9] The *Observer* commented on 'A world crying out for order', arguing that the idea of 'the New World Order was not just over optimistic: it was stupidly misleading. Order was always the last thing that was going to be achieved'.[10] Certainly, from the perspective of the so-called 'developing world', the post-Cold War era was a disaster. Panama, Iraq, Somalia, and Haiti were just some examples of what western peacekeeping and peace-enforcement did for the powerless in the name of global law and order. For those countries, little or nothing changed (Chomsky, 1993 & 1994; Mowlana et al 1992; Peters, 1992).

The notion of a 'New World Disorder' has also been cited as reason for the big powers to exercise their military muscle and boost their defence budgets. This was the most dominant of the two broad worldviews to emerge from media debate about the post-Cold War order. It emphasised the need for the West to keep its existing security structures intact, 'to keep its guard up'. In an uncertain world, instability was the new enemy and it came in a variety of forms. For example, *Newsnight* pointed out the dangers of nuclear weapons falling into the hands of a 'Middle Eastern despot' or a 'deranged Soviet colonel' (BBC2, 8 November 1991). There was also the 'war on drugs', nationalism in the former Soviet republics and the threat of Islamic fundamentalism.

There was an alternative view of a transformed security, economic and political order in the world based on the Helsinki process and tied in with the United Nations. The existing military alliances would atrophy and no one power would assume the task of global policing. This was pushed by the Soviets in the run up to German unification in 1990 but it was never taken seriously by western governments for whom the preservation of the status quo – a US-led Atlantic Alliance – was paramount. And it was never taken very seriously by television news media that continued to approach security issues from the dominant perspective. On the eve of the Malta Summit, December 1989, Gorbachev and Bush made their way to Malta with contrasting opening gambits that provided the news media with the desired imagery. Gorbachev stopped off for an almost messianic state visit to Italy where he was pictured swamped by huge crowds of adoring fans in Rome and Milan, but his PR master-stroke was stepping onto the hallowed anti-Communist ground of the Vatican for an 'historic' reconciliation with the Pope. George Bush sent out a different message. As he landed on the US aircraft carrier, the USS Forrestal, in the Mediterranean, fighter planes were taking off from a base in the Pacific to help quash another attempted insurrection in the Philippines. The point was not lost on the British news media:

[FOOTAGE OF PLANES TAKING OFF FROM AND LANDING ON
THE USS FORRESTAL]
Reporter: On the eve of the Malta Summit, *a display of American military
might.* Just hours after ordering his pilots to support government
troops in the Philippines, George Bush reviewed US air-power in the
Mediterranean...America's action in the Philippines was the first major
military intervention ordered by President Bush and has bolstered his
reputation as a decision-maker. It follows criticism that he failed to
help the recent coup attempt against Panama's General Noriega and
that he's responded weakly to upheavals in Eastern Europe. Now, just
before his meeting with Mr Gorbachev, *Mr Bush has a new, bolder
image* (ITN, 22.00, 1 December 1989; emphases added).

This has the ring of a washing-powder advertisement. Bush is presented
as the 'greenhorn' President still overwhelmed by his new responsibility as US leader and in need of a new image as a bold, hands-on
decision maker. Yet, Noam Chomsky chronicles Bush's past record as
a national security apparatchik in successive administrations since the
1970s, culminating in his post as director of the CIA, and shows that he
had little to learn about projecting US power around the world (1992b,
p. 59–61). Far from needing 'a new, bolder image', Bush was very much an
'old brand' US President. Still, it was a useful public relations strategy and
a persistent one as media coverage of recent US interventions showed.
Two weeks after the Malta Summit, Bush was trying out his new, bolder
image again: invading Panama, capturing its leader, General Manuel
Noriega, an old ally, and installing his new man with a quick oath of
allegiance to God and America. As Noam Chomsky has demonstrated,
the US media response to the operation itself was very favourable,
whatever their complaints about being corralled away from the action
(1992a). In Britain, a *Newsnight* report on the operation began, 'So the
George Bush "wimp factor" disappeared with one big bang in Panama'
(20 December 1989). This after all was the USA's 'backyard' and the
US media pulled out all the stops to: manufacture the crisis; caricature
and demonise General Noriega; and deflect public attention away from
civilian casualties and the real geo-political objectives of the operation
(Chomsky, 1992a, p. 144ff).

Forty-five years of Cold War propaganda and ideology was not simply
put back in the box by *glasnost* and *perestroika*. When it came to reporting

the Soviet Union's response to the invasion some familiar propaganda reflexes helped absorb the impact of international condemnation. For example, a BBC journalist recalled Gorbachev's state visit to Cuba earlier that year. 'The reformist Gorbachev and old-style Communist Fidel Castro have little in common these days', he said. 'At least they didn't until the US invasion of Panama. The reaction by both has been a leap back to Cold War rhetoric' (BBC1, 21.00, 20 December 1989). Yet this and other reports did not seem to see the bigger picture, which was that the Soviet Union and Cuba were but just two voices among the United Nations' clamour to condemn the invasion.

If the US invasion of Panama marked a false Spring for the New World Order, the Gulf Crisis of 1990, when Iraq invaded Kuwait, seemed to demonstrate an unprecedented degree of international opposition, marshaled and led by the UN. But it soon became apparent that the real power emanated from the White House. Far from criticising the US leadership role in the crisis at the expense of the UN, the British media largely endorsed it as proof positive that the US was in an ideal position to direct the New World Order. As US warships headed for the Gulf not to 'free Kuwait' at that stage but to 'defend Saudi Arabia', ITN noted that 'America is once again adopting the role of policeman of the world' (ITN, 22.00, 8 August 1990). But in the first stages of the crisis, it was reported that the option of 'Taking on a war-machine as enormous as Iraq has already, in effect, been ruled out by the defence ministries of the western world', and that 'Foreign Office sources indicate that any military action is now out of the question' (BBC1, 21.00, 2 August 1990). A report on Channel 4 News concluded that despite western involvement in the Iran–Iraq war, 'Any new conflict would be unwinnable' (2 August 1990). Nonetheless, news items were very clear that a solution could only come from the West led by the US. The BBC's John Simpson thought it 'impossible to think that there could be an Arab solution...but if there's to be a solution rather than a compromise it'll come mostly from the West' (BBC1, 21.00, 8 August 1990).

By the end of November, the US was talking of 'freeing Kuwait' even if that meant all out war. To this end it launched a propaganda campaign to forge a military alliance of western and Arab powers, and overcome divisions in western public opinion over the doubling of its forces in the Gulf (MacArthur, 1992). There was much criticism of the way the US hijacked the UN to forge his western–Arab coalition against Saddam

Hussein in the early stages of the crisis but history shows such criticism to be misplaced. Bush simply revived the original and principal purpose of the United Nations: as an agency of enforcement with a hierarchy of leadership and very clear parameters of conduct in the global arena. President Franklin D. Roosevelt set out the blue-print in 1943 when he determined that 'there should be four policemen in the world – the US, Great Britain, Russia, and China...The rest of the world would disarm... As soon as any of the other nations was caught arming they would be threatened first with quarantine and if quarantine did not work they would be bombed'.[11] It was a model of the 'New World Order' that did not translate very well into the grand, idealistic rhetoric of the UN Charter but it was clearly invoked through George Bush's ideas in a speech on the Gulf crisis. He promised that by the time the US dealt with Saddam Hussein they:

> [...] will have taught a dangerous dictator and *any* tyrant tempted to follow in his footsteps that the US has a new credibility, and that what we say goes, and that there is no place for lawless aggression in the Persian Gulf and in this New World Order that we seek to create. And we mean it! And [Saddam Hussein] will understand that when the day is done![12]

When Bush announced the beginning of war, he invoked the New World Order again, this time with the racist undertones that informed much of his bellicose rhetoric against Saddam Hussein. 'We have before us', he said, 'the opportunity to forge for ourselves and for future generations a New World Order, a world where the rule of law, *not the law of the jungle*, governs the conduct of nations' (17 January 1991; emphasis added). Some weeks later, the British Foreign Secretary, Douglas Hurd, endorsed the rhetoric when he told an audience that, 'In the late 20th century nations must be able to conduct affairs by a code more worthy of rational human beings than the law of the jungle'.[13]

Commenting on US media coverage of the Gulf crisis, Edward Said told a BBC documentary that 'the central media failing (was) an unquestioning acceptance of American power', and argued that 'public rhetoric [was] simply undeterred, uncomplicated by any considerations of detail, realism, or cause and effect' in respect to the crisis at hand. The news media simply fulfilled their designated role as they had done so well in their coverage of Vietnam, Grenada and Panama. When the crisis in the Gulf finally gave way to war, Said was just finishing his new work, *Culture and Imperialism*, and he remembered looking again at what he had written:

> Here was a new chapter of the imperial story, with the [US] now at the centre of the world stage instead of France and Britain. And as culture in the form of various narratives of western ascendancy had shaped the nineteenth century imperial dynamic, so it was the media that now played the same role.[14]

Eqbal Ahmad (1992) reflected on how the twentieth century has been 'most remarkable for its simultaneous capacity to promise hope and deliver disappointments', and has ended as it began with 'renewed hopes of a just and peaceable world order...being overwhelmed by politicians and warriors whose political minds remain rooted in the past' (p. 7). He warned that, 'We are being lied to; and we must not be deceived. What we are actually witnessing is a display of imperialism relieved of the limits imposed by superpower rivalry and nuclear deterrence (ibid. p. 10).

The UN sanctions against Iraq for its invasion of Kuwait, shown to been so effective in November 1990, were suddenly no longer effective in January 1991.[15] Diplomacy and negotiations via the UN became 'unhelpful'. And, in a breathtaking display of Orwellian doublethink, Bush's military build-up in the Gulf was read as 'going the extra mile for peace'; his bellicose rhetoric an example of 'extraordinary diplomacy'. A worldwide coalition stood behind the world's only superpower against a pariah state whose leader could not see reason. War had become 'inevitable' (Philo and McLaughlin, 1995). As the bombs fell on Baghdad, some journalists appreciated the wider geo-political implications of this for US military power in the world. David Dimbleby remarked to the US Ambassador to Britain that such a display of military power 'suggests that America's ability to react militarily has really become quite extraordinary, despite all the critics beforehand who said it will never work out like that' (BBC1, 10.00, 18 January 1991). There appeared to be nothing in any of this of a US decline resulting from 'imperial overstretch' (Kennedy, 1989). After the war, Bush declared to the nation: 'It's a proud day for America and, by God, we've kicked Vietnam syndrome once and for all!'[16] At a US army victory cabaret, a senior officer told the troops that the Iraqis 'never had a chance'. Their whole problem, he thought, was their complete ignorance of US military power, 'the lethality, the speed and the vigour of execution that resided in our equipment and in our leadership'. The snag for the US? 'We knew we were good – we didn't know *how* good'.[17]

Somalia 1993: Operation Restore Oil

Bush's successor, President Bill Clinton, also suffered a credibility gap when he eased into office in 1993. The election campaign smears concerning his past still lingered in the public mind and as he prepared to take office from Bush, the crisis in Somalia provided his first major test of leadership. Throughout 1992, television images from Somalia of thousands of starving people in the midst of civil war had brought home to the West the legacy of Cold War, superpower rivalry in the so-called 'Third World'. The superpowers had gone but much of their firepower remained in the hands of rival factions who fought to fill the power vacuum. The images also served as an uncomfortable reminder to all that the concept of a New World Order was conditional only upon the furtherance of western interests. The out-going President Bush and President-elect, Clinton, announced their intention to send in the troops to help the aid agencies distribute food around the country without hindrance or intimidation from the various armed factions. Thus Operation Restore Hope was presented as a mission of mercy rather than an old-fashioned, geo-political, Cold War style invasion. And it would do the image of either President no harm at all.

Yet, according to a *Los Angeles Times* report, there was another aspect to the story that the media in the US, and it seems in Britain, did not include in their coverage: oil. It was oil which motivated the US to launch such a large-scale military operation at a time when it shied away from intervention in comparable crises elsewhere. In what might have been better named 'Operation Restore Oil', The *Los Angeles Times* obtained documents that revealed that 'nearly two-thirds of Somalia was allocated to the American oil giants Conoco, Amoco, Chevron and Phillips in the final years before Somalia's pro-US President Siad Barre was overthrown [...] in January 1991'. This land had the potential to 'yield significant amounts of oil and natural gas if the US-led military mission can restore peace to (Somalia). There was also evidence that the oil company Conoco closely cooperated with the US forces in their 'humanitarian effort' and even leased one of its properties in Mogadishu to serve as a temporary US embassy. The *Los Angeles Times* revealed that the close ties between the US military and the oil companies had 'left many Somalis and foreign development experts deeply troubled...leading many to liken the...operation to a miniature version of Operation Desert Storm'.[18] I looked at several samples of British television news coverage of the story but found no references to links with oil or any other major western interests. However, coverage certainly bore similarities with that of Panama and the Gulf War.

The major US media were alerted in advance to the exact place on a beach near the Somali capital, Mogadishu, where the huge military landing would take place on 9 December, 1992. The day before, the BBC reported that it would be 'an invasion by arrangement, not a dawn raid' and called it 'a humanitarian mission but with muscle' (21.00, 8 December 1992). And the *News At Ten* predicted that 'the gunmen will find out what they're really up against, with the eyes of the world watching' (ITN, 8 December 1992). As in coverage of the Panama and the Gulf War, the show of military might and technology seemed to freeze the critical impulses of the news media in Britain as they launched into the story with gung-ho headlines such as 'Hundreds of American marines storm Mogadishu' (BBC1, 13.00, 9 December 1992), forgetting, it seemed, that this was supposed to be a 'humanitarian' mission of mercy, not *The Sands of Iwo Jima*. This ITN report captures perfectly the tone and mood of coverage in the first critical hours of the operation:

[NEWS FOOTAGE OF US LANDING)
Reporter: D-Day in Somalia. Outlined against the moonlit Indian Ocean, the spearhead force hit the beaches. Giant hovercraft disgorged the American marines of Team Tiger...Out at sea, the warships... Overhead, wave upon wave of helicopters thundered in carrying yet more troops to secure the airport and the docks. The UN peacekeepers who've been holding the fort here just looked on as this huge operation unfolded around them (12.30, 9 December 1992).

A marines' commander told reporters that, 'Our objective here is to come in and display maximum force, to let everyone know that we mean business'. How the warring parties in Somalia received this is unknown but the commander certainly impressed ITN who reported that 'The Somalis have been left in no doubt that these US marines mean business' (12.30, 9 December 1992), and on how 'The Americans show who's in charge in Somalia' (22.00, 9 December 1992). But within a year, the Americans were still in Somalia and they looked anything but 'in charge'. It was at this point that the narrative abruptly changed, from one of US leadership and military clout to one of United Nations failure and incompetence. The crucial point of departure came on 12 June 1993, when 23 Pakistani soldiers were killed in a gun-battle with the forces of Somali 'warlord', General Aideed. UN forces responded with an assault on Aideed's headquarters on 12 June. BBC headlines declared how:

United Nations forces attack the Somali capital in retaliation for the killing of 23 Pakistani peacekeepers. Four arms dumps are destroyed, 200 prisoners taken in an attempt to disarm criminal elements (21.50, 12 June 1993).

The reporter summed it up as 'all part of the UN's latest efforts to bring peace to Somalia' and described it as 'a military success, albeit against a much weaker enemy'. He concluded that 'the real test for the UN now is to win the hearts and minds of the Somali people while keeping up this hard line approach' (ibid.). The next day, 13 June, the tone of coverage changed when Pakistani troops shot dead 20 unarmed Somali protesters. BBC News reported that 'Anger among Somalis *over the actions of the United Nations* is rapidly turning to fury [and]...is losing the UN the sympathy it cannot do without' (BBC1, 18.20, 13 June 1993; emphasis added). ITN showed pictures of wounded civilians being treated in a makeshift operating theatre and reported how 'Somali people are finding it harder and harder to understand the purpose of a humanitarian mission which has turned into a military offensive. [...] Peacekeeping in Somalia has taken on a new and deadly meaning' (ITN, 23.15, 13 June 1993). Another BBC item showed US helicopter guns-ships targeting missiles at mortar batteries in Mogadishu. The reporter said it was part of 'the *UN policy* of destroying weapons here', but reported that 'they're doing it during the day and over busy streets filled with innocent civilians'. He remarked that 'For many Somalis, *hatred for the UN* now overwhelms any animosity against General Aideed'. The item refers to Aideed's comparison of the UN's deeds with those of a dictator and concludes that, 'The sight of French soldiers...planting explosives to destroy a radio station that broadcasts *against the United Nations* does lend force to the comparison' (21.00, 14 June 1993; emphasis added).

Television news pictures of the Battle of Mogadishu, on 3 and 4 October 1993, with the bodies of US Rangers being dragged by a mob through the streets, signaled the end of US resolve to stay the course in Somalia. As the last US troops withdrew on 25 March 1994, ITN broadcast a strongly worded report from Bill Neely that they were getting out 'before good intentions paved the road to hell'. He recalled that, 'When US troops came, there was no government – there is no government now', and that 'what began with a near farcical night-landing under TV lights soon degenerated into an undeclared war'. The US commander told ITN how he prayed that 'the Somali people would raise themselves out of this turmoil and anarchy and to build some kind of society based on love instead of...the gun'. Neely exploded the commander's pious sentiments with the bombshell that 'the US has just given weapons worth £20 million to the Somali police to subdue the clans that America could not subdue' (22.00, 25 March 1994).

The picture of Somalia that came across in the news media, then, was of a country in chaos, its people starving and ruled by warring factions. Its only hope, it seemed, was western aid and military intervention. The country had become a test-bed for the imposition of the 'new world order' President Bush promised during the Gulf Crisis in 1990. However, there were other countries in Africa that experienced total disorder and civil war but which did not figure in western plans for this 'New World Order'; in contrast with Somalia, Rwanda and Sierra Leone were conspicuous by the absence of global policing. During his two terms in office, President Clinton chose to bomb Iraq twice and threaten North Korea over its alleged nuclear weapons programme and its apparent reluctance to allow inspection by the International Atomic Energy Agency. These foreign policy options were designed to help to project his image as a 'new, bolder' US president and again the news media were ready to oblige. For example, when Clinton ordered the first bombing raids on Iraq in January 1993, a BBC reporter noted that 'passing the torch from Bush to Clinton is a time when both men want to show they are not going to be pushed about, so there's a certain amount of domestic and world public relations involved in all this' (BBC1, 21.00, 13 January 1993).[19] A second strike followed in June 1993, this time on the grounds that

Iraq had plotted to assassinate ex-President George Bush. Suspects had been arrested and their trial was still in progress in Kuwait when the US decided its own investigation was proof enough to justify another Cruise missile bombardment of Baghdad. The US President told the world that, 'From the first days of our revolution, America's security has depended on the clarity of this message: don't tread on us!' While he justified the bombing as self-defence under the terms of Article 51 of the UN Charter, he warned Iraq not to do likewise. And he emphatically denied that the bombing had anything to do with image. ITN's newscaster took this up with his Washington correspondent:

> *Newscaster:* Any suggestion that he might have done it to sharpen up his image?
> *Reporter:* Well, he was asked that question today and as you might expect specifically denied it. But officials are not denying that it does give him a boost in those areas where he's seen to be weakest. He's not seen as being a decisive leader or as being a strong military commander. But there was no dithering, no public agonising about this and his statement, 'Don't tread on us', was seen as a very strong, almost Reaganesque warning. (ITN, 22.00, 28 June 1993)

The BBC reported on Clinton's visit two weeks later to South Korea or, to be more precise, on his day 'in and around the demilitarised zone' dressed in military fatigues and threatening North Korea with 'annihilation'. The contradiction of military posturing in a demilitarised zone was apparently lost on the reporter but he was quick to see it was 'clearly designed to sharpen (Clinton's) military image' (BBC1, 22.05, 11 July 1993).

CONCLUDING REMARKS

The rhetoric of a New World Order, therefore, did not stand the test of time, logic or US foreign policy goals. For their part, journalists reporting on wars and conflicts in the Balkans or in parts of Africa, for example, struggled to find a new framework for interpreting, explaining and reporting conflict around the world. The big themes of East versus West, and Totalitarianism versus Freedom and Democracy did not seem to do adequate justice to explanations of 'genocide' (Rwanda, 1994) or 'ethnic cleansing' (Croatia, Bosnia, or Kosovo). Perhaps this ideological deficit explains more than any other factor the tendency for some journalists to seek refuge in ethical or moral attachment to humanitarian causes but the terrorist attacks on America on 11 September 2001 heralded a framework with contours of interpretation and image that once again spoke of a bipolar world of conflict. The next chapter looks at how war correspondents and the media they work for have tried (or not) to negotiate the restrictions and restraints of this framework of interpretation as it has evolved from one of global war on terrorism to the return of the evil empire: Russia.

9

Reporting the 'War on Terror' and the Return of the Evil Empire

We must remember that in time of war what is said on the enemy's side of the front is always propaganda, and what is said on our side of the front is truth and righteousness, the cause of humanity and a crusade for peace.

Walter Lippmann, 1967[1]

This chapter is not a review of the literature that exists on the role of the media in reporting and representation of 9/11, and the so-called war on terror that followed it; nor is it an in depth analysis of the reporting of what have been called the 9/11 wars, that is, Afghanistan and Iraq, fought as part of America's war on terror (see, for example, Carruthers, 2011; Lewis, 2005; Schecter, 2003). Time and resources do not allow for either. Its purpose instead is to develop the thesis proposed in the previous chapter and look at the outlines of the war on terror as a media paradigm for reporting international conflict since 9/11, looking in particular at media responses to the bombing attacks on Madrid in 2004 and London in 2005 in critical comparison with their coverage of America's 'Shock and Awe' bombing of Baghdad in 2003. It will then look at the reporting of the Crimea crisis in 2014 and suggest the possibility that, notwithstanding the hysterical western response to the threat posed by Islamic State (IS), itself fed in part by IS propaganda, we may be looking at the emergence of a paradigm less complex and more sustainable and predictable than the war on terror: a new cold war with a new Evil Empire, Vladimir Putin's Russia.

REPORTING THE WAR ON TERROR

The terrorist attacks on America on 11 September 2001 horrified the world and commanded global media attention. Images of the passenger planes crashing into the twin towers of the World Trade Centre in New York City were endlessly replayed on television and displayed frame by frame in newspaper photo supplements. In Britain, BBC News described the image of the second plane hitting the south tower as 'The face of war in the twenty-first century!' Newspaper front pages across the world the next day were dominated by dramatic photographs of the burning towers; but they differed in their interpretations of what the event represented. Most saw it in obvious terms, as an attack on America: 'U.S. Attacked' (*The New York Times*) 'War On America' (*Daily Telegraph*); 'When War Came To America' (*The Times*); 'A Declaration Of War' (*Guardian*); 'Act of War' (*The New York Post* and *USA Today*). In Britain, *The Sun* described it as 'A Day That Changed The World', while *The Daily Mirror* went so far as to call it a 'War On the World'. With a slight millenarian twist, we also had 'Doomsday America' (*The Independent*) and 'Apocalypse' (*The Daily Mail*).

In an emergency address to a joint session of the US Congress on 20 September, President George W. Bush, mobilised the nation for war against those responsible for the attacks – a sinister worldwide terrorist organisation called Al Qaeda led by an obscure Saudi Arabian construction engineer, Osama bin Laden. This was the moment when Bush first publicly used the phrase 'war on terror' to define America's response to the attacks, marking a shift in tactics from its response to previous terrorist attacks on American interests abroad; such as the bombings of US embassies in Kenya and Tanzania in 1998 (limited military operation against Al Qaeda targets in Afghanistan) and the assault on the USS Cole in 2000 (intelligence investigation). This new response, this new 'war on terror', would start with an aerial bombing campaign against Al Qaeda training camps in Afghanistan but there would be no definitive end until the objective of destroying terror groups all over the world was realised. But Bush was to add a new dimension that suggested something resembling the old Cold War division of the world: '[We] will pursue nations that provide aid or safe haven to terrorism. Every nation in every region now has a decision to make: Either you are with us or you are with the terrorists.' Bush and the neo-conservative ideologues that dominated thinking in his administration were to take the rhetoric to Dr Strangelove-levels in a series of speeches and public statements over the following months. On 29 October 2001, three weeks into 'Operation Enduring Freedom' in Afghanistan, Richard

Perle, Chairman of the US Defense Policy Board Advisory Committee, declared there would be:

> No stages! This is total war. We are fighting a variety of enemies. There are lots of them out there [...] If we just let our vision of the world go forth, and we embrace it entirely, and we don't try to piece together clever diplomacy but just wage total war, our children will sing great songs about us years from now.[2]

And in his State of the Union address to the US Congress on 29 January 2002, Bush divided the world between 'America [and] our friends and allies' and 'regimes that sponsor terror [and] constitute an axis of evil, arming to threaten the peace of the world.'

It is easy in hindsight to dismiss all this as the wild imaginings of a lunatic political fringe but there are three important points to note. The first is that it was part of a carefully calibrated propaganda campaign designed to re-energise and project American power in the Middle East and beyond. The second is that an array of other states happily adopted the war on terror to legitimate their use of overwhelming force against internal threats or nationalist insurgencies (Russia in Chechnya or Israel in the Occupied Territories and Gaza, for example). And the third is that large sections of the western corporate media believed it with little in the way of critical examination. For example, in an interview on 2 December 2001, for NBC's *Meet the Press*, US Secretary of Defense, Donald Rumsfeld lent credence to 'constant discussion' in the British press about Osama bin Laden hiding out in a fantastical 'Secret Cave' somewhere in the mountains of Afghanistan. Referring to a comic-book graphic lifted from *The Times* of London, anchorman Tim Russert's excitement was evident:

> *Russert*: Many Americans have a perception that it's a little hole dug out of the side of a mountain...
> *Rumsfeld*: Oh no!
> *Russert*: [CUT TO GRAPHIC] This is it! This is a fortress! A complex – multi-tiered. Bedrooms and offices on the top as you can see [HELPFUL LABELS ADDED]. Secret exits on the sides and at the bottom cut deep to avoid thermal detection. A ventilation system (!) to allow people to breathe and carry on. Entrances large enough to

drive through trucks and even tanks! Even computer systems and telephone systems! It's a very sophisticated operation!
Rumsfeld: Oh you bet! This is serious business and there's not one of those – there are many of those!

Versions of the graphic from *The Times* also found their way into other elite newspapers such as the *New York Times* and the London *Independent* at a time when Operation Anaconda, to hunt down bin Laden and his followers, was showing no signs of success. It turned out in the end that the perception of many Americans, as Russert put it, was correct – that the caves used by bin Laden and his followers were in fact more akin to 'a little hole dug out of the side of mountain'. In an interview for America's Public Broadcast Service, a US Special Forces sergeant, who was involved in the operation, revealed that 'they weren't these crazy mazes or labyrinths of caves that they described. Most of them were natural caves. Some were supported with some pieces of wood [and were] maybe about the size of a 10-foot by 24-foot room, at the largest. They weren't real big.'[3]

Documentary filmmaker Adam Curtis casts a critical eye on the 'war on terror', propaganda framework. In 'The Rise of the Politics of Fear', the final part of a three-part series, *The Power of Nightmares* (2004), he argues that it was a revival of the Cold War conception of a world divided along bi-polar oppositions of good and evil. Only this new war was being fought against a phantom enemy rather than a nation state in the style of the old Soviet Union. Along with other critics such as Jason Burke (2004), Curtis rejects the conception of Al Qaeda as worldwide terrorist organisation, tightly controlled and funded at the centre by one man, its leader Osama bin Laden. These more considered and informed critiques insist that Al Qaeda, as its literal translation suggests, is more of a world view, a set of ideas around which to inspire a diverse range of political and/or militant, Islamic groups from Africa, the Middle East and Asia. Furthermore, the argument goes, their existence in many cases stands as a legacy of the West's alliance with and funding of the resistance to the Soviet occupation of Afghanistan in the 1980s.

Some commentators have looked at the media coverage of 9/11 in more depth and defined the attacks as the ultimate 'propaganda of the deed', a spectacle of violence and destruction designed to instil terror in a global media audience (Kellner, 2005, pp. 25–75); and to redefine the dominant political discourse (Croft, 2006, pp. 37–83; Moeller, 2004, pp. 59–76). Others such as Liebes and Kampf (2004, pp. 77–95) have argued further that the 'automatic, universal adoption of the genre of breaking news – that is, live marathonic broadcasting during, and in the wake of, a multi-victim attack – facilitates the upgrading of terrorists to superstars' (p. 81). This theory, that the mainstream corporate media in the west serve as unwitting propaganda proxies for terrorist organ-isations, has long been debated in academia but it is a difficult one to prove conclusively. It also assumes that acts of terror like 9/11 seen live on television, or the set-piece TV interview with a terrorist representa-tive, automatically translate into definitional power for that actor. Yet the power to define what constitutes terrorism and the terrorist clearly does not lie with those labelled as terrorists. The Bush administration's propaganda response to 9/11, its rhetoric of a 'war on terror', was backed by the projection of overwhelming military force in Afghanistan and Iraq; and by excessive security measures at home and abroad. This has been equally effective in instilling fear, paranoia and suspicion in the minds of those it claims to protect; and provoking violent retaliation from those it attacks. In both rhetoric and action, the war on terror has been itself a form of terrorism but it is difficult to find any recognition of this in media accounts of various wars and terrorist attacks. This is the key point I want to demonstrate here by comparing the reporting of the bombings of Madrid and London, in 2004 and 2005 respectively, with that of the 'Shock and Awe' bombing of Baghdad in 2003, the curtain raiser to the US invasion.[4] It demonstrates the success of the war on terror as a propaganda framework, one that not only limits under-standing and compassion but that is closed to the possibility of seeing a linkage between the terrorist attacks on Madrid and London with what had been happening in Afghanistan since 2001 and Iraq since 2003.

Madrid and London

In Madrid, on the morning of 11 March 2004, 13 satchels, each containing ten kilograms (or 22 pounds) of explosives, were left on four packed commuter trains. Ten of them detonated, taking the lives of 191 commuters and injuring over 1,800 others. In London, on the morning of 7 July 2005, suicide bombers carrying rucksacks containing between two and five kilograms of explosives, a total of up to 20 kilograms of explosives (or 44 pounds), took the lives of 52 commuters and injured over 700 in explosions on three tube trains and a city bus. These were horrifying attacks on innocent people, bringing the war on terror to Europe for the first time. Of course, Madrid and London had experienced terrorist attacks before, at the hands of the Basque-separatist Euskadi Ta Askatasuna (ETA) and the Irish Republican Army (IRA) respectively. But the scale of these attacks and the deliberate targeting of civilians seemed to be of a new and terrifying dimension; and they appeared to vindicate the repeated warnings of security agencies throughout the continent that such attacks were inevitable.

All but one of the newspapers in the sample, the *Daily Star*, gave the Madrid bombings their front-page lead. *The Times* and *The Independent* headlined it 'Massacre in Madrid', while *The Sun* led with, 'Slaughter of the Innocents'. *The Daily Mail*, *Daily Express*, and the *Guardian* all led with the question of who carried out the attacks. In the days that followed, the question turned into a bitter controversy in Spain and overshadowed the public need for a show of grief and national solidarity. There was a suspicion that the party of government, the Popular Party led by Prime Minister José María Aznar, was deflecting blame from the main suspects, an Al-Qaeda affiliate from Northern Africa, onto the Basque separatist group, ETA. It was seen by many as a vote-winning tactic ahead of the general election in Spain on 14 March, a needless one in fact because the party was comfortably ahead in the opinion polls. It was to ultimately backfire in election defeat. British newspapers were divided in their approach to the question. The *Mail* and *Express* led with a focus on the Al Qaeda angle, but nonetheless posed it as a question:

'Could it be Al Qaeda?' (*Mail*)
'Rail bomb kills 190... Was it Bin Laden?' (*Express*)

The Telegraph and the *Guardian*, on the other hand, presented it as a toss up between the two possibilities:

'192 die as bombs hit commuter trains in Madrid. ETA or al-Qaeda?' (*Telegraph*)
'Massacre in Madrid: ETA or Al-Qaida?' (*Guardian*)

The *Daily Mirror* was the only paper to take a firm and certain line at least in the immediate aftermath of the bombings. Its first edition led with reference to a claim of responsibility from the North African affiliate: 'Al-Qaeda: It was us. Terror Faction Claims Madrid bombs.' But its third edition that day opened up the alternative possibility, that it was ETA. In an article on page twelve, headed 'Carnage Will Bring ETA Reign To An End', the paper's 'Terrorism Expert', Simon Reeve, declared that the attacks bore 'all the hallmarks of the Basque separatist group ETA, and appear to be the death-throes of the terrorist organisation.' In a clue to the source of his analysis, Reeve concluded that the 'bombings will encourage the Spanish government to launch a renewed "war on terror" against ETA and due to the public's revulsion at the massacre, the group is unlikely to survive the carnage of Madrid.'

Few of the newspapers gave front-page space to graphic description of the impact of the explosion on the Madrid commuter trains. *The Independent*'s sub-headline stated that: 'Stations Littered With Body Parts After Butchery On A Brutal Scale Leaves Body Parts On The Platforms, Corpses In Shredded Wreckage.' The *Mail* captioned a photograph of some of the victims: 'Carnage on the commuter line: Horror etched on their faces, victims of yesterday's Madrid railway bombings are treated beside wrecked carriages.' In a special photo feature on page 12 of the paper's third edition – 'An atrocity that touches us all' – a reporter described in graphic, first-hand terms the scene at Madrid's Atocha station:

I saw a baby torn to bits. The trains were all destroyed, with headless corpses. This is so savage you can't even describe it. In shock and disbelief, many in tears, the people of Madrid struggle to come to terms with the horror. Pictures of the devastation tell their own story. Europe's worst terrorist atrocity since Lockerbie has left almost 200 dead, more than 1,400 wounded, a city numbed.

The Times reported an account from a commuter who was on board one of the trains:

'There was a flash at the end of the carriage in front of me. A terrific blast hit us. We were thrown to the floor and then there was another loud bang. I don't know what happened next because I must have passed out.'

When she came to she saw a man whose entire face had been burnt away. 'Everywhere I turned there was blood,' she said. 'The windows were smashed and there was moaning and crying but I couldn't see where it was coming from.'

The headlines in the inside pages of the some of the other newspapers, many of them direct statements from survivors and eyewitnesses, provided a stark picture of the horror, panic and pain on board the trains in the wake of the bombings:

Bloodbath in rush hour: 'Mobiles were still ringing as they carted bodies away. I saw a baby that had been blown to bits.' (*Daily Star*)

'It was butchery on a brutal scale. This catastrophe goes beyond the imaginable', said Juan Redondo, a Madrid fire inspector, as scores of wounded sat on pavements outside the central Atocha station, weeping helplessly at the devastation. (*Express*)

As well as giving readers an impression of the immediate horror of the attacks, the British press sought to provide some insight into the motivations of those responsible. Since there was no certainty at that point about who it might have been, that was always going to be a challenge. If the security consultants and terrorism experts of the world had no hard information, then they could only operate within the realms of speculation; and if they were limited to just that, then the only safe haven lay in the calm waters of wide-sweeping generalisation. What else can a security consultant do when cold-called by a journalist in the immediate aftermath of a terrorist outrage? In an article for *The Independent* – 'Bombers prepared to inflict more shock and harm to grab attention' – Brussels correspondent, Stephen Castle, spoke to a range of diplomats and security experts in the city, many of whom provided insights that were more obvious than expert. For example:

Despite the huge resources devoted to fighting the 'war on terror', bombers are still getting through and causing enormous loss of life by hitting soft targets. 'Terrorists are becoming more indiscriminate and they are having a wider impact on communities,' said Tim Dunne, a Canadian *military analyst and author of a study on terrorism.*

'It looks as if terrorists are becoming more ambitious in their aims. They want to do more damage, inflict more harm and cause more shock – to grab the attention of their public and force governments to react.'

One diplomat who has *specialised in terror issues* said: 'September 11 has set the bar for mass killings and for the shock that could come from them. What we have been worried about is that 9/11 would start a new type of attack: how much horror can you get out of targeting large numbers?' (Emphases added)

Amid the obvious horror of the bombings, the accounts of heroic popular defiance and solidarity; and the editorial rhetoric of freedom and democracy, of no surrender and law and order, a few newspapers brought the threat closer to home:

Security officials ask: Could it happen in Britain? (*Times*)
Britons warned: We may be next! (*Express*)
After Madrid, Britain is next says Al Qaeda (*Mail*)

Critics at the time, mostly on the left, had good reason to cast a cold eye on the national security alerts and scares that western governments had been issuing on a regular basis since 9/11. This was because they had so far come to nothing and, in Britain, seemed to have more to do with Prime Minister Tony Blair's determination to 'stand shoulder to shoulder' with America in its war on terror. Yet just over a year after Madrid, the city of London experienced its own 9/11. On 7 July 2005, the day after the city won the bid to host the 2012 Olympics, a coordinated series of bombing attacks on commuter targets killed 52 innocent commuters and injured over 700. The front-page headlines reflected the sense of fear that they caused throughout the country:

Terror Comes To London (*Independent*)
Al Qaeda Brings Terror To The Heart Of London (*Telegraph*)
London's Day of Terror (*Guardian*)

But also they also provoked the popular press into a defiant stance steeped in the mythical defiance and heroism of Londoners during the Blitz, more than 50 years earlier in the Second World War:

Bastards. Al Qaida Suicide Bombers Blitz London (*Star*)
We Britons Will Never Be Defeated (*Express*)
Bloodied But Not Unbowed (*Mirror*)

Other newspapers offered a more nuanced sense of the public response to what had happened to the city in the previous 24 hours:

From Olympic jubilation to bafflement and horror: First the shock and then a strange, quiet kind of chaos took over London streets (*Guardian*)

A London morning that began tinged with joy and incredulity at victory in securing the Olympic Games was plunged into horrified disbelief as explosives tore through the underground arteries of the city, bringing death and dismay where, a few hours earlier, there had been celebration (*Times*)

As with their coverage of Madrid, there were plenty of headlines in the British papers to sum up the horrific scale and impact of the bombings:

Carnage on our streets (*Star*)
56 Minutes of Hell (*Sun*)
Panic, shoving, fear of fire and bonding below ground (*Times*)
We're going to die! We're going to die! Cries pierce choking air as survivors flee twisted wreckage of Tube (*Mirror*)
Aldgate: Stunned silence, darkness, panic, then calm (*Guardian*)

Copious space was also afforded to editorial and public pronouncements of horror, shock, condemnation and defiance. Yet apart from expressions of solidarity with the people of Madrid, there was very little in this sample of British newspapers to suggest any kind of linkage between what had happened to London and Madrid and what had befallen the people of Afghanistan and Iraq since 9/11. Of the 151 items in this newspaper sample, only two of them made the connection. Both of them were comment pieces for newspapers on opposite ends of the political spectrum: from Andrew Alexander in the conservative *Daily Mail* and from Robert Fisk in the liberal *Independent*. In his column headed 'Revenge was only to be expected', Alexander wrote that:

> Now we know what it must be like to live in Baghdad. Now we see some of the consequences of our decision to let ourselves be hauled along in the wake of the Americans in a bogus cause, steeped in lies and deceit from start to finish and which has had consequences for Iraq – and now for us – which were both predictable and predicted.
>
> We should fear that Tony Blair, flourishing phrases about 'defeating terrorism', will once more follow the George Bush line: we must not give in, we must see things through. Having dug ourselves into a hole, we must dig deeper. Our revenge, unmistakable.

And in his piece for *The Independent* – 'The reality of this barbaric bombing' – Robert Fisk had this to say:

> [It's] no use Mr Blair telling us yesterday that they will never succeed in destroying 'what we hold dear'. 'They' are not trying to destroy 'what we hold dear'. They are trying to get public opinion to force Blair to withdraw from Iraq, from his alliance with the United States, and from his adherence to Bush's policies in the Middle East. [...]
>
> It is easy for Tony Blair to call yesterday's bombings 'barbaric'. Of course they were but what were the civilian deaths of the Anglo-American invasion of Iraq – the children torn apart by cluster bombs, the countless innocent Iraqis gunned down at American military checkpoints? When they die, it is 'collateral damage'; when 'we' die, it is 'barbaric terrorism'.

As devastating as the attacks on Madrid and London seemed, they paled in comparison with the bombing Baghdad and Iraq withstood in 2003 at the hands of a western alliance determined to destroy Saddam Hussein's weapons of mass destruction, which did not exist, and also end his alliance with Al Qaeda, which also did not exist.

BAGHDAD AND IRAQ

From 21 March to early April 2003, the combined air forces of America, Britain and other western and Middle East allies, conducted 29,200 air strikes in Iraq.[5] This was described as the Shock and Awe phase of Operation Iraqi Freedom but Shock and Awe was not merely a neat propaganda moniker for media consumption. It was a component part of a US military doctrine called 'rapid dominance' devised in 1996 by American military planners Harlan K. Ullman and James P. Wade of the National Defense University. Its key aim was to:

> [Affect] the will, perception, and understanding of the adversary to fight or respond to our strategic policy ends through imposing a regime of Shock and Awe [...] against an adversary on an immediate or sufficiently timely basis to paralyze its will to carry on [and to] seize control of the environment and paralyze or so overload an adversary's perceptions and understanding of events that the enemy would be incapable of resistance at the tactical and strategic levels. (1996, pp. 24–25)

While this may make rational sense in the context of a conventional battleground, it has very different connotations when applied against large population centres such as Baghdad.

In this period of three weeks, America and its allies dropped 19, 948 so-called precision weapons on Iraq – of which between 20 and 25 per cent missed their targets – and another 9,251 conventional bombs and missiles. The munitions these weapons delivered included firebombs, cluster bombs and white phosphorous. In both composition and effect, the firebombs used were the same as napalm, a weapon widely used by the US during the Vietnam War and subsequently banned for use against civilian populations by the UN Convention on Certain Conventional Weapons. The use of cluster bombs and white phosphorous against civilians is banned by the Geneva Conventions of War. Coalition forces also deployed armour-piercing weapons containing Depleted Uranium, a toxic contaminant that medical experts have linked to extraordinary levels of birth defects and child mortality in the Iraqi population.[6] It is difficult to obtain precise figures for the civilian casualties of this onslaught but Iraq Body Count estimates a total civilian death toll of 6,716. The total number of civilian deaths at the hands of coalition forces from 2003 to 2011 and the withdrawal of US troops is estimated to be 15,132, or 13 per cent of all violent civilian deaths during the Iraq War.[7]

The devastation that Shock and Awe inflicted on Baghdad and other major cities and towns in Iraq, including the high civilian casualty rates and the destruction to vital civilian infrastructure such as power plants, and water and sewage systems, was not the 'collateral damage of war' as apologists might insist. By its own definition as a military doctrine, Shock and Awe was a deliberate campaign of terror designed to weaken the country for a land invasion. It was also illegal and it was opposed by large sections of public opinion in the west. Yet very few in the western media seemed to see it like that.

Unlike the Gulf War 1991, which had almost unanimous public and political support, the bombing and invasion of Iraq in 2003 divided world opinion and was deeply controversial from beginning to end, not least because of its violent impact on the Iraqi population and its very dubious aims and objectives. British newspaper coverage certainly reflected these divisions but in the curious way that characterised British politics at the time. The most critical coverage came from the liberal left newspapers that were normally supportive of the Labour government of the day – the *Guardian*, *The Independent* and the *Daily Mirror* – while the right wing press gave it full and largely unwavering support. The contrast is illustrated at its most stark extreme by the front pages of the *Daily Mirror* and *The Sun* over the first two days of the Shock and Awe campaign, 21 and 22 March:

The World Watched in Shock and Awe (*Sun*)
1000 Bombs in One Night (*Sun*)

Shocking and Awful – America's Shameful 'Shock and Awe' Attack on Baghdad last night (*Mirror*)
Mass Destruction (*Mirror*)

The *Daily Star* saw the opportunity for tasteless humour with the 'Bangdad 2' (21 March); but the rest of the newspapers led with headlines and photographs that left readers in no doubt as to the scale and enormity of what Shock and Awe represented:

Firestorm (*Mail*)
The Sky Falls In on Baghdad (*Mail*)

Bombs And Cruise Missiles Bring Death And Destruction to Baghdad
In Biggest Blitz Of The City In 12 Years. Shocked and Awed (*Express*)
Blitz Sets Baghdad Ablaze (*Telegraph*)
Carrier Launches 'Cataclysmic Bomb' Campaign (*Telegraph*)
The Blitzing of Baghdad (*Times*)
A Modern Day Blitzkrieg (*Guardian*)
Bubbles of Fire Tore Into the Sky Above Baghdad (*Independent*)

However, much of the uncritical coverage of Shock and Awe adopted
the official, western propaganda line that the bombing was aimed not
at the people of Iraq but at Saddam Hussein and his brutal regime. *The
Daily Mail* themed its whole coverage as 'War on Saddam', and the other
pro-war newspapers consistently reported with a nod to the official line:

War Planes Target Saddam's House in Blitz on Baghdad (*Telegraph*)
Iraqi Tyrant Dead or Wounded. Son is Killed (*Star*)
Saddam's Home and Palaces Hit as The Iraqi Capital Comes Under
Intense Fire From Cruise Missile Attack on the First Full Day of
Hostilities (*Express*)

But there was no focus in the pro-war papers on the impact that Shock
and Awe might have on the people of Baghdad and Iraq; there were no
stories of heroic acts or speeches of defiance; no tributes to the Iraqi
emergency services; and no reporting of the horror, panic and fear that
the people were experiencing under this sustained and overwhelming
assault. In other words, the very basic human angle that defines their
coverage of most terrorist attacks against civilian targets was absent in
their treatment of Shock and Awe. This might be explained or excused
in part by the impossibility or difficulty western reporters would have
in trying to report the bombings from the point of view of Baghdad's
citizens. However, I would argue that it is made all the more impossible
or difficult when the story is told within the unreal world of the war on
terror, a world divided in two between gods and monsters, friends and
enemies, and good and evil; and where, as Robert Fisk argued in the
aftermath of the London bombings, attacks on 'us' constitute terrorism
but attacks on 'them' are explained away with the almost meaningless
label, 'collateral damage'.

In many ways, the war on terror paradigm has been as leaky as the
new world order paradigm that preceded it in the 1990s. There is no

doubt that militant Islam still represents a threat to western interests and civilian populations – witness the various attacks in 2015, including that on Paris. And the paradigm does offer up certain patterns of thought reminiscent of the Cold War: the splitting of the world into blocs of 'us' versus 'them'; the projection of threat and fear; and the policing of public opinion and behaviour by regimes of censorship and surveillance. What is required for a more structured and permanent paradigm of inter-pretation like that of the old cold war, one that will produce consistent and apparently rational solutions for thought and action, is a global, inter-state conflict. This would involve a predictable game in which the players adhere to an agreed set of rules and preferable outcomes. There would be brinkmanship and crises for sure but these would be contained or resolved by a set of built-in safety mechanisms, including deterrence, diplomacy and hotlines. Each side would have a clearly defined sphere of global influence in which it would be allowed to do what it pleases without interference from the enemy. There would be espionage, sanctions and spy-swaps; and there would be set-piece summits, rhetorical confronta-tion and even periods of détente and cooperation.

THE RETURN OF THE EVIL EMPIRE

There are signs amid the apparent chaos and confusion of terror and disorder in the world today of certain nostalgia for the relative certainties and predictability that a new, cold war order like this might offer. All that is needed is a suitable enemy and there have been a few candidates, the most obvious among them being Russia, China and Iran. While occasional tensions with the latter two countries over territorial ambitions in the case of China and nuclear power in the case of Iran, these have only offered the west pieces in the Cold War jigsaw puzzle. Russia's annexation of the Crimean peninsula during the Ukrainian crisis in 2014, on the other hand, appeared to offer the complete set.

The Crimea crisis in brief

The crisis over Crimea emerged in February 2014 against the backdrop of political instability in Ukraine. Growing protests on the streets of the capital, Kiev, forced from office the Russian-friendly but corrupt

President, Victor Yanukovych, which resulted in turn in the resignation of the government. The formation of a new, more nationalist and right-wing administration was viewed with suspicion and growing anxiety among the country's ethnic Russian minority, especially in the Crimea, a region that was originally part of Russia but 'gifted' to Ukraine in 1954, during the Soviet era. It was also viewed with some consternation in Moscow, whose interests in the Crimea were significant. The region's capital, Sevastopol, was the base for Russia's Black Sea fleet and a garrison of 25,000 troops. As tensions in the region mounted over the following weeks, with confrontations in the capital between pro-Russian and pro-Ukrainian demonstrators, Russia's President, Vladimir Putin, appeared to lend tacit support for a return of the region to Russian jurisdiction by way of a referendum. On 2 March, a small force of Russian troops, without military identification or insignia, entered the region and took control of its two principal airports, a development that turned the situation into an international crisis. However, it quickly became apparent that the response from the US, Britain, NATO and the European Union was going to be limited to threats of economic and diplomatic sanctions. On 16 March, the people of Crimea voted in a referendum and returned a 95.5 per cent vote in favour of a return to Russian jurisdiction, a result received in the west with suspicion and derision. On 17 March, a triumphant President Putin welcomed the result in parliament and moved immediately to sign it into law.

The following case study analysis of how British newspapers reported the crisis is based on a sample period from 23 February, just after the fall of the Ukrainian government, to 20 March 2014 inclusive, taking in the immediate aftermath of the Crimean referendum. The search of the Nexis database used the key words 'Putin' and 'Crimea', and generated a sample of 541 news and editorial items. The analysis reveals the construction of the classic Cold War enemy image as personified by Russian President, Vladimir Putin, and the outline formation of a new, Cold War paradigm for reporting and explaining the crisis.

The Putin lexicon: a new enemy

The language used to depict the Russian leader and his actions and policies during the crisis produced a profile that if based on a clinical examination might justify a split diagnosis of a condition ranging from paranoid-schizophrenia to psychopathy. I will offer a flavour of it here but for a complete list of words and phrases see Appendix 7 and Appendix 8. The weight of content lies with the so-called elite newspapers – especially *The Times* and the *Guardian*, for whom international stories sit high in their news agendas. With the exception of *The Daily Mail* and *Mail on Sunday*, coverage in the popular press – the *Sun*, the *Daily Mirror* and the *Daily Star* – was minimal and produced little other than very bad headline puns on the name of the Russian leader: for example, 'Vlad's troops go Russian in!' (*The Sun*, 2 March); 'The Vladfather' (*Sun* 17 March); and 'Putin our place' (*Daily Mirror*, 19 March).

Among the elite newspapers, the most negative and subjective portrait by a long way was that of the *Guardian*, an ironic finding indeed when one considers that this was the newspaper of the great Morgan Philips Price, whose reporting of the Russian Revolution in 1917, and the ensuing allied intervention the following year, distinguished him from the majority of western journalists too ready to toe the propaganda line. The *Guardian* characterised the Russian president throughout the sample period as a 'pugnacious', 'triumphant' but 'frustrated' leader with a 'nostalgia for Soviet times'; he was a cross between an 'unrepentant Cold War warrior' and a 'pre-1917 imperial nationalist'; a 'KGB professional' prone to 'zero-sum thinking', 'flights of apparent fancy', 'bombast', 'bile' and 'paranoia'. The 'irredentist adventure' in the Crimea was 'a carve-up' and a 'land grab' by a man at the head of an 'expansionist', 'de facto dictatorship'. The *Guardian*'s sister paper, the *Observer* (Sunday), described Putin as 'unpleasant' and 'ruthless man' who demonstrated 'calm calculation' in his handling of the wider crisis in the Ukraine. For the *Daily Telegraph*, Putin was a 'steely', 'determined', 'strong man'; 'exerting power in the shadows' and advancing his cause in Crimea using 'a covert network of influence'; his 'paranoia' and 'macho politics', as well as his 'territorial aggression', explained the motivations for his 'land grab', or 'annexation', of the Crimean peninsula. Putin was described in *The Times* as 'Vlad the invader', 'chairman of the world's unofficial Autocrat's Club' and a 'master of the dark arts'; he was an 'aggressive' and 'enraged' politician in the pursuit of 'power games' and 'brinkmanship'. *The Sunday Times* described him as a man of 'ruthless clarity of purpose' and 'permanent rage', ready to promote his policies by way of 'bribery', 'bluff' and 'threat'. *The Daily Mail* saw him as a 'bogey man' and a 'puppet master' whose public demeanour was 'defiant', 'aggressive' and 'emotional'; it, too, described the return of Crimea to Russia as a 'land grab', an 'annexation' and, alluding to Hitler's annexation of Austria in 1938, a 'Russian anschluss'.[8] *The Sun* depicted him as a 'tyrant' and 'classic Bond villain' engaged in a 'titanic game of bluff' in the Crimea; while the *Daily Mirror* referred to him as a 'hard man' and the new 'Rasputin'.

Among the elite newspapers, *The Independent* was the most sober in its assessment of Putin, describing him as a 'confident', 'business-like' if somewhat 'prickly' leader in his dealings with the media. The paper's strongest characterisation of his actions was to describe them, at best, as empty 'sabre-rattling'; at worst, as post-Soviet 'revanchism'; its sister paper, *The Independent on Sunday*, depicted him as a man of 'calm calculation' if somewhat 'unpleasant' and 'ruthless' by nature. Mary Dejevsky, columnist and chief editorial writer for the paper, has long experience of reporting on Russia, going back to her time as Moscow correspondent for *The Times* during the Soviet era. In an interview for this book,[9] she explained the various misconceptions about Putin that seemed to drive this negative media coverage, 'some of them deliberate and some of them not':

The non-deliberate misconception is that he somehow imposed himself on Russia and that he's not by any manner or means democratically elected. [...] Nonetheless, Putin had huge amounts of support even before the annexation of Crimea. And to my mind, Putin is the legitimate President of Russia because he's managed somehow to sense, like any good politician, where the centre of Russian opinion is at any particular point and he adjusts accordingly. So I think for all sorts of reasons he's legitimate so to denounce him as illegitimate, a dictator, an autocrat, or whatever, that that's actually wrong.

Another misconception is to see him as a dictator or latter-day Tsar, which is to over-estimate his real power in the country. As Dejevsky explains:

[While] Putin is strong personally, his power is very strong in the Kremlin, in the country at large he's actually a weak leader because it's very difficult for anybody in the Kremlin to have all the levers of power at his disposal. This great idea that Putin can sit in the Kremlin and snap his fingers and...people all turn around and do exactly as he says – that is completely wrong. Russian power is extraordinarily fragmented – there are a lot of regional interests, a huge amount of corruption. One of Putin's biggest problems ever since he became leader, and it's only a little less now I would say, is that his writ doesn't rule across Russia.

The surprisingly negative sometimes extreme image of the Russian leader in the *Guardian* might be explained, she suspects, by a recent change of editorial personnel in the paper, with the more sympathetic, left-of-centre Jonathan Steele giving way to Luke Harding, whose recent, negative experience of reporting post-Soviet Russia may be driving the paper's more hard-line stance.

Of course, the composite portrait of Putin in the British press that I have presented here does not amount to a psychological or clinical profile based on scientific method and evidence; although that did not stop the US-based website, *Psychology Today*, lending Putin's enemy image some spurious legitimacy. In a piece entitled, 'The Danger that Lurks Inside Vladimir Putin's Brain', Professor Ian H. Robertson of Trinity College Dublin concluded that 'contempt is key to Putin's troubling psychological profile'. Posted on 17 March 2014, the day after the referendum, Robertson explained that Putin's contempt for international leaders, institutions and the rule of law is rooted in his 'Marxist-Leninist worldview', which treats such things as 'instruments of capitalist or bourgeois oppression'; and in a national or political culture 'where the ends justified the means'. Without a shred of clinical evidence, Robertson declared that 'there can be little doubt that [Putin's] brain has been neurologically or physically changed so much that he firmly and genuinely believes that without him, Russia is doomed'. In his closing section, sub-headed, 'How to handle a man like Putin', the professor offers a prognosis using language more typical of a neoconservative ideologue than a professional psychologist:

> *I have little doubt* that Putin feels personally humiliated by the fall of the Soviet Union and its empire and that, fuelled by power and with a blindness to risk, he will work ever harder to make good that humiliation through further dangerous adventures. He will be all the more driven by his feeling of personal and national superiority to the contemptibly weak, decadent and cowardly western powers – as he probably sees them.

So how should the West respond? *Psychologically speaking,* the very worst response would be appeasement because this will simply fuel his contempt and strengthen the justification for his position. Strong consequences have to follow from his contempt for international law and treaties. This will cost the West dearly, economically speaking, but the longer-term costs of appeasement will make the costs of strong, early action appear trivial in retrospect.[10] (Emphases added)

What this kind of pop psychology and media coverage represents is a symphony of hysteria in the service of propaganda. In past conflicts, such as the Gulf War 1991 and the Iraq War 2003, similar language to describe the Iraqi leader, Saddam Hussein, as a 'monster' and a 'new Hitler', functioned as the drumbeats of war, softening domestic publics for the 'inevitable' conflict to come (see, for example, Philo and McLaughlin, 1995; Miller, 2004; Tumber and Palmer, 2004). The caricature of Putin as psychopath during the Crimea crisis, on the other hand, appeared to serve two different purposes. The first was to deflect from western responsibility for helping to provoke the crisis in the first place; and the second, intentionally or by default, was to distract from western impotence in the face of a military force they were not ready or willing to confront. This was apparent in the editorial and opinion pages of the newspapers examined in this case study.

Return of the Evil Empire and a new Cold War?

Beyond the extreme characterisations of the Russian leader, there was a clear difference of opinion within and between the newspapers about what the crisis actually represented in the context of wider, international relations. Some headlines made explicit reference to the possibility or danger that developments could lead to a new Cold War order:

Russia and NATO face off over Ukraine (*Daily Telegraph,* 27 February)
The crisis in Crimea could lead the world into a second Cold War (*Observer,* 2 March)
Europe's peace at risk in new Cold war (*The Daily Mail,* 3 March)
And so the Cold War starts again (*The Sunday Times,* 16 March)
Crimea 'could spark a new Cold War' (*Daily Express,* 19 March)

Others added classic Cold War enemy imagery into the mix. A *Sunday Telegraph* analysis of the economic implications of the crisis was headed, 'Don't mess with the Bear' (9 March). While NATO could observe only limited Russian troop movements near the border with Ukraine, *The Daily Mail*, reported otherwise. Never a newspaper to allow rumour or baseless information to get in the way of a good scare story, it picked up a grossly exaggerated warning from 'a senior security chief in Kiev', that the Russian army was about to invade, and headlined it as fact: 'Red Army masses on Ukraine border' (13 March).

As the crisis mounted, culminating in the referendum and the return of Crimea to Russian jurisdiction, other newspaper items pinned responsibility for ensuing international tensions on Russia and Putin alone. In the wake of the 95.5 per cent 'Yes' vote, the *Guardian*'s editorial was headed, 'Mr Putin and the threat of a new Cold War' (17 March); while *The Times* reported on Putin's triumphant speech in parliament, declaring the return of Russia to its rightful place on the world stage, with the headline, 'Strutting Putin stokes a new Cold War as Crimea returns to the fold' (*The Times*, 19 March).

Some editorial content provided a measure of perspective and warned against western over-reaction, not all of it exclusive to the liberal press. In *The Daily Mail*, for example, Steven Glover questioned the doublethink at the heart of western rhetoric. 'Aren't we guilty of hypocrisy?' he asked:

When Russia was too weak for its complaints to be taken seriously, Britain and America bombed its regional ally Serbia in 1999, and then confiscated the Serbian enclave of Kosovo (which, by the by, remains a basket case bankrolled by the West). Why was that right and moral, whereas the return of Crimea to Russia with the approval of most of its population is wicked? I suggest that when it suits us we do what we think we can get away with, but that when the Russians act on the same principle we accuse them of violating moral norms and interna-tional law. ('Yes, Putin is a bully but aren't we guilty of moral hypocrisy on Crimea?' 20 March)

Three column pieces in particular appeared in the *Guardian*, offering critical counterpoint to the newspaper's negative news coverage. In a guest column headed, 'This is no Cold War II' (1 March), historian Tarik Cyril Amar argued that 'talk of a return to the Cold War [in the West] is wide of the mark. Putin is not aggressive because he feels unchallenged by a flabby west. Since the end of the Soviet Union, the European Union and NATO have enlarged at the impressive clip of roughly one new member every two years.' On that basis, he argued, the ongoing crisis in Ukraine, encouraged by the west, was from Putin's point of view 'a massive political defeat'.

In separate articles, senior *Guardian* journalists, Jonathan Steele and Seamus Milne highlighted the hype and hypocrisy at the heart of the west's response. With long experience reporting on Russian affairs, Steele pointed readers to NATO's role in provoking the crisis in Ukraine and the Crimea:

> The fact that NATO insists on getting engaged reveals the elephant in the room: underlying the crisis in Crimea and Russia's fierce resistance to potential changes is *NATO's undisguised ambition to continue two decades of expansion* into what used to be called 'post-Soviet space'. At the back of Pentagon minds, no doubt, is t*he dream that a US navy will one day replace the Russian Black Sea fleet in the Crimean ports.* ('Not too late for wisdom', 3 March; emphases added)

On 6 March, Seamus Milne opened his column with the remark that: 'Diplomatic pronouncements are renowned for hypocrisy and double standards. But western denunciations of Russian intervention in Crimea have reached new depths of self-parody.' With a swipe at the rhetoric of US Secretary John Kerry and his loud insistence that countries like Russia cannot just invade other countries on 'a trumped up pretext', Milne commented:

> That the states which launched the greatest act of unprovoked aggression in modern history on a trumped-up pretext – against Iraq, in an illegal war now estimated to have killed 500,000, along with the invasion of Afghanistan, bloody regime change in Libya, and the killing of thousands in drone attacks on Pakistan, Yemen and Somalia, all without UN authorisation – should make such claims is beyond absurdity. ('The clash in Crimea is the fruit of western expansion', 6 March)

In a column for *The Independent*, Mary Dejevsky highlighted the dangers of thinking about the crisis within a Cold War framework, 'one of the greatest, and least recognised (of which is) misreading Russia.' She explained that:

> Already a Western consensus has gained hold, according to which Vladimir Putin has spent his 14 years in power just waiting for the chance to rebuild the Soviet empire, and here he is now, gleefully seizing it with both bloodied hands.
>
> [...] But what if building a new Russian empire is not actually what Putin is about? Western leaders, egged on especially by those European countries that were scarred, and no wonder, by their bitter experience of Soviet domination, have created a Cold War bogey of Putin and Putin's Russia that is lodged in their collective brain. Putin's every move and every utterance is slotted into that logic and judged in that frame. The result is a predisposition to take literally what might not be meant literally, and all too often to discount what Putin and his officials actually say. ('This aggression is more a cry to be heard than an attempt to invade a sovereign nation', 7 March)

This knee-jerk foreign policy response to Russia's actions seems to forget that the country today is very different in size and reach than when it was the hegemonic power of the Soviet Union during the Cold War. For a start, it is much smaller and less powerful; but, more importantly, it is only now coming to terms with the new geopolitics of the post-Soviet era and negotiating to secure its borders with its neighbours to the south (for example, the Transcauceses and Central Asia). For that reason alone, Dejevsky rejects 'the idea that Putin is an expansionist. It seems to me that [he] is much more concerned with Russia's security inside its post Cold War borders and I think the West has completely ignored that.'[11]

CONCLUDING REMARKS

Whether or not this new Cold War framework hardens or not into something more coherent and persistent will depend on the future direction of Russia's relationship with the west, on changes of leadership in Russia and the US, and whether that in turn leads to a softening or hardening of foreign policy stances. But if there is to be a real and existing new Cold War, then the kind of reporting we have seen in respect to Russia in the Crimean crisis does not promise great hope for a balanced, nuanced understanding of this most important international power play. The reporting of terrorism and terrorist attacks, of diplomatic crises, of inconvenient friends and unreliable enemies, must surely go beyond hysterical reaction, the projection of irrational fear and, as Mary Dejevsky puts it, deliberate and non-deliberate misconception. That, of course, will depend not just on the disposition, knowledge and understanding of the individual war or foreign correspondents but also on the editorial policies of the news organisations they work for.

10

Conclusions:
'Telling Truth to Power' – the Ultimate Role of the War Correspondent?

This book has presented a critical, historically grounded analysis of the role of the war correspondent. It has highlighted the risks, the problems and the failures that have defined the role but it has also given credit where that is due and acknowledged the inspirational example of correspondents such as William Howard Russell, Morgan Philips Price, Martha Gellhorn, Wilfred Burchett, John Pilger and Robert Fisk. Their work seems to bear testament to the ideal beloved of all journalists and writers, of 'telling truth to power'. But as Arundhati Roy has argued, 'Power owns the truth [and] knows the truth just as well if not better than the powerless know the truth' (2004, p. 68). In view of everything that has gone before in this book, I think she is right.

Telling truth to power does not change or lessen the risks and dangers that accompany the journalist in the war zone. And as we have seen, the risks are not equal; the level of special training, protection and institutional support journalists receive depends on the size and wealth of their media employer. It may be difficult to address such inequality at a structural level but it could at least be ameliorated by way of a central fund supported by the major international media and run by journalist organisations such as the International Press Institute (IPI) or the Committee for the Projection of Journalists (CPJ). There are other more avoidable, contentious risks that have troubled war reporters and various representative organisations. The CPJ has long campaigned to end the culture of impunity that surrounds the deliberate targeting and killing of journalists by various militaries. The essential difference between the regular armies of the USA or Israel, for example, and paramilitary organisations such as IS, is the degree to which they are bound by the obligations of democratic legitimacy and accountability. In cases where there is substantial evidence that state combatants have killed or injured journalists, there should be independent judicial inquiry, not 'internal investigations' that rarely lead to prosecution, trial or conviction.

Telling truth to power depends on having a strong and direct voice that will be heard. Yet the constraints of objectivity and impartiality often dampen rather than amplify the voice of the war correspondent. In any case, the possibility of being objective and impartial in the warzone, in the face of horror and atrocity, varies according to the nature of the conflict, the level of public consensus or controversy abroad, or the extent of military censorship and restrictions in place. In other words, it is unlikely that the Journalism of Attachment that Martin Bell advocated during the Bosnian civil war would ever be possible or likely in the reporting of controversial conflicts such as Israel–Palestine or in the highly-organised wars we have seen in Afghanistan and Iraq. Nonetheless, Bell was brave enough to cast off the metaphorical helmet and flak jacket to express what he thought, and felt as a human being before being a war correspondent, and incurred the wrath of those who preferred that he would be silent. The journalist may not be privy to all of the truth all of the time in such situations, but we might expect that he or she will be honest. Indeed, Chapter 3 of this book closed by asking how the western media can presume to report with impartiality an overwhelmingly asymmetrical conflict such as Israel–Palestine. Some might think it a naive question but I would suggest that the level of public ignorance and misunderstanding of that long running, bloody conflict, as so powerfully demonstrated by Greg Philo and Mike Berry (2004 and 2011), is down in part to the media's failure to properly explain the asymmetries of the conflict in terms of history, military force and capability, political and diplomatic power and, most disturbing of all, civilian casualties, especially among children. If being objective and impartial makes explanation and context impossible or impractical in such cases then that is to effectively elide part of the truth.

As the advance of media technologies continues apace, telling truth to power should be easier and more impactful than ever before yet these technologies present the war reporter with a double-edged sword. The speed of communication is compressed into much shorter periods of time so that, while the difference between sending and receiving news of war by pony dispatch and telegraph in the nineteenth century was a matter of days, the difference between sending and receiving via satellite-cable in the late twentieth century and social media in the twenty-first is a matter of hours and seconds respectively. The opportunities this presents for reporting conflict with new urgency and immediacy are obvious but that in turn pressurises journalistic routines of fact checking and verification. Just like the telegraph, the social media may revolutionise the reporting of war but they may also empower the individual citizen to take a more direct, immediate and interactive part in the story of war in unpredictable and not always desirable ways. And as we have seen, combatant states and terrorist organisations have been just as wise to the immense propaganda potential of social media. The distance between speaking the truth and hearing the truth amid so much online noise may be virtually unbridgeable.

Part II of this book put into the long historical perspective of 160 years the relationship between the war correspondent and the military, a relationship that offers the journalist the most direct and obvious opportunity for telling truth to power. But the strategies and tactics that the military have developed to control and restrict reporting are designed not to answer to the truth but to deflect or even silence it, to create a control culture in which the majority of journalists conform to the restrictions in return for military lies, disinformation and propaganda. In this sense, the relationship has changed very little in the last century and a half. The military learn the lessons of the last war and then plan better ways to control the media in time for the next war, more often than not with a high degree of media cooperation. Most war correspondents seem to forget the lessons in time for the next war, reserving regret and protest for their post-retirement memoirs. Independent journalists, the so-called 'unilaterals', can range beyond the confines of the army personnel carrier or the media briefing centre and seek out alternative stories and sources of information. They can fill in the information gaps, get to the hidden stories of war or expose the manipulation and propaganda that often frame the official briefing. This exposes them to considerably more risk than their embedded colleagues and while we might ask legitimate questions about their effectiveness we cannot doubt their honesty, their integrity and their courage.

Telling truth to power is also subject to ideological constraint – to those political and cultural assumptions that socialise and discipline the journalist to make certain choices, to prefer one interpretative frame over another. The book closed with an examination of two ideological frameworks that have been used to explain complex conflicts and crises, 'Cold War' and 'war on terror', the seductive power to which war correspondents are as susceptible as any other intellectual tribe. After all, it seems easier, more convenient, to tell stories of a global conflict between military and economic superpowers, or a worldwide alliance against terrorism and extremism, than to explain much more complex and uncertain realities. These narratives serve as a form of propaganda as effective as formal censorship, because they reduce our understanding to the lowest common denominators of friends and enemies, monsters and terrorists, heroes and psychopaths. In the wake of 9/11, the concept of a war on terror dominated public debate about conflict and security, constructing a regime of fear, self-censorship and passive consent in public life that has had its effect on media and journalism. But just as in the Cold War, with the peace and anti-nuclear movements, the war on terror has also met with a significant and heartening level of public resistance to the point where it has recently been dropped from official discourse (Burke, 2015, p. 169). We should not be complacent, though, because we are already seeing a possible replacement as the west enters into a new Cold War with Russia. If the reporting of the Crimean crisis of 2014 is anything to go by, there is little hope that truth will trump the fear and hysteria whipped up to control our responses and, as Herman and Chomsky (1988) would put it, 'manufacture' our consent.

The point I am making here, then, is that if we want to identify the ultimate role of the war correspondent, something practical and achievable, then the romantic notion of 'telling truth to power' falls rather short of the mark in most respects. The great war correspondents I have mentioned in this chapter have shown that the best the journalist can do in a time of war is not so much tell truth *to* power but spell out the truth *about* power.

Appendices

Appendix 1
International Press Institute:
Recommendations to News
Organisations for Improving
Journalists' Safety

a. 'Preservation of human life and safety is paramount. Staff and freelancers should be made aware that unwarranted risks in pursuit of a story are unacceptable and must be strongly discouraged. Assignments to war zones or hostile environments must be voluntary and should only involve experienced newsgathering practitioners.'

b. 'All staff and freelancers asked to work in hostile environments must have access to appropriate safety training and retraining. Employers are encouraged to make this mandatory.'

c. 'Employers must provide efficient safety equipment to all staff and freelancers assigned to hazardous locations, including personal-issue Kevlar vests or jackets, protective headgear and properly protected vehicles, if necessary.'

d. 'All staff and freelancers should be afforded personal insurance while working in hostile areas, including coverage against death and personal injury.'

e. 'Employers should provide and encourage the use of voluntary and confidential counselling for staff and freelancers returning from hostile areas, or after the coverage of distressing events. (This is likely to require some training of media managers in the recognition of the symptoms of post-traumatic stress disorder).'

f. 'Media companies and their representatives are neutral observers; they don't carry firearms in the course of their work.'

g. 'Media groups should work together to establish a data bank of safety information, including the exchange of up-to-date safety assessments of hostile and dangerous areas.'

(Source: Richard Tait, 2001, 'Unacceptable Danger', International Press Institute Report No. 1)

Appendix 2
The 'Surviving Hostile Regions' Course for War Correspondents

AKE was the first company in the UK to design and deliver a course specifically for journalists.

Length: Courses are one to five days. The length and content of the courses are specifically tailored to type of business, area of operation and support available.

Cost of course: US$1,400.

Number of participants: Around 500 journalists have attended the course.

Staff: The course is taught by former British Special Air Service (SAS) personnel.

The three principles of the course: the awareness, anticipation, avoidance of unnecessary danger.

Types of courses: specialist training, team building, security, medical.

Specialist training includes a course called Surviving Hostile Regions. This course trains journalists for surviving hostile regions and environments: weather, disease and war.

The Surviving Hostile Regions syllabus:
- weapons and effects
- casualty assessment
- weapon types (small arms)
- airway clearance
- weapons employment
- cardio-pulmonary
- resuscitation
- control of bleeding

- heavy weapons
- treatment of burns
- target awareness
- fractures theory
- military-media relations
- map-reading techniques
- venomous animals
- personal protection
- common diseases
- mines and booby traps
- climatic conditions
- self-sufficiency
- public disorder
- the trauma casualty
- hostage survival
- planning
- exercise

The company's website allows participants to register online and purchase equipment such as individual trauma belt packs and medical-team belt kits.

It is located in Hereford, UK, but also offers courses in the United States.

Company website: www.akegroup.com.

(Source: Report 1.01, International Press Institute, Vienna, 2001)

Appendix 3
British Ministry of Defence (MoD) Green Book Guidelines for the British Media Reporting the Gulf War, 1991

Restricted subjects (at the discretion of the Joint Information Bureau, Riyahd):

a. Composition of the force and the locations of ships, units and aircraft.
b. Details of military movements.
c. Operational orders.
d. Plans or intentions.
e. Casualties.
f. Organisations.
g. Place names.
h. Tactical details, e.g. defensive positions, camouflage methods, weapon capabilities or deployments.
i. Names or numbers of ships, aircraft, or military units.
j. Names of individual service men.

Appendix 4
US Military Ground Rules for Media Reporting of the Gulf War, 1991

The following information was restricted because its release could 'jeopardize operations and endanger lives':

a. 'Specific numerical information on troop strength'.
b. 'Details of future military plans, operations or strikes, including postponed or cancelled operations'.
c. 'Information, photography or imagery that would reveal specific location of military forces or show the level of security at military bases or encampments'.
d. 'Rules of engagement details'.
e. 'Information on intelligence collection activities, including targets, methods, and results'.
f. 'Specific information on friendly force troop movements tactical deployments, and dispositions that would jeopardize operational security or lives'.
g. 'Identification of mission aircraft points of origin'.
h. 'Information on the effectiveness or ineffectiveness of enemy camouflage, cover, deception, targeting, direct or indirect fire, intelligence collection, or security measures'.
i. 'Specific identifying information on missing or downed aircraft or ships while search and rescue operations are planned or underway'.
j. Special operations forces' methods, unique equipment or tactics'.
k. 'Specific operating methods and tactics'.
l. 'Information on operational or support vulnerabilities that could be used against US forces such as details of major battle damage or major personnel losses'.

(Source: Hughes, 1992, p. 460ff)

Appendix 5
US Department of Defense (DoD)
Public Affairs Guidance (2003)
for Embedded Reporters

DoD Public Affairs Guidance on Embedding Media During Possible Future Operations/Deployments in the US Central Command's Area of Responsibility

Sections:

1. Purpose

2. Policy
   'We need to tell the factual story – good or bad – before others seed the media with disinformation and distortions. [...] To accomplish this, we will embed media with our units. These embedded media will live, work and travel as part of the units with which they are embedded to facilitate maximum in-depth coverage of US forces in combat and related operations.'

3. Procedures

4. Ground rules
   'Violation of the ground rules may result in the immediate termination of the embed and removal from the AOR [Area of Responsibility].'
   4.F. Categories of 'releasable' information:
   4.f.1. Approximate friendly force strength figures.
   4.f.2. Approximate friendly casualty figures. Embedded media may within OPSEC (Operational Security) limits confirm unit casualties they have witnessed.
   4.f.3. Confirmed figures of enemy personnel detained or captured.
   4.f.4. Size of friendly force participating in an action or operation ...using approximate terms.

4.f.5.   Information and location of military targets may be released when it no longer warrants security protection.

4.f.6.   Generic description of origin of air operations such as 'land-based'.

4.f.7.   Date, time, or location of previous conventional military mission, as well as mission results, are releasable only if described in general terms.

4.f.8.   Types of ordnance expended if described in general terms.

4.f.9.   Number of aerial combat or reconnaissance missions or sorties flown in CentCom's area of operation.

4.f.10. Type of forces involved.

4.f.11. Allied participation by type of operation.

4.f.12. Operational code names.

4.f.13. Names and home towns of US military units.

4.f.14. Service members' names and home towns with the individuals' consent.

4.G. Categories of information that are not releasable since their publication or broadcast could jeopardize operations and endanger lives.

4.g.1.   Specific number of troops in units below corps/MEF [Marine Expeditionary Force] level.

4.g.2.   Specific number of aircraft in units at or below the air expeditionary wing level.

4.g.3.   Specific numbers regarding other equipment or critical supplies.

4.g.4.   Specific numbers of ships in units below the carrier battle group level.

4.g.5.   Names of military installations or specific geographic locations of military units in the CentCom [AOR] unless specifically released by the [DoD] or authorized by the CentCom Commander.

4.g.6.   Information regarding future operations.

4.g.7.   Information regarding force protection measures [...] except those that are readily apparent.

4.g.8.   Photography showing level of security at military installations or encampments.

4.g.9.   Rules of engagement.

4.g.10. Information on intelligence collection activities.

4.g.11. Extra precautions in reporting will be required at the commencement of hostilities to maximize operational surprise.

4.g.12. During an operation, specific information on friendly force troop movements, tactical deployments, and dispositions that would jeopardize operational security or lives. Information on on-going engagements will not be released unless authorized for release by on-scene commander.

4.g.13. Information on special operations units.

4.g.14. Information on effectiveness of enemy electronic warfare.

4.g.15. Information identified postponed or cancelled operations.

4.g.16. Information on missing or downed aircraft or missing vehicles while search and rescue operations are being planned or underway.

4.g.17. Information on effectiveness of enemy camouflage, cover, deception, targeting, direct or indirect fire, intelligence collection, or security measures.

4.g.18. No photographs or other visual media showing an enemy prisoner of war or detainee's recognizable face, nametag, or other identifying feature or item may be taken.

4.g.19. Still or video imagery of custody operations [...].

4.H. Procedures and policies applying to coverage of wounded, injured, and ill personnel.

5. Immunizations and personal protective gear.

6. Security.

7. Miscellaneous/Coordinating instructions.

(Source: US Department of Defense, 2003)

Appendix 6
British Ministry of Defence (MoD) Green Book, 2013: Working Arrangements with the Media for Use Through the Full Spectrum of Conflict

Section 22. The embed system:
The purpose of embedding correspondents with units and formation headquarters is to enable the media to gain a deeper understanding of the operation in which they are involved, particularly through access to personnel and commanders. They will be afforded all possible briefings and other facilities, including the opportunity to accompany British troops during war-fighting operations. Their individual requirements will be met wherever possible. In return, they are likely to be subject to some military orders and training, both for their own safety and that of the unit.

Section 29. Briefing release caveats: MOD and military spokesmen will offer these briefings at various levels under one of the following terms. The conditions of any briefing will be stated in advance:

- Attributable: The information is for use and can be quoted in full. It will be either "directly attributable" (where the spokesman can be identified by name), or "indirectly attributable" (where the person providing the information cannot be identified by name but can normally be described as "a MOD official", "a UK military spokesman", etc).
- Unattributable: The information may be used but may not be attributed to a named source, either an individual or the organisation involved. Hence, for example, "military sources", or "Whitehall sources", but not "Ministry of Defence sources", or "1st Armoured Division sources".

- Background: the information is given to aid greater understanding. It will be stated at the time whether it may be used but, if used, may not be attributed in any way, except as though from a journalist's own knowledge.
- Not for Use: The information may not be published and is given only to aid greater understanding. The term "off the record", is sometimes misinterpreted, misunderstood and misused. It should not be employed.

(Source: Joint Service Publication 580, Version 8, 31 January 2013)

Appendix 7
British Newspaper Descriptions of President Putin During the Crimea Crisis, 21 February–20 March 2014

(Frequency of more than one occurrence in brackets)

- Afraid
- Aggressive
- Alpha male
- Ambitious
- Anti-democrat   (2)
- Autocrat

- Bogeyman
- Brutal
- Bully   (2)
- Business-like

- Chairman of the world's unofficial Autocrat's Club
- Classic Bond villain
- Competitive
- Confident
- Contemptuous soul
- Cunning

- Decisive
- Defiant   (4)

- Emboldened
- Emotional
- Enraged
- Expansionist

- Frustrated

- Hard man
- Imperial
- Incapable of calm calculation
- KGB professional
- Loathsome
- Macho
- Master of the dark arts
- Menacing
- Nimble
- Opportunist
- Paranoid
- Pariah
- Pre-1917 imperial nationalist
- Prickly
- Pugnacious
- Puppet master (2)
- Rambling
- Rasputin
- Reckless
- Ruthless (2)
- Steely (2)
- Strongman (2)
- Strutting
- Suspicious
- Swaggering
- Tetchy
- Triumphant
- Tsar
- Tyrant (2)
- Uncompromising (2)
- Unpleasant
- Unrepentant Cold war warrior
- Vindictive

- Vlad-father
- Vlad the Invader

- Wooden

(The survey of newspapers for the stated period was based on a search of the Nexis newspaper database using the search terms 'Putin' and 'Crimea'. The resulting sample of 541 news and editorial items included London editions of the *Daily Telegraph, Times, Daily Mail, Daily Express, Guardian, Independent, Sun, Daily Mirror, Daily Star, Sunday Times, Sunday Telegraph, Independent on Sunday, Observer, Mail on Sunday* and *Sunday Express*. To avoid unwarranted duplication of results, the sample excluded editions in Scotland, Northern Ireland and Ireland.)

Appendix 8
British Newspaper Descriptions of President Putin's Policies and Actions During the Crimea Crisis, 21 February–20 March 2014

(Frequency of more than one occurrence in brackets)

- Acting defensively
- Aggression   (4)
- Aggrieved party
- Anger
- Annexation   (4)

- Bile
- Bitterness
- Bluff
- Bravura
- Bribery
- Brinkmanship   (2)
- Bombast
- Bullying

- Calm calculation
- Carve-up
- Covert network of influence
- Cynicism

- De facto dictatorship
- Determination

- Exerting power in the shadows

- Flights of apparent fancy

- Irredentist adventure

- Land grab   (7)

- Machinations
- Macho politics
- Muscle flexing (2)

- Nazi tactics
- Nostalgia for Soviet times

- Paranoia
- Patriotic bluster
- Permanent rage
- Pitiless pragmatism
- Politics of grievance
- Power games
- Propaganda
- Putsch (2)

- Raising the stakes
- Revanchism
- Revanchist foray
- Russian anschluss
- Ruthless clarity of purpose
- Ruthless determination

- Sabre rattling (4)
- Strong-arm threats

- Threat
- Titanic game of bluff
- Territorial ambitions

- Unadulterated militarism
- Unprovoked aggression

- Whim

- Zero-sum thinking

(The survey of newspapers for the stated period was based on a search of the Nexis newspaper database using the search terms 'Putin' and 'Crimea'. The resulting sample of 541 news and editorial items included London editions of the *Daily Telegraph*, *Times*, *Daily Mail*, *Daily Express*, *Guardian*, *Independent*, *Sun*, *Daily Mirror*, *Daily Star*, *Sunday Times*, *Sunday Telegraph*, *Independent on Sunday*, *Observer*, *Mail on Sunday* and *Sunday Express*. To avoid unwarranted duplication of results, the sample excluded editions in Scotland, Northern Ireland and Ireland.)

Notes

CHAPTER 1: INTRODUCTION

1. 'Sheer folly', *Media Guardian*, 15 October 2001.
2. 'Adie fury as error follows error in BBC row', *Guardian*, 11 October 2001.
3. See for example, *Berlin Correspondent* (dir. Eugene Forde, 1942); *Circle of Deceit* (dir. Volker Schlöndorff, 1981); *Salvador* (dir. Oliver Stone, 1983), *Under Fire* (dir. Roger Spottiswoode, 1983); *The Killing Fields* (dir. Roland Joffé, 1984); and *Welcome to Sarajevo* (dir. Michael Winterbottom, 1999).

CHAPTER 2: THE WAR CORRESPONDENT: RISK, MOTIVATION AND TRADITION

1. For the purposes of clarity and simplicity, I have taken the IPI and CPJ as my principal sources for information on the risks and dangers of war reporting. However, this is not to ignore the work of similar organisations such as Reporters Without Borders and the Freedom Foundation.
2. See IPI website: www.freemedia.at
3. See CPJ website: www.cpj.org
4. "Who killed my dad?' – The death of Terry Lloyd', ITV, ITN Productions, 21 March 2013.
5. Jim Boumelha (2010) 'US must deliver justice on friendly fire', Comment is Free in *Guardian*, 10 April (www.theguardian.com, consulted July 2014).
6. See: 'War Spin: Saving Private Lynch', *Correspondent*, BBC2, 18 May 2003.
7. Source: 'Collateral Murder', online article (https://collateralmurder.wikileaks.org, consulted July 2014).
8. The most cited sources in news reports appear to be the United Nations and the UK-based Syrian Observatory for Human Rights (SOHR). The United Nations (UN) decided to stop monitoring the ongoing death toll at the end of 2013 because of the attendant dangers of doing so.
9. Source: Naomi Hunt, 'Syrian Journalists Association: 100 media activists & journalists killed in Syrian conflict', IPI article, 3 December 2012 (http://www.freemedia.at/newssview/article/syrian-journalists-association-100-media-activists-journalists-killed-in-syrian-conflict.html, consulted July 2014).

10. Source: Roy Greenslade 'Marie Colvin killed in Syria', *Guardian Media*, 22 February 2012 (http://www.theguardian.com/media/greenslade/2012/feb/22/sundaytimes-syria, consulted July 2014); see also Paul Conroy's own account of what happened (Conroy, 2013); and a collection of Marie Colvin's most recent war reporting (Colvin, 2012).

11. Source: Shadi Alkasim, 'Increasing numbers of journalists kidnapped in Syria', IPI article, 2013 (http://www.freemedia.at/newssview/article/increasing-number-of-journalists-kidnapped-in-syria.html, consulted July 2014).

12. See Ploughshares' Armed Conflicts Report, 'Philippines-Mindanao (1971 – first combat deaths)', updated 2009, (http://www.justice.gov/eoir/vll/country/armed_conflict_report/Philippinesmm_Mindanao.pdf, consulted July 2014).

13. Source: Scott Griffen, 'Justice Delayed: The Maguindanao Massacre, Two Years On', IPI article, 23 November 2011 (http://www.freemedia.at/home/singleview/article/justice-delayed-the-maguindanao-massacre-two-years-on.html, consulted July 2014).

14. Elena Shmaraeva, 'Politkovskaya killers sentenced, but who hired them?', openDemocracy, 18 June 2014 (http://opendemocracy.net/od-russia/elena-shmaraeva/who-really-killed-anna-politkovskaya, consulted July 2014).

15. http://www.cpj.org/europe/russia/ (consulted July 2014).

16. From John Blair (dir.), 'Dying to tell a story', *Reporters at War*, Vol. 1, True Vision Films, 2003.

17. See Steele's 2002 memoir, *War Junkie: One Man's Addiction to the Worst Places on Earth* (London: Transworld Publishers).

18. Lloyd was to fight his way back to recovery and return to life as a war reporter. On assignment in Syria, 2014, he was captured, beaten and shot by a warlord he had cultivated as a source, but managed to escape.

19. 'The Boer War: The First Media War', *Timewatch*, BBC2, 1998.

20. The first edition of this book gave costs of up to US$1,400 for such courses, but I have been unable to get updated costs for 2014.

21. http://www.akegroup.com/insurance (consulted July 2014).

22. http://www.akegroup.com/sectors/media/ (consulted July 2014).

23. Nicholson; interview with the author, Surrey, 25 October 1999.

24. Lindsey Hilsum, Diplomatic Editor, Channel 4 News; interview with the author, London 26 October 1999.

25. Lindsey Hilsum, Diplomatic Editor, Channel 4 News; interview with the author, London, 26 October 1999.

26. Nik Gowing, Diplomatic Editor, BBC World; interview with the author, London, 28 November 1999.

27. Mark Laity, interview with the author, London, 18 November 1999. Laity is now a press officer at the North Atlantic Treaty Organization (NATO) Headquarters.
28. 'Tales From the Gulf', *The Late Show*, BBC2, 19 July 1991.
29. Ibid.
30. Alex Thomson; interview with the author, London, 29 November 1999.
31. Michael Nicholson; interview with the author, Surrey, 25 October 1999.
32. Ibid.
33. Amanpour; email correspondence with the author, 5 December 1999.
34. Simpson; telephone interview with the author, 9 December 1999.
35. O'Kane; telephone interview with the author, 29 February 2000.
36. Nicholson; interview with the author, Surrey, 25 October 1999.
37. Urban; interview with the author, London, 25 October 1999.
38. Pilger; telephone interview with the author, 4 February 2000.
39. Bell; interview with the author, London, 27 October 1999; see also Ben Brown, as interviewed in Katovsky and Carslon (2004, pp. 217–21).
40. Fisk; interview with the author, Belfast, 18 October 1999.
41. Ibid.
42. Brittain; telephone interview with the author, 2 November 1999.
43. Thomson; interview with the author, London, 29 November 1999.
44. Brittain; telephone interview with the author, 2 November 1999.
45. Fisk; interview with the author, Belfast, 18 October 1999.
46. Gowing; interview with the author, London, 28 November 1999.
47. Pilger; telephone interview with the author, 4 February 2000.
48. Simpson; telephone interview with the author, 4 February 2000.
49. Laity; interview with the author, London, 18 November 1999.
50. Bell; interview with the author, London, 27 October 1999.
51. Hilsum; interview with the author, London 26 October 1999.
52. Pilger; telephone interview with the author, 4 February 2000.
53. Brittain; telephone interview with author, 2 November 1999.
54. O'Kane; telephone interview with the author, 29 February 2000.
55. Thomson; interview with the author, London, 29 November 1999.
56. Nicholson; interview with the author, Surrey, 25 October 1999.
57. Gowing; interview with the author, London, 28 November 1999.
58. The programmes were: 'Saving Private Ryan', part of BBC2's current affairs strand *Correspondent*, 2003; and 'The War We Didn't See', Channel 4, 2003.

CHAPTER 3: JOURNALISM, OBJECTIVITY AND WAR

1. *True Stories: Babitsky's War*, Channel 4, 25 March 2000.
2. See Glasgow University Media Group 1976; Parenti, 1993.

3. Pilger; telephone interview with the author, 4 February 2000.

4. See, for example: Didion, 1983; Kapuscinksy, 1982, 1983 and 2001; and Thompson, 2011.

5. Nicholson; interview with the author, Surrey, 25 October 1999.

6. Nicholson's story was eventually fictionalised in the film *Welcome to Sarajevo* (dir. Michael Winterbottom, 1999).

7. Fisk; interview with the author, Belfast, 18 October 1999.

8. O'Kane; telephone interview with the author, 29 February, 2000.

9. Thomson; interview with the author, London, 29 November 1999.

10. Amanpour; email correspondence with the author, 5 December 1999.

11. 'Courage under fire', *Guardian*, 20 September 1999; In 2001, Marie Colvin went on to report on the civil war in Sri Lanka, where she lost an eye from a shrapnel wound. On 21 February 2012, she was killed reporting from Homs in Syria.

12. Brittain; telephone interview with the author, 2 November 1999.

13. 'Courage under fire', *Guardian*, 20 September 1999.

14. Brittain; telephone interview with the author, 2 November 1999.

15. O'Kane; telephone interview with the author, 29 February, 2000; see also *Guardian*, 26 May 2000.

16. Urban; interview with the author, London, 25 October 1999.

17. Simpson; telephone interview with the author, 9 December 1999.

18. Ibid.

19. Fisk; interview with the author, Belfast, 18 October 1999.

20. Hilsum; interview with the author, London, 27 October 1999.

21. Fisk; interview with the author, Belfast, 18 October 1999.

22. While the peace process has seen a dramatic drop in the level of violence in Northern Ireland, sectarian tension persists at a low level, boiling over periodically over issues pertaining to identity and the violence of the past.

23. Cited by *Al Jazeera* online: Ben Piven, 'Iran and Israel: Comparing military machines', 24 April 2012 (www.aljazeera.com/indepth/features/2012/03/20 12326131343853636.html, consulted, July 2014).

24. INSS, Middle East Military Forces, 2012 (www.inss.org.il, consulted, July 2014).

25. Thomson; telephone interview with the author, 7 July 2015.

26. Ibid.

27. Bell; interview with the author, London, 27 October 1999.

28. Interviewed in 'Tales from Sarajevo', *Late Show*, BBC2, 23 January 1993.

29. Ibid.

30. The problem of the media cheerleading for military interventions in civil conflicts and humanitarian crises was most particular to the ideological confusions and falsities of the post-cold war, 'end of history' era of the 1990s

and one which I have covered comprehensively in the first edition of this volume (McLaughlin, 2002a, pp. 182–98).

CHAPTER 4: FROM LUCKLESS TRIBE TO WIRELESS TRIBE: THE IMPACT OF MEDIA TECHNOLOGIES ON WAR REPORTING

1. Cited in Paul Mason (2013), p. 14.
2. See, for example, Ofcom's Communications Market Report, UK, 2014 (stakeholders.ofcom.org.uk/market-data-research/market-data/communications-market-reports/cmr14/uk/, accessed February 2015). For the US, see K. V. Matsa and A. Mitchell, '8 Key Takeaways about Social Media and News', Pew Research Centre, 26 March 2014 (www.journalism.org/2014/03/26/8-key-takeaways-about-social-media-and-news/, accessed February 2015).
3. *Late Show*: 'Tales from the Gulf', BBC2 19 July 1991; for the detailed back story of the photograph and the photographer, Kenneth Jarecke, see Torie Rose Deghett, 'The war photo no one would publish', *The Atlantic* (online), 8 August 2014 (www.theatlantic.com/international/archive/2014/08/the-war-photo-no-one-would-publish/375762/, consulted July 2015).
4. 'The First Media War', *Timewatch*, BBC2, 1995.
5. O'Kane; telephone interview with the author, 29 February 2000.
6. Thomson; interview with the author, London, 29 November 1999.
7. Hilsum; interview with the author, London, 26 October 1999.
8. Gowing; interview with the author, London, 28 November 1999.
9. Ibid.
10. Ibid.
11. Simpson; telephone interview with the author, 9 December 1999.
12. Ibid.
13. See also, Shaw, 1996b, *Civil Society and the Media in Global Crises*.
14. Gowing; interview with the author, London, 28 November 1999.
15. Ibid; see also Gowing, 1996, 1997 and 1998.
16. Caryn James, 'A public flooded with images from friend and foe alike', *The New York Times*, 10 October 2001.
17. Ariel Peled, 'The first social media war between Israel and Gaza', *Guardian Media Network*, 6 January 2012 (www.theguardian.com/media-network/media-network-blog/2012/dec/06/first-social-media-war-israel-gaza, accessed February 2014).
18. Thomson; telephone interview with the author, 7 July 2015.

19. Peter Preston, 'Twitter is no substitute for proper war reporting – just look at Libya', *Guardian*, 27 February 2011 (www.theguardian.com/media/2011/feb/27/twitter-war-reporting-peter-preston, consulted February 2014).

CHAPTER 5: GETTING TO KNOW EACH OTHER: FROM CRIMEA TO VIETNAM

1. See Phillips Price, 1997, pp. 141–49.
2. Pilger; telephone interview with the author, 4 February 2000.
3. Leslie; email response to the author, 22 August 2001; see Leslie's memoirs in Leslie, 1995.
4. Ibid.
5. See Hallin, 1996; MacArthur, 1992; Pilger, 2001; Williams, 1993.

CHAPTER 6: LEARNING AND FORGETTING: FROM THE FALKLANDS TO THE GULF

1. Cited in Fialka (1992, p. 62).
2. Nicholson; interview with the author, Surrey, 25 October 1999.
3. William Boot is the pen name of Christopher Hanson of the *Seattle Post-Intelligencer.*
4. Sherman, director of the US Navy's PR office in Los Angeles, was nicknamed 'Hollywood Mike' for his consultancy work on movies like *Top Gun*, *The Hunt for Red October* and *Flight of the Intruder.* (Thomson, 1992, p.40).
5. Fisk; interview with the author, Belfast, 18 October 1999.
6. Fisk in *The Late Show*, 'Tales from the Gulf', BBC2, 19 July 1991.
7. Maggie O'Kane remembers how this reached its nadir during the US invasion of Haiti in 1994 when journalists, crazed by the competition the pooling system engendered, embarked on something of a witch hunt for reporters who made it to the island unaccredited and by unorthodox means; telephone interview with the author, 29 February 2000.
8. Fisk; interview with the author, Belfast, 18 October 1999.
9. 'Tales from the Gulf'.
10. Bell; interview with the author, London, 27 October 1999.
11. Urban; interview with the author, London, 25 October 1999.
12. Nicholson; interview with the author, Surrey, 25 October 1999.
13. Urban; interview with the author, London, 25 October 1999.
14. Bowen recounts this episode in his memoirs, *War Stories*; see Bowen (2006, pp. 83–89).
15. Nicholson; interview with the author, Surrey, 25 October 1999.

CHAPTER 7: GOODBYE VIETNAM SYNDROME:
THE EMBED SYSTEM IN AFGHANISTAN AND IRAQ

1. From 'DoD Public Affairs Guidance on embedding media during future operations/deployments in the US Central Command's Area of Responsibility'; see Appendix 5 of this book for details of reporting restrictions.
2. See *Correspondent*: 'War Spin: Saving Private Lynch', BBC2, 18 May 2003.
3. For Castro's account of the incident, see 'The War We Never Saw', Channel 4, 5 June 2003; the programme was part of a special series on the Iraq War, *The True Face of War.*
4. Thomson: telephone interview with the author, 7 July 2015.
5. From *Correspondent*: 'War Spin: Saving Private Lynch', BBC2, 18 May 2003.
6. Ibid.
7. Ibid.
8. 'War Spin: Saving Private Lynch'.
9. See Coneta (2004).
10. 'War Spin: Saving Private Lynch'.
11. The analysis is based on a sample of British and American television news programmes from 12–19 April 1999: BBC News at 13.00, 18.00, 21.00 and BBC2 Newsnight at 22.30; ITN bulletins at 12.30, 18.30, 23.00, and Channel 4 News at 19.00; the sample of American programmes comprised of CNN and NBC bulletins at 17.00 on each day of the sample period.
12. Ibid.
13. Shea; telephone interview with the author, 2 February 2000.
14. Thomson; interview with the author, London, 29 November 1999.
15. Lynch; interview with the author, London, 1 December 1999.
16. Shea; telephone interview with the author, 2 February 2000.
17. Ibid.
18. Ibid.
19. Ibid.
20. Lynch; interview with the author, London, 1 December 1999; for a fuller discussion of the 'new Labourisation' of information during the Kosovo crisis, see Philip Hammond (2000) and Campbell (1999).
21. Laity; interview with the author, London, 18 November, 1999.
22. Fisk; interview with the author, Belfast, 18 October 1999.
23. Shea; telephone interview with the author, 2 February 2000.
24. Fisk; interview with the author, Belfast, 18 October 1999.
25. Shea; telephone interview with the author, 2 February 2000.
26. Cited in Paterson (2014, pp. 21–22).

CHAPTER 8: REPORTING THE COLD WAR
AND THE NEW WORLD ORDER

1. Chomsky (2002, pp. 20–21).
2. All these press references are dated 2 June 1988.
3. See Simpson (1990).
4. Thomson; interview with the author, London, 29 November 1999.
5. Simpson; telephone Interview with the author 9 December 1999.
6. Submission to the US Congressional Joint Economic Committee; *Daily Telegraph*, 11 November, 1989.
7. The Huw Wheldon Lecture by John Simpson, BBC2 1993.
8. McCrystal, Cal, 'The world at war', *Independent on Sunday* (Review, pp. 39–41), 14 March 1991.
9. Young, Hugo, 'A year of no world order', *Guardian*, 31 December 1992.
10. Comment, *Observer*, p. 18, 26 December 1993.
11. Channel 4, Critical Eye: 'Proud Arabs and Texas Oilmen', 1993.
12. 'The Audit of War', *Dispatches*, Channel 4, January 1992.
13. Hurd in a speech at Blaby, 2 February 1991, cited in Gittings (1991, p. 22); for a detailed discussion of race and gender in Gulf War rhetoric and imagery, see Enloe (1992) and Farmanfarmaian (1992).
14. Said in 'Culture and Imperialism', *Arena*, BBC2, 1993.
15. The *Guardian* was alone among the British press in arguing against using force and quoted a CIA report that sanctions had stopped 97% of Iraqi exports (15 January 1991). A BBC News item referred to the success of sanctions in wrecking not just Iraq's economy but those of its neighbours, especially Jordan. It interviewed an American economist, who estimated that sanctions were having, 'More than ten times the impact (than on) economies in past episodes, where sanctions have *succeeded* in achieving their goal' (BBC1, 21.00, 14 January 1991).
16. 'Uncle Sam's Last Stand', *Assignment*, BBC2, 1991.
17. 'The Audit of War', *Dispatches*, Channel 4, January 1992.
18. Fineman, M. 'The oil factor in Somalia', *Los Angeles Times*, 18 January 1993; see also Jensen (1994).
19. Greg Philo and Greg McLaughlin, 'ITN passes the Tebbit Test', *New Statesman and Society*, 29 January 1993.

CHAPTER 9: REPORTING THE WAR ON TERROR
AND THE RETURN OF THE EVIL EMPIRE

1. Walter Lippmann, 'Peace talks thwarted by matter of semantics', *The Free Lance Star*, 11 January 1967, p. 4; Lippmann was commenting in this article

on how the semantics of propaganda were being deployed to limit public understanding of tentative peace talks in Vietnam.

2. Cited in John Pilger, 'A New Pearl Harbour', *New Statesman* (online) 16 December 2002 (www.newstatesman.com/node/144428, accessed February 2015.

3. From 'Campaign Against Terror', *Frontline*, Public Broadcast Service (date unavailable) (www.pbs.org/wgbh/pages/frontline/shows/campaign/interviews/572.html, accessed March 2015).

4. The case study analyses in this chapter are based on samples of British newspapers. Unless otherwise stated, these were generated using keyword searches of the Nexis newspaper database to include the London editions of the *Daily Telegraph*, *Times*, *Daily Mail*, *Daily Express*, *Guardian*, *Independent*, *Sun*, *Daily Mirror*, *Daily Star*, *Sunday Times*, *Sunday Telegraph*, *Independent on Sunday*, *Observer*, *Mail on Sunday* and *Sunday Express*. To avoid unwarranted duplication of results, the samples excluded editions published in Scotland, Northern Ireland and Ireland.

5. Cited in the anti-war website 'War is a Crime' (http://warisacrime.org/iraq#_edn19, accessed March 2015).

6. Cited in *War Is A Crime*.

7. For a detailed breakdown of casualty figures and the methodologies used to compile them, see the Iraq Body Count website (www.iraqbodycount.org/analysis/numbers/2011/).

8. The *Daily Mail* was publicly supportive of Hitler's expansionism in Europe up until the invasion of Poland in 1939 and Britain's declaration of war against Germany.

9. Dejevsky: telephone interview with the author, 6 July 2015.

10. See the full post at: Ian H. Robertson, 'The danger that lurks inside Vladimir Putin's brain', 17 March 2015, *Psychology Today* blog (www.psychologytoday.com/blog/the-winner-effect/201403/the-danger-lurks-inside-vladimir-putins-brain, accessed March 2015).

11. Dejevsky: telephone interview with the author, 6 July 2015. Elsewhere, Dejevsky draws intriguing parallels between the situation in Ukraine and Northern Ireland. See: 'Forget the Cuban Missile Crisis and Sudetenland; Northern Ireland Offers the Best Parallel for Eastern Ukraine', *The Spectator*, 10 February 2015.

Bibliography

Adams, Valerie (1986) *The Media and the Falklands Campaign* (London: Macmillan).

Ahmad, Eqbal (1992) 'Portent of a New Century', in Bennis, Phyllis and Michel Moushabeck (eds) *Beyond the Storm: A Gulf Crisis Reader* (Edinburgh: Canongate), pp. 7–21.

Allen, Stuart and Barbie Zelizer (eds.) (2004) *Reporting War: Journalism in Wartime* (London: Routledge).

Althusser, Louis (1971) 'Ideology and ideological state apparatuses (Notes towards an investigation'), in Louis Althusser, *Lenin and Philosophy and Other Essays* (London: New Left Books), pp. 121–76.

Arnett, Peter (1996) 'The Clash of Arms in Exotic Locales', *Media Studies Journal: Journalists in Peril*, Vol. 10, No. 4, Fall.

Aubrey, Crispin (ed.) (1982) *Nukespeak: The Media and the Bomb* (London: Comedia/Minority Press Group).

Aucoin, James L. (2001) 'Epistemic Responsibility and Narrative Theory: The Literary Journalism of Ryszard Kapuscinski', *Journalism*, Vol. 2, No. 1, April, pp. 5–21.

Ayres, Chris (2005) *War Reporting for Cowards* (London: John Murray).

Baker, James (1996) 'Report First, Check Later', *Harvard International Journal of Press/Politics*, Vol. 1, No. 2, pp. 3–9.

Baudrillard, Jean (1995) *The Gulf War Did Not Take Place* (Bloomington, IN: Indiana University Press).

Baudrillard, Jean (2002) *The Spirit of Terrorism: And Requiem for the Twin Towers* (London: Verso).

Bell, Martin (1993) 'Testament of an Interventionist', *British Journalism Review*, Vol. 4, No. 4, pp. 8–11.

Bell, Martin (1997) 'TV News: How Far Should We Go?', *British Journalism Review*, Vol. 8, No. 1, pp. 7–16.

Bell, Martin (1998) 'The Truth is Our Currency', *Harvard International Journal Press/Politics*, Vol. 3, No. 1, pp. 102–09.

Bjork, Ulf Jonas (1994) 'Latest from the Canadian Revolution: Early War Correspondence in the New York Herald, 1837–1838', *Journalism Quarterly*, Vol. 71, No. 4, pp. 851–58.

Blanchard, Margaret (1992) 'Free Expression and Wartime: Lessons from the Past, Hopes for the Future', *Journalism Quarterly*, Vol. 69, No. 1, Spring, pp. 5–17.

Boot, William (1990) 'Wading Around in the Panama Pool', *Columbia Journalism Review*, March/April, pp. 18–20.

Boot, William (1991) 'The Pool', *Columbia Journalism Review*, May/June, pp. 24–27.

Borovik, Artyom (1990) *The Hidden War: A Russian Journalist's Account of the Soviet War in Afghanistan* (London: Faber & Faber).

Bourdieu, Pierre (1971) 'Systems of Education and Systems of Thought', in Young, Michael F.D. (ed.) *Knowledge and Control: New Directions for the Sociology of Education* (London: Collier-Macmillan), pp. 189–207.

Bowen, Jeremy (2006) *War Stories* (London: Simon and Schuster).

Boyd-Barrett, Oliver (2004) 'Understanding: the second casualty', in Allen, Stuart and Barbie Zelizer (eds.) *Reporting War: Journalism in Wartime* (London: Routledge), pp. 25–42.

Braestrup, Peter (1983) *Big Story: How the American Press and Television Reported and Interpreted the Crisis of Tet 1968 in Vietnam and Washington* (London: Yale University Press).

Braestrup, Peter (1985) *Battle Lines: Report of the Twentieth Century Fund Task Force on the Military and the Media* (New York, NY: Priority Press).

Brothers, Caroline (1997) *War and Photography: A Cultural History* (London: Routledge).

Brown, Charles H. (1967) *The Correspondents War: Journalists in the Spanish-American War* (New York, NY: Charles Scribner's Sons).

Burchett, Wilfred (1980) *At the Barricades* (London: Quartet).

Burke, Jason (2004) *Al Qaeda: The True Story of Radical Islam* (London: Penguin Books).

Burke, Jason (2011) *The 9/11 Wars* (London: Allen Lane).

Burke, Jason (2015) *The New Threat From Islamic Militancy* (London: Bodley Head).

Burns, John C. (1996) 'The Media as Impartial Observers or Protagonists: Conflict Reporting or Conflict Encouragement in Former Yugolsavia', in Gow, James, Richard Paterson and Alison Preston (eds) *Bosnia by Television* (London: BFI), pp. 92–100.

Burrowes, John (1984) *Frontline Report: A Journalist's Notebook* (Edinburgh: Mainstream).

Butler, David (1995) *The Trouble with Reporting Northern Ireland* (Aldershot: Avebury).

Callinicos, Alex (1991) *The Revenge of History: Marxism and the East European Revolutions* (Cambridge: Polity Press).

Cameron, James (1967) *Point of Departure* (London: Oriel Press).

Campbell, Alistair (1999) 'Communications Lessons for NATO, the Military and Media', *Royal United Services Institute Journal*, Vol. 144, No. 4, pp. 31–36.

Carr, E. H. (1986) *What is History?*, 2nd edition (London: Macmillan).

Carruthers, Susan L. (1995) *Winning Hearts and Minds: British Governments, the Media and Colonial Counterinsurgency, 1944–60* (London: Leicester University Press).

Carruthers, Susan L. (2011) *The Media At War: Communication and Conflict in the Twentieth Century*, 2nd edition (London: Palgrave Macmillan).

Chandler, David (2000) 'Western Intervention and the Disintegration of Yugoslavia', in Hammond, Philip and Edward S. Herman (eds) *Degraded Capability: The Media and the Kosovo Crisis* (London: Pluto Press), pp. 19–30.

Chang, Wong Ho (1991) 'Images of the Soviet Union in American Newspapers: A Content Analysis of Three Newspapers', in Dennis, Everette E., George Gerbner and Yassen N. Zassoursky (eds) *Beyond the Cold War: Soviet and American Media Images* (London: Sage), pp. 65–83.

Chomsky, Noam (1989) *Necessary Illusions* (London: Pluto Press).

Chomsky, Noam (1992a) *Deterring Democracy* (London: Vintage).

Chomsky, Noam (1992b) "What We Say Goes' - the Middle East in the New World Order', in Peters, Cynthia (ed.) *Collateral Damage: The New World Order at Home and Abroad* (Boston, MA: Southend Press), pp. 49–92.

Chomsky, Noam (1993) *Year 501: The Conquest Continues* (Boston, MA: Southend Press).

Chomsky, Noam (1994) *World Orders, Old and New* (London: Pluto Press).

Chomsky, Noam (1999) *The New Military Humanism: Lessons From Kosovo* (London: Pluto Press).

Chomsky, Noam (2002) *Media Control: The Spectacular Achievements of Propaganda*, 2nd edition (New York, NY: Seven Stories Press).

Collier, Richard (1989) *The Warcos: The War Correspondents of the Second World War* (London: Weidenfeld and Nicolson).

Colvin, Marie (2012) *On the Front Line: The Collected Journalism of Marie Colvin* (London: Harper Press).

Coneta, Carl (2004) 'Disappearing the Dead: Iraq, Afghanistan, and the Idea of a 'New Warfare'', Project on Defense Alternatives Research Monograph #9, 18 February (Cambridge, MA: Commonwealth Institute).

Conroy, Paul (2013) *Under the Wire: Marie Colvin's Final Assignment* (New York, NY: Weinstein Books).

Croft, Stuart (2006) *Culture, Crisis and America's War on Terror* (Cambridge: Cambridge University Press).

Crozier, Emmett (1959) *American Reporters on the Western Front, 1914–1918* (New York, NY: Oxford University Press).

Cumings, Bruce (1992) *War and Television* (London: Verso).

Darrow, Siobhan (2000) *Flirting with Danger: Confessions of a Reluctant War Reporter* (London: Virago Press).

Dennis, Everette E., George Gerbner and Yassen N. Zassoursky (eds) (1991) *Beyond the Cold War: Soviet and American Media Images* (London: Sage).

Dickson, Sandra (1994) 'Understanding Media Bias: The Press and the US Invasion of Panama', *Journalism Quarterly*, Vol. 71, No. 4, Winter, pp. 809–19.

Didion, Joan (1983) *Salvador* (London: Chatto & Windus).

Dimbleby, Jonathan (1975) *Richard Dimbleby: A Biography* (London: Hodder and Stoughton).

Dorman, William A. and Mansour Farhang (1987) *The US Press and Iran: Foreign Policy and the Journalism of Deference* (London: University of California Press).

Dunsmore, Barry (1996) 'The Next War: Live?' *Harvard International Journal Press/Politics*, Vol. 1, No. 3, pp. 3–5.

Elwood-Akers, Virginia (1988) *Women War Correspondents in the Vietnam War, 1961–1975* (Methuen, NJ: Scarecrow Press, Inc.).

Enloe, Cynthia (1992) 'The Gendered Gulf', in Peters, Cynthia (ed.) *Collateral Damage: The New World Order at Home and Abroad* (Boston, MA: Southend Press), pp. 93–110.

Entman, Robert M. and Andrew Rojecki (1993) 'Freezing out the Public: Elite and Media framing of the US Anti-Nuclear Movement', *Political Communication*, Vol. 10, No. 2, pp. 155–73.

Ewing, Joseph H. (1991) 'The New Sherman Letters', in Matthews, Lloyd J. (ed.) *Newsmen and National Defense: Is Conflict Inevitable?* (New York, NY: Brassey's), pp. 19–29.

Farmanfarmaian, Abouali (1992) 'Did You Measure Up?: The Role of Race and Sexuality in the Gulf War', in Peters, Cynthia (ed.) *Collateral Damage: The New World Order at Home and Abroad* (Boston, MA: Southend Press), pp. 111–38.

Farrar, Martin J. (1998) *News From the Front: War Correspondents on the Western Front 1914–18* (London: Sutton Publishing).

Fialka, John J. (1992) *Hotel Warriors: Covering the Gulf War* (Washington, DC: Woodrow Wilson Center Press).

Fisk, Robert (1990) *Pity the Nation: Lebanon at War* (Oxford: Oxford University Press).

Fisk, Robert (2001) *Pity the Nation: Lebanon at War*, 3rd edition (Oxford: Oxford University Press).

Fisk, Robert (2006) *The Great War for Civilisation: The Conquest of the Middle East* (London: Harper Perennial).

Fleming, Dan (2001) 'The Kosovo Conflict on the Web: A Case Study', in Fleming, Dan (ed.) *Formations: A 21st Century Media Studies Text Book* (Manchester: Manchester University Press), pp. 116–19.

Foden, Giles (1999a) 'The First Media War', *The Mail & Guardian* (Johannesburg), 7 October.

Foden, Giles (1999b) *Ladysmith* (London: Faber and Faber).

Fox, Robert (1988) 'Foreign Bodies: Part 4', *The Listener*, 9 June, pp. 14–15.

Franco, Victor (1963) *The Morning After: A French Journalist's Impressions of Cuba Under Castro* (London: Pall Mall Press).

Thussu, Daya Kishan and Des Freedman (2004) (eds) *War and the Media: Reporting Conflict 24/7* (London: Sage).

Fukyama, Francis (1989) 'The End of History?' in *The National Interest*, No. 16, pp. 3–18.

Fukyama, Francis (1992) *The End of History and the Last Man* (London: Hamish Hamilton).

Gellhorn, Martha (1993) *The Face of War* (London: Granta Books).

Gellhorn, Martha (1994) 'The Invasion of Panama', in Granta Books (eds) *The Best of Granta Reportage* (London: Granta Books), pp. 269–87.

Gerbner, George (1991) 'The Image of Russians in American Media and the "New Epoch"', in Dennis, Everette E., George Gerbner and Yassen N. Zassoursky (eds) *Beyond the Cold War: Soviet and American Media Images* (London: Sage), pp. 31–35.

Gitlin, Todd (1980) *The Whole World is Watching: The Mass Media in the Making and the Unmaking of the New Left* (Berkley, CA: University of California Press).

Gittings, J. (ed.) (1991) *Beyond the Gulf War: The Middle East and the New World Order* (London: CIIR).

Glasgow University Media Group (1976) *Bad News* (London: Routledge & Kegan Paul).

Glasgow University Media Group (1985) *War and Peace News* (Milton Keynes: Open University Press).

Glasser, Theodore L. (1992), 'Objectivity and News Reporting', in Cohen, E. (ed.) *Philosophical Issues in Journalism* (Oxford: Oxford University Press), pp. 176–83.

Goff, Peter (2000) 'Introduction', in Goff, Peter (ed.) *The Kosovo News and Propaganda War* (Vienna: International Press Institute), pp. 13–34.

Goodman, Walter (1991) 'Arnett', *Columbia Journalism Review*, May/June, pp. 29–31.

Goodwin, Jan (1987) *Caught in the Crossfire: A Woman Journalist's Breathtaking Experiences in War-torn Afghanistan* (London: Macdonald).

Gourevitch, Philip (1998) *We Wish To Inform You That Tomorrow We Will Be Killed With Our Families: Stories from Rwanda* (London: Picador).

Gowing, Nik (1995) 'This Reporter Can Never be a Footnote', *British Journalism Review*, Vol. 6, No. 4, pp. 67–71.

Gowing, Nik (1996) 'Real-time TV Coverage from War: Does it Make or Break Government Policy?', in Gow, James, Richard Paterson and Alison Preston (eds) *Bosnia By Television* (London: BFI), pp. 81–91.

Gowing, Nik (1997) *Media Coverage: Help or Hindrance in Conflict Prevention*, report to the Carnegie Commission on Preventing Deadly Conflict, New York, NY: Carnegie Corporation.

Gowing, Nik (1998) 'Dispatches from Disaster Zones: The Reporting of Humanitarian Emergencies', conference paper, *New Challenges and Problems for Information Management in Complex Emergencies*, London, 27–28 May.

Halberstam, David (1979) *The Powers That Be* (London: Chatto & Windus).

Halberstam, David (1991) 'Television and the Instant Enemy', in Sifry, Micah L. and Christopher Cerf (eds) *The Gulf War Reader: History Documents, Opinion* (New York, NY: Times Books) pp. 385–88.

Halliday, Julian, Sue Curry Jansen and James Schneider (1992) 'Framing the Crisis in Eastern Europe', in Raboy, Mark and Bernard Dagenais (eds) *Media, Crisis and Democracy: Mass Communication and the Disruption of Social Order* (London: Sage), pp. 63–78.

Hallin, Daniel C (1989) *The 'Uncensored War': The Media and Vietnam* (London: University of California Press).

Hallin, Daniel C. and Paolo Mancini (1989) *Friendly Enemies* (Perugia: Perugia Press).

Halloran, Richard (1991) 'Soldiers and Scribblers: A Common Mission', in Matthews, Lloyd J. (ed.) *Newsmen and National Defense: Is Conflict Inevitable?* (New York, NY: Brassey's), pp. 39–59.

Hammond, Philip (1999) 'Reporting Kosovo: Journalists versus Propaganda', in Goff, Peter (ed.) *The Kosovo News and Propaganda War* (Vienna: International Press Institute), pp. 62–67.

Hammond, Philip (2000) 'Third Way War: New Labour, the British Media and Kosovo', in Hammond, Philip and Edward S. Herman (eds) *Degraded Capability: The Media and the Kosovo Crisis* (London: Pluto Press), pp. 123–31.

Hammond, William M. (1991) 'The Army and Public Affairs: A Glance Back', in Matthews, Lloyd J. (ed.) *Newsmen and National Defense: Is Conflict Inevitable?* (New York: Brassey's), pp. 1–18.

Hankinson, Alan (1982) *Man of Wars: William Howard Russell of The Times* (London: Heinemann).

Harris, Robert (1983) *Gotcha! The Media, the Government and the Falklands Crisis* (London: Faber).

Hawkins, Desmond (1985) *War Report: D-Day to VE Day* (London: BBC).

Hedges, Chris (1991) 'The Unilaterals', *Columbia Journalism Review*, May/June, pp. 27–29.

Herman, Edward S. and Noam Chomsky (1988) *Manufacturing Consent: The Political Economy of the Mass Media* (Pantheon Books: New York).

Herman, Edward S. and David Petersen (2000) 'CNN's Selling NATO's War Globally', in Hammond, Philip and Edward S. Herman (eds) *Degraded Capability: The Media and the Kosovo Crisis* (London: Pluto Press), pp. 111–22.

Herr, Michael (1978) *Dispatches* (London: Picador).

Hertsgaard, Mark (1988) *On Bended Knee: The Press and the Reagan Presidency* (New York, NY: Schocken Books).

Hickman, Tom (1995) *What Did You Do in the War, Auntie? The BBC at War 1939–45* (London: BBC Books).

Hilsum, Lindsey (1997) 'Crossing the Line to Commitment', in *British Journalism Review*, Vol. 8, No. 1, pp. 29–33.

Hindle, Wilfred (ed.) (1939) *Foreign Correspondent: Personal Adventures Abroad in Search of the News by Twelve British Journalists* (London: Harrap & Co.).

Hoffman, Fred S. (1991) 'The Panama Press Pool Deployment: A Critique', in Matthews, Lloyd J. (ed.) *Newsmen and National Defense: Is Conflict Inevitable?* (New York, NY: Brassey's), pp. 91–109.

Hollowell, John (1977) *Fact and Fiction: the New Journalism and the Non-Ficiton Novel* (Chapel Hill, NC: University of North Carolina Press).

Holme, Christopher (1995) 'The Reporter at Guernica', *British Journalism Review*, Vol. 6, No. 2, pp. 46–51.

Hughes, Mark (1992) 'Words at War: Reflections of a Marine Public Affairs Officer in the Persian Gulf', *Government Information Quarterly*, Vol. 9, No. 4, pp. 431–71.

Hume, Mick (1997) *Whose War is it Anyway? The Dangers of the Journalism of Attachment* (London: BM Inform Inc.).

Huntington, Samuel (1993) 'The Clash of Civilizations?' in *Foreign Affairs*, Vol. 72, No. 3, pp. 22–49.

Huntington, Samuel (1996) *The Clash of Civilizations and the Remaking of World Order* (New York, NY: Simon & Schuster).

Huntington, Samuel (2011) *The Clash of Civilizations and the Remaking of World Order*, 2nd edition (New York, NY: Simon & Schuster).

Jensen, C. /Project Censored (1994) *Censored: The News that Didn't Make the News and Why* (New York, NY: Four Walls Eight Windows).

Kapuscinksi, Ryszard (1982) *Shah of Shahs* (London: Picador).

Kapuscinksi, Ryszard (1983) *The Emperor* (London: Picador).

Kapuscinksi, Ryszard (2001) *The Shadow of the Sun: My African Life* (London: Allen Lane/The Penguin Press).

Katovsky, Bill and Timothy Carlson (eds.) (2004) *Embedded – The Media at War in Iraq: An Oral History* (Guildford, CT: Lyon's Press).

Keane, Fergal (1995) *Season of Blood: A Rwandan Journey* (London: Viking).

Keeble, Richard (1999) 'A Balkan Birthday for NATO', *British Journalism Review*, Vol. 10, No. 2, pp. 16–20.

Keeble, Richard (2004) 'Information warfare in an age of hypermilitarism', in Allen, Stuart and Barbie Zelizer (eds.) *Reporting War: Journalism in Wartime* (London: Routledge), pp. 43–58.

Keeble, Richard and John Mair (eds.) (2010) *Afghanistan, War and the Media: Deadlines and Frontlines* (Bury St Edmunds: Arima Publishing).

Kellner, Douglas (2005) *Media Spectacle and the Crisis of Democracy: Terrorism, War and Election Battles* (London: Paradigm Publishers).

Kennedy, Paul (1989) *The Rise and Fall of the Great Powers: Economic Change and Military Conflict from 1500–2000* (London: Fontana).

Kirtley, Jane E. (1992) 'The Eye of the Sandstorm: The Erosion of First Amendment Principles in Wartime', *Government Information Quarterly*, Vol. 9, No. 4, pp. 473–90.

Knightley, Phillip (1988) 'Foreign Bodies: Part 3', *The Listener*, 2 June, pp. 12–13.

Knightley, Phillip (1995) 'The Cheerleaders of World War II', in *British Journalism Review*, Vol. 6, No. 2, pp. 40–5.

Knightley, Phillip (2004) *The First Casualty: The War Correspondent as Hero and Myth Maker from the Crimea to Iraq*, 3rd edition (London: The Johns Hopkins University Press).

Kolbenschlag, George R. (1990) *A Whirlwind Passes: Newspaper Correspondents and the Sioux Indian Disturbances of 1890–91* (Vermillion, SD: University of South Dakota Press).

Laband, John and Ian Knight (1996) *The War Correspondents: The Anglo-Zulu War* (London: Bramley Books).

Lambert, Andrew and Stephen Badsey (1994) *The Crimean War: The War Correspondents* (London: Sutton).

Lambert, Derek (1987) *Just Like the Blitz: A Reporter's Notebook* (London: Hamish Hamilton).

Lande, Nathaniel (1996) *Dispatches from the Front: A History of the American War Correspondent* (New York, NY: Oxford University Press).

Lawrence, Anthony (1972) *A Foreign Correspondent* (London: Allen and Unwin).

Leslie, Jacques (1995) *The Mark: A War Correspondent's Memoir of Vietnam and Cambodia* (New York, NY: Four Walls Eight Windows).

Lewis, Jeff (2005) *Language Wars: The Role of Media and Culture in Global Terror and Political Violence* (London: Pluto Press).

Levy, Gideon (2010) *The Punishment of Gaza* (London: Verso).

Lichtenberg, Judith (1996) 'In Defense of Objectivity Revisited', in Curran, James and Martin Gurevitch (eds) *Mass Media and Society*, 2nd edition (London: Edward Arnold).

Liebes, Tamar and Zohar Kampf (2004) 'The PR of Terror: How New-style Wars Give Voice to Terrorists', in Allen, Stuart and Barbie Zelizer (eds.) (2004) *Reporting War: Journalism in Wartime* (London: Routledge), pp. 77–95.

Lippman, Walter (1992) 'Stereotypes, Public Opinion and the Press', in Cohen, E. (ed.) *Philosophical Issues in Journalism* (Oxford: Oxford University Press), pp. 161–75.

Livingston, Steven (1997) 'Clarifying the CNN Effect: An Examination of Media Effects According to Type of Military Intervention', Research Paper R-18 (Harvard: Joan Shorenstein Center Press/Politics/Public Policy).

Lloyd, Anthony (2007) *Another Bloody Love Letter* (London: Headline Review).

Lloyd, Anthony (1999) *My War Gone By, I Miss It So*, 1st edition (London: Doubleday).

Lukosiunas, Marius A. (1991) 'Enemy, Friend, or Competitor? A Content Analysis of the *Christian Science Monitor* and *Izvestia*', in Dennis, Everette E., George Gerbner and Yassen N. Zassoursky (eds) *Beyond the Cold War: Soviet and American Media Images* (London: Sage), pp. 100–10.

MacArthur, John (1992) *Second Front: Censorship and the Gulf War* (London: University of California Press).

MacGregor, Brent (1997) *Live, Direct and Biased? Making Television News in the Satellite Age* (London: Edward Arnold).

Mason, Paul (2013) *Why it's Still Kicking off Everywhere: The New Global Revolutions*, 2nd edition (London: Verso).

Massing, Michael (1991) 'Another Front', *Columbia Journalism Review*, May/June, pp. 23–24.

Matthews, Herbert L. (1971) *A World in Revolution: A Newspaperman's Memoir* (New York, NY: Scribner's).

Matthews, Lloyd J. (ed.) (1991) *Newsmen and National Defense: Is Conflict Inevitable?* (New York, NY: Brassey's).

McLaughlin, Greg (1993) 'Coming In from the Cold: British TV Coverage of the East European Revolutions', in Aulich, James and Tim Wilcox (eds) *Europe Without Walls: Art, Posters and Revolution 1989-93* (Manchester: Manchester City Art Galleries), pp. 189–99.

McLaughlin, Greg (1999) 'Refugees, Migrants and the Fall of the Berlin Wall', in Philo, Greg (ed.) *Message Received* (London: Longman), pp. 197–209.

McLaughlin, Greg (2002a) The *War Correspondent*, 1st edition (London: Pluto Press).

McLaughlin, Greg (2002b) 'Rules of engagement: TV journalism and NATO's "faith in bombing" during the Kosovo crisis', in *Journalism Studies*, Vol. 3, No. 2, pp. 257–66.

McLaughlin, Greg and Stephen Baker (2010) *The Propaganda of Peace: The Role of Media and Culture in the Northern Ireland Peace Process* (Bristol: Intellect Books).

McLaughlin, Greg and Stephen Baker (2015) *The British Media and Bloody Sunday* (Bristol: Intellect Books).

McNair, Brian (1988) *Images of the Enemy* (London: Routledge).

McNair, Brian (1994) *News and Journalism in the UK* (London: Routledge).

McNair, Brian (2010) *Journalists in Film: Heroes and Villains* (Edinburgh: Edinburgh University Press).

McNulty, Mel (1999) 'Media Ethnicisation and the International Response to War and Genocide in Rwanda', in Allen, Tim and Jean Seaton (eds) *The Media of Conflict: War Reporting and Representations of Ethnic Violence* (London: Zed Books) pp. 268–86.

Mercer, Derek, Geoff Mungham and Kevin Williams (1987) *The Fog of War: The Media on the Battlefield* (London: Heinemann).

Mickiewicz, Ellen (1991) 'Images of America', in Dennis, Everette E., George Gerbner and Yassen N. Zassoursky (eds) *Beyond the Cold War: Soviet and American Media Images* (London: Sage), pp. 21–30.

Miller, David (1994) *Don't Mention the War: Northern Ireland, Propaganda and the Media* (London: Pluto Press).

Miller, David (ed.) (2004a) *Tell me Lies: Propaganda and Media Distortion in the Attack on Iraq* (London: Pluto Press).

Miller, David (2004b) 'The propaganda machine', in Miller, David (ed.) *Tell Me Lies: Propaganda and Media Distortion in the Attack on Iraq* (London: Pluto Press), pp. 80–99.

Misser, Francois and Yves Jaumain (1994) 'Death By Radio', *Index on Censorship*, Vol. 23, September/October, pp. 72–74.

Moeller, Susan D. (1990) *Shooting War: Photography and the American Experience of Combat* (New York, NY: Basic Books).

Moeller, Susan D. (2004) 'A moral imagination: the media's response to the war on terrorism', in Allen, Stuart and Barbie Zelizer (eds) *Reporting War: Journalism in Wartime* (London: Routledge), pp. 59–76.

Morrison, David and Howard Tumber (1988) *Journalists at War: The Dynamics of News Reporting During the Falklands War* (London: Sage).

Mowlana, Hamid et al. (eds) (1992) *Triumph of the Image: The Media's War in the Persian Gulf* (Oxford: Westview Press).

Nash, William L. (1998) 'The Military and the Media in Bosnia', *Harvard International Journal Press/Politics*, Vol. 3, No. 4, pp. 131–5.

Neuman, Johanna (1995) *Lights, Camera, War!* (New York, NY: St Martin's Press).

New Left Review (ed.) (1982) *Exterminism and Cold War* (London: Verso).

Nicholson, Michael (1993) *Natasha's Story* (London: Pan Books).

Page, Charles A. (1898) *Letters of a War Correspondent* (Boston, MA: LC Page & Co.).

Parenti, Michael (1993) *Inventing Reality: The Politics of the News Media*, 2nd edition (New York, NY: St Martin's Press).

Paterson, Chris (2014) *War Reporters Under Threat: The United States and Media Freedom* (London: Pluto).

Pax, Salam (2003) *The Baghdad Blog* (London: Atlantic Books/Guardian).

Pedelty, Mark (1995) *War Stories: The Culture of the Foreign Correspondent* (London: Routledge).

Perry, William J. (1996) 'The Pentagon and the Press', *Harvard International Journal of Press/ Politics*, Vol. 1, No. 1, pp. 121–26.

Peters, Cynthia (ed.) (1992) *Collateral Damage: The New World Order at Home and Abroad* (Boston, MA: Southend Press).

Peters Talbott, Shannon (1996) 'Early Chechen Coverage Tests Print Journalists' Independence', *Transition*, 9 August, pp. 48–51.

Philips Price, Morgan (1997) *Dispatches from the Revolution, Russia 1916–18*, Tania Rose (ed.) (London: Pluto Press).

Philo, Greg and Greg McLaughlin (1995) 'The British Media and the Gulf War', in Philo, Greg (ed.) *The Glasgow Media Group Reader. Vol. 2: Industry, Economy, War and Politics* (London: Routledge), pp. 146–56.

Philo, Greg and Mike Berry (2004) *Bad News from Israel* (London: Pluto).

Philo, Greg and Mike Berry (2011) *More Bad News from Israel* (London: Pluto).

Philo, Greg (2012) 'Pictures and public relations in the Israeli-Palestinian conflict', in Freedman, Des and Daya Kishan Thussu (eds) *Media and Terrorism: Global Perspectives* (London: Sage), pp. 151–64.

Pilger, John (2001) *Heroes* (London: Vintage), pp. 254–65.

Politkovskaya, Anna (2001) *A Dirty War: A Russian Reporter in Chechnya* (London: The Harvill Press).

Politkovskaya, Anna (2004) *Putin's Russia* (London: The Harvill Press).

Politkovskaya, Anna (2008) *A Russian Diary: With a Foreword by Jon Snow* (London: Vintage).

Politkovskaya, Anna (2011) *Is Journalism Worth Dying For? Final Dispatches* (New York, NY: Melville House Books).

Prochnau, William (1995) *Once Upon A Distant War* (New York, NY: Times Books).

Ramsey, Stuart (2010) 'The case for the honest embed', in Keeble, Richard and John Mair (eds.) *Afghanistan, War and the Media: Deadlines and Frontlines* (Bury St Edmunds: Arima Publishing), pp. 23–32.

Reed, John (1926) *Ten Days That Shook the World* (London: Martin Lawrence).

Richter, Andrei G. (1991) 'Enemy Turned Partner: A Content Analysis of *Newsweek* and *Novoye Vremya*', in Dennis, Everette E., George Gerbner and Yassen N. Zassoursky (eds) *Beyond the Cold War: Soviet and American Media Images* (London: Sage), pp. 91–99.

Roth, Mitchel P. (ed.) (1997) *Historical Dictionary of War Journalism* (London: Greenwood Press).

Roy, Arundhati (2004) *The Chequebook and the Cruise Missile: Conversations with Arundhati Roy*, interviews by David Barsamian (London: Harper Perennial).

Royle, Trevor (1989) *War Report: The War Correspondent's View of Battle from the Crimea to the Falklands* (London: Gratton Books).

Rutland, Peter (1996) 'Russian Television and the Chechen War', *OMRI Analytical Brief*, No. 331, 10 September.

Sabey, Ruth (1982) 'Disarming the Disarmers', in Aubrey, Crispin (ed.) *Nukespeak: The Media and the Bomb* (London: Comedia/Minority Press Group), pp. 55–63.

Sarkesian, Sam C. (1991) 'Soldiers, Scholars and the Media', in Matthews, Lloyd J. (ed.) *Newsmen and National Defense: Is Conflict Inevitable?* (New York, NY: Brassey's), pp. 61–69.

Schechter, Danny (2003) *Media Wars: News At A Time of Terror* (New York, NY: Rowman and Littlefield).

Schlesinger, Philip (1987) *Putting 'Reality' Together: BBC News* (London: Methuen).

Schorr, Daniel (1995) 'Ten Days that Shook the White House', in Hiebert, R.E. (ed.) *Impact of Mass Media: Current Issues* (White Plains, NY: Longman), pp. 53–57.

Schudson, Michael (1978) *Discovering News* (New York, NY: Basic Books).

Sebba, Anne (1994) *Battling For News: The Rise of the Women Reporter* (London: Sceptre).

Shakespeare, Nicholas (1998) 'Martha Gellhorn', *Granta 62: What Young Men Do*, Summer, pp. 215–35.

Shaw, Martin (1996a) 'The Kurds Five Years On', *New Statesman*, 5 April.

Shaw, Martin (1996b) *Civil Society and Media in Global Crises* (London: Pinter).

Sheehan, Neil (1989) *A Bright Shining Lie: John Paul Vann and America in Vietnam* (New York, NY: Vintage).

Simpson, John (1990) *Dispatches From the Barricades: An Eyewitness Account of the Revolutions that Shook the World, 1989-90* (London: Hutchinson).

Smith, Vaughan (2010) 'The "brittle" compact between the military and the media', in Keeble, Richard and John Mair (eds.) *Afghanistan, War and the Media: Deadlines and Frontlines* (Bury St Edmunds: Arima Publishing), pp. 42–47.

Southworth, Herbert R. (1977) *Guernica! Guernica! A Study of Journalism, Diplomacy, Propaganda and History* (Berkeley: University of California Press).

Steele, Jon (2002) *War Junkie: One Man's Addiction to the Worst Places on Earth* (London: Transworld Publishers).

Stenbuck, Jack (1995) *The Typewriter Battalion* (New York, NY: William Morrow & Co. Inc.).

Streckfuss, Richard (1990) 'Objectivity in Journalism: A Search and a Reassessment', *Journalism Quarterly*, Vol. 67, No. 4, pp. 973–83.

Sweeney, Michael S. (1998) '"Delays and Vexations": Jack London and the Russo-Japanese War', *Journalism & Mass Communications Quarterly*, Vol. 75, No. 3, Autumn, pp. 548–49.

Tait, Richard (2001) 'Unacceptable Danger', International Press Institute, Vienna, Report No. 1.

Teichner, Martha (1996) 'No Sense at All', in *Media Studies Journal: Journalists in Peril*, Vol. 10, No. 4, Fall.

Thompson, Edward (1982) 'Notes on Exterminism, the Last Stage of Civilization', in New Left Review (ed.) *Exterminsim and Cold War* (London: Verso), pp. 1–34.

Thompson, Hunter S. (2011) *Fear and Loathing at Rolling Stone: The Essential Writing of Hunter S. Thompson* (Jann S. Wenner, ed.) (New York, NY: Simon and Schuster Paperbacks).

Thomson, Alex (1992) *Smokescreen: The Media, the Censors, the Gulf* (Tunbridge Wells: Laburnham and Spellmount).

Thomson, Alex (2010) 'The rough guide to roughness', in Keeble, Richard and John Mair (eds.) *Afghanistan, War and the Media: Deadlines and Frontlines* (Bury St Edmunds: Arima Publishing), pp. 13–22.

Tuchman, Gaye (1972) 'Objectivity as Strategic Ritual: An Examination of Newsmen's Notions of Objectivity', *American Journal of Sociology*, Vol. 77, No. 4, pp. 660–70.

Tumber, Howard and Jeffrey Palmer (2004) *Media at War: the Iraq crisis* (London: Sage).

Ullman, Harlan K. and James P. Wade (1996) *Shock and Awe: Achieving Rapid Dominance* (Defense Group Inc.: National Defense University).

Vulliamy, Ed (1993) 'This War Has Changed My Life', *British Journalism Review*, Vol. 4, No. 2, pp. 5–11.

Wagner, Lydia (1989) *Women War Correspondents of World War II* (New York, NY: Greenwood Press).

Wakefield, Dan (1974) 'The Personal Voice and the Impersonal Eye', in Weber, R. (ed.) *The Reporter As Artist: A Look at the New Journalism Controversy* (New York, NY: Hastings House), pp. 39–48.

Ward, Stephen J. (1998) 'An Answer to Martin Bell: Objectivity and Attachment in Journalism', *International Journal Press/Politics*, Vol. 3, No. 3, pp. 121–25.

Washburn, Stanley (1982) *On the Russian Front in WWI: Memoirs of an American War Correspondent* (New York, NY: Robert Spellar & Sons).

Waugh, Evelyn (1938) *Scoop: A Novel About Journalists* (London: Penguin Books).

Weschler, Lawrence (1990) 'The Media's One and Only Freedom Story', in *Columbia Journalism Review*, March/April, pp. 25–31.

Whitman, Bryan (2004) 'The Birth of Embedding as Pentagon War Policy' in Katovsky, Bill and Timothy Carlson (eds.) *Embedded – The Media at War in Iraq: An Oral History* (Guildford, CT: Lyon's Press); pp. 203–08.

Williams, Kevin (1993) 'The Light at the End of the Tunnel: The Mass Media, Public Opinion and the Vietnam War', in Eldridge, John (ed.) *Getting the Message: News, Truth, Power* (London: Routledge), pp. 305–30.

Williams, Pete (1995) 'The Pentagon Position on Mass Media', in Hiebert, Ray Eldon (ed.) *Impact of Mass Media: Current Issues*, 3rd edition (White Plains, NY: Longman), pp. 327–34.

Williams Walsh, Mary (1990) 'Mission: Afghanistan', *Columbia Journalism Review*, January/February, pp. 27–36.

Wilson, Andrew (1982) 'The Defence Correspondent', in Aubrey, Crispin (ed.) *Nukespeak: The Media and the Bomb* (London: Comedia/Minority Press Group), pp. 33–37.

Wolfe, Humbert (1930) *The Uncelestial City* (London: Gollancz).

Wright, Evan (2004) 'Our Warrior Youth', in Katovsky, Bill and Timothy Carlson (eds.) *Embedded – The Media at War in Iraq: An Oral History* (Guildford, CT: Lyon's Press), pp. 329–39.

Woofinden, Bob (1988) 'Foreign Bodies: Part 1', *The Listener*, 19 May, pp. 14–15.

Zassoursky, Yassen N. (1991) 'Changing Images of the Soviet Union and the United States', in Dennis, Everette E., George Gerbner and Yassen N. Zassoursky (eds) *Beyond the Cold War: Soviet and American Media Images* (London: Sage), pp. 11–20.

Zizek, Slavoj (2012) *Welcome to the Desert of the Real* (London: Verso).

Index